Rabbis and their Community

Rabbis and their Community

Studies in the Eastern European Orthodox
Rabbinate in Montreal, 1896–1930

IRA ROBINSON

© 2007 Ira Robinson

University of Calgary Press
2500 University Drive NW
Calgary, Alberta
Canada T2N 1N4
www.uofcpress.com

No part of this publication may be reproduced, stored in a retrieval system or transmitted, in any form or by any means, without the prior written consent of the publisher or a license from The Canadian Copyright Licensing Agency (Access Copyright). For an Access Copyright license, visit www.accesscopyright.ca or call toll free 1-800-893-5777.

Library and Archives Canada Cataloguing in Publication

Robinson, Ira, 1951–
  Rabbis and their community : studies in the Eastern European Orthodox rabbinate in Montreal, 1896–1930 / Ira Robinson.

Co-published by the Concordia University Institute for Canadian Jewish Studies.
Includes bibliographical references and index.
ISBN 978-1-55238-186-1

1. Rabbis–Québec (Province)–Montréal–Biography. 2. Orthodox Judaism–Québec (Province)–Montréal–History–20th century. 3. Jews, East European–Québec (Province)–Montréal–Biography. 4. Jews–Québec (Province)–Montréal–History–20th century. I. Concordia University. Institute for Canadian Jewish Studies. II. Title.

BM750.R62 2007   296.8'32092271428
C2007-904073-X

The University of Calgary Press acknowledges the support of the Alberta Foundation for the Arts for our publications. We acknowledge the financial support of the Government of Canada through the Book Publishing Industry Development Program (BPIDP) for our publishing activities. We acknowledge the financial support of the Canada Council for the Arts for our publishing program.

COMMITTED TO THE DEVELOPMENT OF CULTURE AND THE ARTS

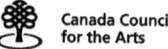

Cover design by Melina Cusano
Page design and typesetting by zijn digital

To my father, Jacob Robinson
(1917–1998)

and to my mother, Hannah L. Robinson
(1912–2007).

Their memory is a blessing.

Contents

Preface
ix

· 1 ·
Introduction:
The Yiddish-speaking Orthodox Rabbinate in
North America and its Importance
1

· 2 ·
"Pa Is a Mussolini":
A Portrait of Rabbi Hirsh Cohen
21

· 3 ·
Rabbi Simon Glazer:
A Rival for the Chief Rabbinate
35

· 4 ·
Rabbi Yudel Rosenberg:
Kabbalist and Communal Leader
57

· 5 ·
Rabbis and *Shohtim*: The Cases of Getsel Laxer and Hyman Crestohl
69

· 6 ·
The Founding of the Jewish Community Council of Montreal (*Va'ad ha-'Ir*)
87

· 7 ·
The Kosher Meat Wars of the 1920s and their Aftermath
103

· 8 ·
New Thoughts from an Ancient Source: Hirsh Wolofsky's Commentary on the Torah
119

· 9 ·
Afterword
127

Glossary
129

Notes
133

Index
159

Preface

This book originated in a series of lectures held at the Jewish Public Library of Montreal on successive Monday nights from October 30 to December 11, 2000. It was co-sponsored by the Library and the Concordia University Institute for Canadian Jewish Studies. My thanks go to people at both institutions: to Professor Norman Ravvin, Professor of Canadian Jewish Studies and Director of Concordia's Institute for Canadian Jewish Studies, for agreeing to the idea and providing the funding; to Eva Raby, executive director of the Jewish Public Library, and Claire Stern and Eirann Harris of its staff for making it all happen so smoothly and apparently effortlessly. Finally, and most importantly, to all those who attended these lectures, for providing a sounding-board for the ideas ultimately expressed in this book. Chapter 8 was not originally part of the lecture series but is included because of its close relationship to the other chapters of the book.

This book had its genesis in my research on Rabbi Yudel Rosenberg, whom you will meet in Chapter 4. I have been working on a comprehensive biography of Rabbi Rosenberg for well over a decade. That I have not yet completed this biography is due in part to numerous complicating factors in my academic and personal life. More important, however, has been the fact that in order to do the best job possible in depicting the life and times of Rabbi Rosenberg, I needed to investigate not only him, but his colleagues, rivals, and communities. Thus, for example, I could not responsibly describe Rabbi Rosenberg's claim to be the chief rabbinate of Montreal without first looking carefully at his predecessor in this claim,

Rabbi Simon Glazer,[1] and his arch-rival, Rabbi Hirsh Cohen.[2] Since neither had received adequate scholarly study, I found that I had to do much of the preliminary work myself. This book, therefore, is a culmination of this work.

Taken as a whole, however, this book constitutes much more than a mere preliminary to Rabbi Rosenberg's biography. It also serves to sketch in a portrait of the Eastern European immigrant rabbinate of Montreal in the first three decades of the twentieth century. While it is true that Eastern European rabbis in North America have been getting considerably more scholarly attention in the past few years, one finds that most of the extant scholarly studies tend to concentrate on only one rabbi at a time. Thus the context in which that rabbi worked and the interaction of that rabbi with his colleagues is necessarily portrayed in a one-sided manner. In order to obtain the fullest possible understanding of the dynamics of the Eastern European Orthodox rabbinate in North America, we must attempt to examine carefully the multifaceted interrelationship between a number of rabbis sharing the same communal turf. While this book is not a substitute for an exhaustive, full-scale study of the Montreal rabbinate of this era, I believe that it does go farther toward that end than previous studies of one or another figure. I further believe that this study will have implications for research on the North American Orthodox rabbinate of this era in other major North American Jewish communities.

The book begins with a chapter on why the Yiddish-speaking Orthodox Rabbinate in North America is of importance in our study of North American Jewry as a whole, and why it has been neglected. The next chapter creates a portrait of Rabbi Hirsh Cohen, who was the dominant Eastern European immigrant rabbi of Montreal in the first half of the twentieth century. Chapter 3 speaks of Rabbi Simon Glazer, who from 1907 to 1918 was Rabbi Cohen's main rival for the chief rabbinate of Montreal. When Rabbi Glazer left Montreal, he was succeeded by Rabbi Yudel Rosenberg, whose life in Montreal was marked by his rivalry with Rabbi Cohen, as well as his scholarly work on kabbala. His story is told in Chapter 4. Chapter 5 deals with two rabbis, Getsel Laxer and Hyman Crestohl, who became rabbis in small-town Quebec, and later moved to Montreal, but who did not achieve the power and position of Rabbis Cohen, Glazer, or Rosenberg. They rather functioned as ritual slaughterers [*shohtim*], a position of less communal prestige. Chapter 6 details the founding of the Jewish Community Council of Montreal (*Va'ad ha-'Ir*) in 1922, an attempt on the part of the immigrant Jewish community and its rabbinate to unite, while the next chapter discusses the Kosher Meat War, which nearly killed the Jewish Community Council in its early years and pitted rabbi against rabbi. Chapter 8 discusses Hirsh Wolofsky, Yiddish journalist and community leader, who was instrumental in the founding and fortunes of the Jewish Community Council through the perspective of a commentary on the Torah he wrote and published in this period. A short chapter on the implications of the findings of this book for the subsequent history of North American Orthodox Judaism concludes the book.

In my research for this book, I have to thank the archivists at the National Archives of Canada in Ottawa, the Archives of the Jewish Public Library of Montreal, the Canadian Jewish Congress National Archives of Montreal, and the American Jewish Archives in Cincinnati, Ohio. I also have to especially thank Janice Rosen for many helpful suggestions, and the late Henriette Kallus for research assistance in the early stages of this research. Eve Lerner read the entire manuscript. Her sharp eye was most useful. Lastly, I am grateful to the University of Calgary Press for believing in this book and for sending it for evaluation to two discerning anonymous readers. Their numerous suggestions have made this a much better book.

Parts of this book were originally published in the journals *Canadian Ethnic Studies*, *Canadian Jewish Studies*, and *Jewish Political Studies Review*. My thanks to the editors of all these publications for their permission to use the material.

Montreal
July 11, 2006

· 1 ·

The Yiddish-Speaking Orthodox Rabbinate in North America and its Importance

We want to extend our brotherhood and respect to the old-fashioned rabbi for whom American life is an unbroken series of disappointment and sorrow. – Rabbi Leo Jung (1929)[1]

This book will examine the Yiddish-speaking immigrant Orthodox rabbinate in Montreal, Canada, at the beginning of the twentieth century. In its pages, we will analyze and attempt to understand the deeds and motivations of rabbis who are, for the most part, forgotten men in the Jewish community they helped to shape. It is inevitable that personalities, factors, and trends from both the late nineteenth century and the middle of the twentieth century will be brought into our discussion for purposes of illustration. Nonetheless it is in the first three decades of the twentieth century in particular that the personalities who made up the Eastern European immigrant rabbinate in Montreal, the issues they faced, and the institutions they created, most particularly the Jewish Community Council of Montreal [*Va'ad ha-'Ir*],[2] were factors of fundamental importance for the development of the Jewish community of Montreal as a whole.

Taking into account all the changes stemming from Quebec's Quiet Revolution and the Sephardic immigration of the postwar years, the contemporary Montreal Jewish community is still recognizably descended from the community set up by Jewish immigrants from Eastern Europe in the period 1880–1930.[3] However, when historians came to chronicle the history of this community, or any other North American Jewish community for that matter, the men of the Eastern European rabbinate and the synagogues in which they preached and prayed were often marginalized, if not entirely neglected.[4] There are important structural reasons for that neglect. Before concentrating on the story of the Montreal rabbis and their community, therefore, it will be important for us to understand the institution of the Eastern European immigrant Orthodox rabbinate from a much wider perspective. Why did these rabbis become forgotten men? Perhaps the best way to begin considering this issue is by recounting an incident that took place slightly outside the temporal and geographical frame of this book, but which nonetheless graphically illustrates both the problems and the potential of research in this subject.

Early in 1943, it was apparent to anyone in North America who had eyes to see, and who was carefully reading the newspapers, particularly the Yiddish press,[5] that something tremendously horrible was happening to the Jews of Nazi-occupied Europe. The exact nature and proportions of what would come to be known as the Holocaust were still unknown, but disturbing reports from a number of sources had begun reaching people at the World Jewish Congress and the United States State Department, among others, that the Germans were systematically killing all the Jews within the territory under their control.

There is presently a debate among historians of American Jewry regarding the appropriateness of the response of the American Jewish communal leadership to this news.[6] These historians have asked the following questions:

1. Could that leadership have done more to protest?
2. Would open and public protest by that leadership have made any difference in the end result?

One American Jewish group that did engage in a vehement public protest was the Agudath ha-Rabbonim of the United States and Canada. The Agudath ha-Rabbonim was an organization of immigrant Orthodox rabbis in North America, founded in 1902.[7] The rabbis of Agudath ha-Rabbonim decided to go to Washington on October 6, 1943, just prior to Yom Kippur, the most solemn day in the Jewish calendar, to attempt to meet with President Roosevelt and to plead with him to do something to save the Jews of Europe.[8] Approximately four hundred rabbis gathered in Washington to demonstrate. Nearly all of them were European-born. They were most comfortable expressing themselves in the Yiddish language, though most had lived in various North American cities for two decades and more, and many had become fluent in English as well. The group's demonstration in Washington was covered by the major newspapers and newsreels of the day. Despite this publicity, however, the rabbis did not get what they really desired – the chance to see President Roosevelt. When the president found out about the rabbis' request for an appointment, he turned to one of his most trusted advisors, Samuel Rosenman. Rosenman told FDR that he did not have to see the group, for, as he stated to the president in his memorandum, "they are a group of rabbis who have just recently left the darkest period of the medieval world. They really represent no one."[9] Rosenman's political sense had told him that these rabbis, and the issues they represented, were marginal and could be ignored with impunity. Rosenman was not alone in his evaluation of these rabbis. In this, he most probably represented a large portion of American Jewish public opinion.

The reasons for this negative evaluation of the rabbis of the Agudath ha-Rabbonim by Samuel Rosenman are not dissimilar to the reasons they have not received an adequate evaluation in the histories of North American Jewry. The history of the Jewish community in this period has often been written by people who felt about these rabbis something similar to what Samuel Rosenman felt: that they represented the "darkest period of the medieval age"; that even though they were living *in* the twentieth century, they were not *of* that century; and that these were people who did not and should not have a say in either the Jewish present or future.

Seeking the reasons behind this negative evaluation brings us to some of the major issues of the great Eastern European Jewish migration to North America, which, in turn, are intimately tied to the revolution inherent in Jewish modernity. This revolution engendered, among its other major effects, a historiography whose predominant characteristic has been an emphasis on transformation and change[10] in Jewish life in the past two centuries, and a corresponding de-emphasis on continuity and tradition during this period. In evaluating this historiography, it is of crucial importance to understand who is doing the writing. As Michael Kazin has written, in a different context:

Historians, like most people, are reluctant to sympathize with people whose political opinions they detest. Overwhelmingly cosmopolitan in their cultural tastes and liberal or radical in their politics, scholars of modern America have largely eschewed research projects about past movements that seem to them either bastions of a crumbling status-quo or the domain of puritanical, pathological yahoos.[11]

It is reasonably clear that a number of historians of American Judaism have, in the past, succumbed to a "whiggish" interpretation of American Jewish history in which Orthodoxy was kindly and conveniently consigned to the dustbin.[12] In this they follow most contemporary observers of the early twentieth century, for whom the future of Judaism in North America belonged, depending upon the observer's ideological persuasion, to the Zionists, the socialists, the communists, the Yiddishists, the Hebraists, to Reform Judaism, to Conservative Judaism ... in other words, to anyone but the Orthodox. Until quite recently, therefore, few historians of North American Jewry seemed interested at all in the experiences of those who in the first half of the twentieth century struggled against great odds to transplant the age-old culture of rabbinic Judaism, as they perceived it, to the New World.[13] Thus, for every word historians have written about Eastern European immigrant rabbis and their synagogues in the historiography of the North American Jewish community, there are arguably twenty or even thirty words about such subjects as the influence of the Jewish labour movement and secular yiddishist education within the immigrant Jewish community.

Indeed, in the face of this situation, more than one historian of Orthodox Judaism in North America has come to the conclusion that the world of the Orthodox rabbi in North America at the end of the nineteenth and the beginning of the twentieth centuries is less well known and less intensely studied than the Jewish world of thousands of years ago. Louis Bernstein, working a mere two decades ago, in introducing his study of the Rabbinical Council of America, thus stated, "The historian working in the Jewish catacombs of Rome or in Philo's Alexandria may have more material at his disposal than a researcher of American Orthodoxy."[14]

This silence with respect to the Orthodox rabbinate is not confined to the historiography of North American Jewry. It is very much the case as well in descriptions of the Eastern European homeland of these rabbis. Thus Dan Miron, a prominent scholar of nineteenth-century Yiddish literature, in an article entitled "The Literary Image of the Shtetl," presented an analysis of the Jewish world of Eastern Europe as portrayed by the renowned nineteenth-century Yiddish writer, Shalom Abramovits, who wrote under the *nom de plume* Mendele Mokher Seforim. Miron asserts that, as far as Mendele's contemporaries and successors were concerned, his works "covered" the complete spectrum of life in the shtetl. This was so despite the fact that, as Miron stated, "[Mendele's] novels have almost nothing to say about Hasidism and the Hasidic way of life, in spite of the fact that the Ukrainian shtetl society upon which the writer focussed was largely dominated by Hasidism.... For that matter, the entire rabbinic tradition of learning receives very little attention."[15] The religious establishment of the Jewish Ukraine is missing in Mendele's "complete" portrayal of Eastern European Jewish life. Rabbis and hasidic rebbes may have been denigrated by Mendele, but not portrayed. They had become invisible in the literary shtetl he had built.

Given this situation, it should not be entirely surprising to hear that, when I set out to research the Eastern European Orthodox rabbinate of Montreal in the period of the early twentieth century, I found relatively little written on it in the histories of Canadian or North American Jewry. The rabbis and their community are, relatively speaking, missing in Simon Belkin's pioneering history of the immigrant community of Montreal in its crucial formative years. His heroes are the members of the *Poalei Tsiyyon* [Labour Zionists] of Montreal.[16] The same is true of Israel Medresh's sketches of this era in *Montreal fun Nekhtn* and *Tsvishn Tsvei Velt Milhomes*,[17] and in Hirsh Wolofsky's memoirs.[18] Pierre Anctil, in his introduction to his translation of Belkin, has observed that the *Poalei Tsiyyon* had a sense of themselves as pioneers who were making history. They also felt that this history needed to be preserved for future generations. With Belkin's work, they succeeded in having their self-conception perpetuated.[19] Medresh also seems to have thought of the incidents and people he portrayed as worthy of perpetuation.[20]

The rabbis, unlike the *Poalei Tsiyyon*, did not seem to have a sense that they were doing something new and extraordinary, even though their attempted implantation of Eastern European Orthodox Judaism in North America was as revolutionary an experiment as any made by the *Poalei Tsiyyon*. It is certainly true that these rabbis may have been tilting at windmills and attempting the impossible, but not any more so than the educators of the *Poalei Tsiyyon* who hoped that Yiddish language and culture could be successfully implanted in the Jewish youth of North America.[21] The rabbis were engaged in a noble experiment – win or lose – at least on a par with their Yiddishist brethren.

The rabbis of whom we are speaking have also suffered, at least in part, because, unlike the activists of *Po'alei Zion*, they were not, by and large, chronicled from within their ranks. The culture of Rabbinic Judaism, whose contemporary representatives these rabbis were, did not particularly care to emphasize history or historiography – whether its own or anyone else's. The Eastern European rabbis in North America, whatever else they stood for, perceived themselves to be heirs to a culture in which the recording of post-Biblical history was not considered a terribly significant activity. North American Orthodox rabbis wrote and published voluminously in areas that were of interest to them, such as sermons, Biblical and Talmudic commentaries, and responsa.[22] We can and will learn much about their story from all of these writings. However, the one thing that they almost never did was to consider that their story was important to record as such.[23] For the most part, they had no sense that what they were doing was so special that they needed to write down what happened in narrative form. As the historian Yosef Haim Yerushalmi has written, insofar as rabbinic Judaism has retained a hold in the modern world, its curriculum does not give more than a minor place to history.[24]

The Orthodox rabbis of North America, to repeat, did not especially benefit from historical examination because, on the one hand, they did not tell their own story, and, on the other hand, they did not "fit" into the story mainstream historians chose to tell. "Progressive" Jews, on the other hand, such as those identified with the Jewish labour movement, were chronicled, from within their own movement as well as by mainstream historiography, and were generally seen as a better "fit" in the master narrative of the unravelling of the Judaic tradition in North America.[25] Interestingly, even Orthodox scholars have contributed to the neglect of the contribution of pre-World War II Orthodoxy in their emphasis on the postwar Orthodox "resurgence." Once again, I will cite Louis Bernstein:

Sixty years ago few observers gave Orthodox Judaism a meaningful chance to become an important factor on the American Jewish scene. But since World War II, Orthodoxy has become a significant component of American life.[26]

Thus, in attempting an analysis of the history of rabbinic culture in Montreal itself, or elsewhere in Canada,[27] I found that I needed to begin with a lot of digging and sifting of primary sources. In contextualizing these primary sources, one must begin with the thesis propounded by Jeffrey Gurock, which states that the members of the Eastern European immigrant rabbinate can be understood through classification on a spectrum of "accommodationists" vs. "resisters" to "America" and all it stood for.[28] Gurock's insight is most useful, for both accommodation and resistance were part of the common experience of these rabbis. However, Gurock's classification scheme needs to be further refined to account for the fact that there are numerous cases of rabbis who were "resisters" in some aspects of their lives – such as dress and language – and yet "accommodators" in other areas, such as halakhic leniency.[29] Furthermore, in assimilating Gurock's thesis to this research, it must be carefully noted that there was no Eastern European Orthodox rabbi who was so "accommodationist" that he ceased being countercultural with respect to mainstream North American mores, and there was no "resister" who was not changed in significant ways by his encounter with "America."

As well, prior to commencing the story of the Montreal rabbinate, a word needs to be said concerning periodization. The mass immigration of Eastern European Jews to North America and elsewhere had its beginnings in the 1870s, and received a great impetus from the Russian pogroms of 1881 and the Russo-Japanese War of 1904–5. Interrupted by World War I, this mass immigration lasted into the 1920s, at which time it was crippled by United States immigration restriction policies and given its deathblow by the onset of the Great Depression. This migration, spanning over half a century, is all too often looked upon as a unit, with the implication that there was uniformity in the migration, its motivations, and its consequences whether in the 1880s or the 1920s. However, even a cursory analysis will show that there were basic differences between those Jews migrating in the 1880s and those migrating in the 1920s, which greatly affected the fortunes of Orthodox Judaism. A brief personal anecdote will serve to illustrate. My great-grandfather, Moshe Nochum Segal, left Lithuania for New York in 1882. He stayed in New York for a few months and came to the conclusion that this was no place for Jewish people to live, and so he left for home. My great-grandfather died in Lithuania, but his widow and her children wound up in New York a few years later. He had plenty of company within the circles of Orthodoxy, both in his conclusions and in his and his family's actions.[30] In the late nineteenth century, one of the greatest of the Eastern European rabbis of that era, Rabbi Jacob Willowsky, widely known as the Ridbaz, coined a phrase that echoes down the ages, "In America, even the stones are *treyf*." He also wound up coming to America and settling for a number of years in Chicago.[31] The greatest of rabbinic leaders of Eastern Europe, Rabbi Israel Meir ha-Kohen, more widely known as the Hofets Hayyim, wrote a book for the benefit of the Eastern European Jewish emigrants entitled *Nidchei Yisroel* [*The Scattered Ones of Israel*].[32] This book, which contained halakha for travellers as well as moral encouragement and exhortation, ended with a plea: Don't go to America. If you go, don't stay there. Don't bring your family there. Leave them safe at home where there is the possibility of a full Jewish life.[33] Despite these sentiments, there is a report that the Hofets Haim had stated, toward the end of his life, that if he were a young man, and not in ill health, he would go to America.[34] What had been unthinkable a few decades before had come within the realm of possibility. There is a trend that is discernible: North America may indeed have started out in the 1880s as an "impossible" place for Jews to observe the traditions and lifestyle characteristic of Orthodox Judaism. Yet, within a relatively short period of time, Jews in their hundreds of thousands and their millions came to North America and established themselves and their institutions. In other words, there are basic differences between the situation of Orthodox Jews in America in the 1880s and in the 1920s that historians have to consider.[35]

By the end of World War I, a lot of important Orthodox institution building had been accomplished. Eastern European Orthodox rabbis had arrived and organized the Agudath ha-Rabbonim (though they could hardly be called united, as we will see). Jewish schools and yeshivas, on both elementary and advanced levels, had been founded. The Union of American Orthodox Congregations, an attempt to unite and strengthen American Orthodoxy, had been established. Without at all minimizing the difficulties of Orthodox Jewish life in the 1920s, it is fair to say that the makings of an institutional, educational, and organizational basis for Orthodox Jewish life, which had been lacking at the onset of the great migration, had been established.

The difficulties that remained as obstacles to Orthodox life in North America were nonetheless quite significant. The most important of these difficulties was the absence of the possibility for most Jews in America to live in "Jewish time," which, for an Eastern European Orthodox Jew, was normative. In Eastern Europe, Jews had been more or less able to live their lives according to their own calendar with Sabbath and holiday periods differentiated from the workaday week.[36] It did not particularly matter whether individual Eastern European Jews were ideologically committed to this religious lifestyle. Even many of those who were relatively or totally nonobservant often acquiesced, at least in public, with Sabbath or holiday observance. On the contrary, one had to be ideologically motivated *not* to join in the general communal observance of "Jewish time." Thus doctrinaire Marxists, like the members of the Jewish socialist Bund, were ideologically motivated in this way and did not choose to observe "Jewish time" in a way satisfactory to the Orthodox. However, the ordinary Eastern European Jew in the street did tend to go along with what has been called *"milieu frommigkeit."* In other words, he or she would be observant of "Jewish time" because that observance was generalized in Jewish society. In North America, during the period of mass immigration, we witness the reverse phenomenon: one had to be ideologically motivated to observe "Jewish time." In many cases even those desiring to do so found it to be practically impossible. The reasons for this stem largely from economic determinants.

In Eastern Europe, even non-Jews understood that Jewish businesses were going to be closed on Saturdays and Jewish holidays and accommodated to that practise.[37] Indeed there were some cases in Eastern Europe in which the parish priest, in making communal announcements after Sunday mass, informed his parishioners that a Jewish holiday was coming up and that therefore the Jews' stores would be closed for business.[38] When the Eastern European Jews came to America, however, they found it to be nearly impossible to live in "Jewish time" in this way. Non-Jews would not accommodate them. Even in instances where both Jews and non-Jews, who had had commercial relations in the Ukraine, came to the same place in America and resumed the same economic relationship, "Jewish time" did not survive the crossing. Jewish stores in America tended overwhelmingly to remain open on Sabbath and holidays. It could be and often was the case that, in the first generation of immigration, the owners of these stores were observant of the halakha in every other way but this. The economics of "making it" in America had overwhelmed them. The only important vestige of "Jewish time" in North America came on the High Holidays of Rosh ha-Shana and Yom Kippur. Jews, who otherwise kept their stores open on Jewish Sabbaths and holy days, felt obligated to close their stores at this time.

This was particularly the case in small towns. The following is a specific example of what was a much wider phenomenon. In the 1920s, Rabbi Joshua Halevi Herschorn of Montreal got a question from North Bay, Ontario, from the local teacher and *shohet*. The question concerned the possibility of reading from a Torah scroll in the local synagogue on Saturday morning in the absence of a minyan of males over thirteen years of age. Rabbi Herschorn's response was a gently put "no."[39] That the question needed to be asked raises the issue: where were the adult males of the North Bay Jewish community on Saturday mornings? They were obviously in their stores. What happened in North Bay occurred in other North American towns and cities – including Montreal – as well. The problem of getting jobs for Sabbath-observant Jews, even in the greatest North American Jewish centre of all, New York, was always quite difficult. Owners of garment factories knew very well that if they wanted to hire good labour cheap, they could promise the observant workers that they would not have to work on Saturdays. To take a cut in pay in order to observe "Jewish time" was accepted as normal. Jews thus had to be motivated to observe "Jewish time," particularly when their economic situation as new immigrants was very "hand to mouth" and a governmental "social safety net" was almost completely absent.[40]

Another important difference between the Jewish experience in Europe and North America was that, in Eastern Europe's towns and cities, Judaism was manifestly a public presence in the synagogues and study halls. In America, on the contrary, Jews tended to keep their observances mostly at home, rather than in synagogues. Thus, for the most part, such Judaic observances as survived, survived mainly in the home. *Kashrut*, the system of Judaic dietary laws, was a home observance not affected by the restriction of "Jewish time," and thus remained more or less observed by the immigrant generation.[41] This created important new dynamics between men, whose traditional primary domain was in public, and women, whose primary domain was the home. This is one reason, among others, that Jewish women became an especial target for satire: they had become so much more important in the transmission of Judaism.⁴²

There were, of course, sizeable Jewish communities, such as Montreal and New York, with an "internal" Jewish economy. Within this economy it was possible to observe "Jewish time" in the most complete manner possible. Within this economy it was also possible to get along with next to no English, though, even for the most isolated Jews within this internal Jewish economy, Yiddish rapidly became anglicized. Thus, when Rabbi Jacob Joseph came to New York in 1882, it was noticed by Yiddish journalist Abraham Cahan that, very soon after his arrival, his sermons began to feature English words:

It was only his second or third sermon since his arrival and already he was making a clumsy attempt to accommodate himself to his audience by using American Yiddish. Once he used the word "clean" for *"rein"* and it was easy to see this was purposely done to show he was not a greenhorn.⁴³

As we will see, however, jobs in the internal Jewish economy were relatively few and not at all simple to obtain. One of the most prestigious jobs within this internal economy was that of rabbi. Many of the people we will be dealing with in this book had achieved, or were fighting for, such privileged positions. Slightly down the scale of prestige was the job of *shohet*, who killed animals according to the Judaic laws of *kashrut*. We will be speaking of men in this position as well, and their relations with the rabbis. One of the great realities in the situation of Orthodox rabbis in North America in this era is that it was only from the supervision of the kosher meat industry that rabbis were able to make anything approaching a decent living. Certainly, as we will see, whatever salary they received from their congregations was not sufficient to make ends meet. The journalist Abraham Cahan, a keen observer of the immigrant Jewish scene in New York at this time, thus stated:

Here there are hundreds of congregations, one in almost every street, for the Jews come from many different cities and towns in the old country, and the New York representatives of every little place in Russia must have their congregations here. Consequently, the congregations are for the most part small, poor and unimportant. Few can pay the rabbi more than three or four dollars a week, and often instead of having a regular salary he is reduced to occasional fees for his services at weddings, births, and holy festivals generally.[44]

All the factors we have mentioned will be of significance when we consider the case of the development of the Jewish community of Montreal. In 1871, the first Dominion of Canada census counted only 409 Jews in Montreal. In 1901, with the mass Eastern European Jewish migration to Canada already established, there were practically 7,000 Jews in the city. In the next thirty years, the Jewish population went from 7,000 to 58,000. In the next thirty years, from 1931 to 1961, Jewish Montreal increased from 58,000 to 102,000. The major increase in Jewish population in Montreal, therefore, began in the latter part of the nineteenth century. From 400 to 7,000 is a quantum leap. From 7,000 to 58,000 is no less a quantum leap. What this means is that Montreal at the beginning of this immigration was a Jewish community that, although it was the largest by far in the Dominion of Canada, was by any standard quite miniscule. It means as well that practically all the population increase was accounted for by the Eastern European immigrants and their children. Thus, by 1931, the average Jew in Montreal was either foreign-born or the child of foreign-born parents and was either Yiddish-speaking or the child of parents whose mother-tongue was Yiddish.[45] The older, more acculturated Jewish community of Montreal was certainly not eliminated. It undoubtedly retained an important communal influence. However, its influence was much less proportionately than that of the established, acculturated Jewish communities of New York and Chicago, where, even prior to this mass migration, the Jewish community numbered in the tens of thousands.[46]

Montreal at the beginning of the era of Eastern European Jewish migration was a city of three synagogues. One of them was founded in 1768: Shearith Israel, the Spanish and Portuguese Congregation. It was formally Orthodox in its service, which was in the Sephardic tradition, though, at this point, there were very few true Sephardim in the congregation. Most of the members were of Ashkenazi descent who, for reasons of social prestige and other factors, wished to be affiliated with the oldest congregation in Montreal and in Canada.[47] Until 1846, Shearith Israel was the only synagogue in Montreal. In that year, a congregation was formed calling itself the Congregation of English, German, and Polish Jews. It was ultimately named Shaar Hashomayim.[48] The name of this congregation tells us some important things. The congregation, first of all, defined itself as "English." This indicates something significant about the nature of Jewish immigration to Canada at that date. Prior to the 1880s, most of the Jewish immigrants to Canada did not arrive there directly from continental Europe; they were rather funnelled through England. They thus liked to consider themselves "English" Jews, however short their stay in the mother country. Whatever their ultimate origins, they also wished to assert their connection with England in a Canada that was still very closely tied with the mother country well into the twentieth century.

In 1882, Temple Emanu-El was founded. Interestingly enough, this Reform congregation was founded by Jews coming to Montreal from the United States where, by the 1870s, Reform Judaism had become the dominant Jewish religious expression. Though it represented a religious interpretation of Judaism that seemed quite foreign to them, the rabbis we will be discussing would develop an interesting, and by no means completely hostile, relationship with Temple Emanu-El.[49]

When the Eastern European Jews began arriving in Montreal en masse, they thus saw two "orthodox" synagogues and one Reform temple. In the two congregations with an Orthodox ritual, both had retained the ritual but had combined it with a genteel, acculturated ambience that was entirely beyond the experience of the Eastern European Jews, who, as early as 1882,[50] had began to set up their own religious institutions. Prominent among them was B'nai Jacob (1886), which inherited Shaar Hashomayim's old building. There were tensions involved in this new founding of congregations by the Eastern European Jews. Some people in the established congregations wanted to know why it was that the immigrant Jews did not join the older synagogues and put obstacles in their way.[51] However, it was clear to most that the cultural and economic gap between the members of the different communities was too great to be bridged. Moreover, the rabbis of these established congregations did not particularly wish to make room for other rabbis who may have had superior Talmudic learning, but whose general cultural attainment would have been deemed by them to be inferior.

How were these newly founded immigrant synagogues going to find their spiritual leadership? The short answer is from Eastern Europe, first and foremost from Lithuania. The "Godfather" of the Eastern European immigrant rabbinate in North America was Rabbi Isaac Elchanan

Spector, one of the most prominent Lithuanian rabbis of his generation.[52] If one examines the biographies of the earliest Eastern European rabbis of North America, one will find that a very large proportion of these men were his direct students and received their *semikha* [rabbinic ordination] from him.[53] It is not happenstance that when Eastern European immigrant rabbis founded a yeshiva in New York, they named it the Isaac Elchanan Theological Seminary, which eventually became the cornerstone of Yeshiva University.[54]

The rabbis who came to North America in the early decades of the Eastern European immigration were of two sorts. First of all, there were rabbis in financial trouble, unable to make ends meet at home. In the Eastern European milieu, being a rabbi was often not a particularly advantageous position. Rabbis in general were not well paid, even in some of the larger cities. In smaller places, especially, rabbis often got along in a decidedly hand-to-mouth way. Thus in many a community the rabbi's wife was customarily given a monopoly for the sale of such things as candles and yeast. There were also stipulated times of year, such as Purim, when the rabbi was given gifts by those members of his community who could afford to do so. That is why the rabbinate was most often not the first career path chosen by young men. Indeed, one could speak of a stereotypical rabbinical biography. A young man showed prowess in Torah study at an early age. After marriage, he continued studying Torah for a time. Then he started a business and *failed* at that business. That is the point at which he became a rabbi.[55]

A famous example of the rabbi who could not make it financially at home is Rabbi Jacob Joseph of Vilna, whom we have already met. He came to New York in the 1880s, a time when traditional Judaism in that city was said by its critics to be in almost complete disarray.[56] The reason that Rabbi Joseph, who had an honoured position in Vilna, came to such a place at all was that he was heavily in debt and the position promised him in New York would allow him to get out of debt. He lived to regret his decision.[57]

Those rabbis who did not come because they were heavily in debt tended to be young, inexperienced, and adventurous. It is particularly important for us to note the relative youth of many of the rabbis we will meet in this book because, if the rabbis of the generation I am speaking of are remembered at all, it is as venerable, elderly men with white beards. They are not remembered in their vigorous twenties, thirties, and forties.

How can we understand the mostly young rabbis who came to North America in this era and the problems they faced? Perhaps the best way to begin to understand their situation is to pose the question: Who is a rabbi? The answer to this question is both simple and complicated. The simple definition of an Orthodox rabbi is a man who has received rabbinic ordination [*semikha*]. What does "ordination" mean, however? To begin answering that question one has to contend with the complicated history of rabbinical ordination.[58] In the classical rabbinic literature – the Mishna and Gemara – *semikha* is the according of an authority that was understood as having begun with Moses at Sinai and continued down the generations, transmitted by masters to disciples, as detailed in the opening chapter of the Mishnaic tractate *Avot*. This particular *semikha*, however, was interrupted during the Roman persecution of Judaism in the second century. In the absence of this true *semikha*, the spiritual and intellectual leaders of rabbinic Judaism, though they were still called rabbis, found it impossible to establish a solid hierarchy and understood that, in the present day, they did not possess the authority to do such things as levy fines [*kenasot*].[59] There was an interesting attempt in the sixteenth century in Safed to renew the ancient, authoritative form of *semikha*. Among the people who received *semikha* during this attempt was Rabbi Joseph Karo, author of the *Shulḥan 'Arukh*. This experiment was not universally accepted, however. After a great debate, which made its mark on the responsa literature of the time, the attempt was abandoned.[60]

As it was practised among Ashkenazic Jews in the modern era, rabbinical ordination was essentially anarchic, with no universally accepted procedures or standards of competence required of candidates. *Semikha*, essentially, consisted of a piece of paper, signed by someone calling himself a rabbi, attesting to the fact that someone else was worthy to be considered a rabbi. To be more precise, it is a statement by a rabbi stating that a certain person is worthy of adjudicating Jewish law. The usual formula in Hebrew in the ordination document was and is *yoreh yoreh*: "Can he give instruction [in the law]? He can give instruction [in the law]." On a more advanced level, there is the statement *yadin yadin*: "Can he serve as a judge [of rabbinic law]? He can serve as a judge." But, once again, there is no particular authority given to a person merely because of the fact of his having received such a document. The attestation of the ordination document does not even necessarily mean that a person possesses any more Torah learning than others in the community. It fact, particularly in Eastern Europe in the nineteenth century, there were often men in the community who did not possess a *semikha* document and yet were able to vie with the official rabbis in terms of their Torah learning. Indeed, many such Jews, who possessed enormous learning, never bothered to obtain *semikha*. Thus the Hofets Hayym never obtained *semikha* until late in his life, in the 1920s, when he did so for the purpose of obtaining a passport.[61] In North America, on the other hand, the rabbi was not merely likely to be pre-eminent in his congregation in terms of his Torah learning; he was often the only one in the congregation to possess such learning.

To sum up, *semikha* is nothing more or less than the statement of a rabbi that someone else is worthy to be considered a rabbi. That made it problematic. Nineteenth-century Lithuanian rabbi Eliezer Gordon, who made an unsuccessful attempt to institutionalize the Eastern European rabbinate, recognized that "there is great neglect in the granting of rabbinical ordination, and many who are unworthy of ordination are ordained, and this is a stumbling block and an obstacle for the Jews."[62] One of the greatest rabbis to emigrate from Eastern Europe to the United States in this period, Rabbi David Willowsky [Ridbaz], described the situation in this way:

No reliance should be placed on such [ordination] certificates granted in recent years. It was given to any young man who desired it, in order to encourage him to continue his studies ... every young man who studied some *Yoreh Deah* was granted ordination. I have done so myself.[63]

Prominent rabbis were undoubtedly confronted with prospective candidates for *semikha* dozens of times a year. These young men were given tests in halakha in matters of practical, everyday concern, such as admixtures of meat and milk. If the young men gave cogent answers, then the rabbi would write a letter giving *semikha*. Once the man possessing this *semikha* crossed the ocean, however, he soon found that it was not unassailable. Partisans of a given rabbi could indeed boast of the quality of the *semikha* of their rabbi. His opponents, on the other hand, could and would cast aspersions and doubt on such claims. Thus in any conflictual situation between rabbis – and there would be many – there were those who chose to assert that their opponents were in fact not rabbis at all, whatever their credentials said.[64]

This was particularly true, as we will see, when the fight was over who constitutes a "chief rabbi." Who or what is a "chief rabbi"? There is no classical Judaic source for such a position, but in the absence of a generally recognized authority structure, rabbis wishing to be thought of as having a position of leadership often sought to be distinguished by the title "chief rabbi." There is a story that is told of New York in the 1920s, in which a passerby saw a sign proclaiming a certain rabbi Widrevitch as "Chief Rabbi of America." Upon being asked who made him chief rabbi, the rabbi is supposed to have replied, "The sign painter." Sometimes it was also the printer who printed the letterhead who could confer the title of chief rabbi. In the face of an authority vacuum, authority could be and was manufactured.

In such a chaotic situation, what was to be done? How could the Eastern European immigrant rabbinate react to the radically new conditions in which it found itself? Given that the rabbinate was theoretically a monopoly, how did it react to the rules of laissez-faire capitalism that prevailed in North America? As an anonymous rabbi commented in 1902, "The rabbinate has become a business. This one sells a *heter* [permissive ruling] while the other peddles an *issur* [prohibition]."[65] One major answer to this problem was an attempt to organize. The previously mentioned Agudath ha-Rabbonim was a union formed by many of the immigrant Orthodox rabbis in North America in order to attempt to create order out of this chaos. The group's leadership asserted, to no avail, that only the members of their organization were authentic rabbis and that all other claimants, particularly those who claimed to have done their rabbinical studies in America, were somehow not up to their standard. They also attempted, unsuccessfully, to gain control of the Rabbi Isaac Elchanan Theological Seminary, the main Orthodox institution in America preparing students for the Orthodox rabbinate.[66] They were nonetheless never able to make good their desire to restrict and control *semikha*, which remained a somewhat ambiguous term throughout our period.

Agudath ha-Rabbonim was also never able to arrive at a satisfactory answer to the major issue of territoriality in the North American rabbinate. Traditionally, in Europe, a rabbi was called *"mara de-atra"* – literally "the master of a place," a piece of geographical territory, such as a city or town, as opposed to a congregational building. European rabbis coming to America tried very hard to retain this territorial component of the rabbinate. Thus the Agudath ha-Rabbonim in its constitution mandated that a member coming to a city where a member was already present had to prove that there was no encroachment on the colleague before he could take up his rabbinate in that city.[67] The attempt to restrict rabbinical territoriality was an abject failure and led to numerous rabbinical conflicts over who was the rabbi of what city, district, or slaughterhouse.

A second major issue these rabbis had to face was *kashrut*. When is meat kosher and when is it not? Why is meat kosher for some rabbis and not in the opinion of others? Though in its broad parameters the rules of what made foods kosher or not were understood and agreed upon, there remained nonetheless many legal "grey areas" that required interpretation and in which rabbis often differed. Because of the lack of agreed-upon lines of rabbinic authority, disputes all too often wound up publicized in the press and decided in secular courts.[68] Often it seemed that *kashrut* in North America was the prisoner of "lower standards ... and cheaper prices," while supervision of major slaughterhouses seemed to be the prime prize to be captured in numerous kosher meat wars.[69]

A final challenge to the rabbis of whom we will be speaking in this book was Jewish education, in which area there were also basic and important changes taking place in the period we are investigating. There was a growing realization among all North American Jews – Orthodox or not – that Eastern European methods of Jewish education could work only if one had seventy hours per week to try to teach children, which was the case in the nineteenth-century Eastern European *ḥeder*.[70] If one only has ten or twelve hours a week, or even less, to teach a child the rudiments of Judaic knowledge, then one needs to strategize pedagogically. This means that all too often early attempts to transplant the Eastern European *ḥeder* to North America proved to be a failure.[71] Thus, there was a change in Jewish educational thinking in North America, which resulted in the concept of the Talmud Torah, a "modern" school designed to teach Torah to North American Jewish children in the hours after public school. Among the major issues that had to be resolved was the language of instruction in the Talmud Torah. Were the texts to be studied to be read in Hebrew and then translated into Yiddish, as had been the case in Europe? Was English to have a role, or was Hebrew alone [*ivrit be-ivrit*] to predominate in the classes? At the beginning of the twentieth century, all of these questions and more faced the Eastern European immigrant rabbinate.

    The rabbis we will be dealing with in this book all possessed knowledge of the Torah in a society that did not particularly value that knowledge in the way traditional Jewish societies had done. They needed to make their way in a society which, it seemed, had repudiated nearly all that they stood for. It was a society that seemed to need them only insofar as they could be called upon to declare food to be kosher. Even then, there always seemed to be another rabbi ready to proclaim the opposite conclusion. How, then, did these immigrant, Eastern European Orthodox rabbis attempt to build a community in these adverse circumstances? The chapters of this book, which examines the rabbinate of Montreal at the beginning of the twentieth century, will provide approaches to the answers to these questions.

· 2 ·

"Pa Is a Mussolini":
A Portrait of Rabbi Hirsh Cohen

[W]ith his patriarchal appearance, with his silver-white beard which extends to the belt and with the eyes which peer deep into the soul of each person, [Rabbi Cohen] makes a strong impression on everyone who comes into contact with him. (1930)[1]

Rabbi Hirsh Cohen will play an important role in most of the chapters of this book. Telling the story of Montreal's Eastern European Orthodox rabbinate would be inconceivable without accounting for the presence and personality of Rabbi Cohen; without detailing who he was and what he stood for. Other rabbis came and went, but Rabbi Cohen remained a fixture in the leadership of the Montreal rabbinate from the beginning of the twentieth century until the time, in the late 1940s, when he suffered a debilitating stroke and became unable to fulfill his duties.[2] He was born in Budwicz, near Vilkomir in Russian Poland, in the early 1860s, and attended the yeshiva of Volozhin.[3] In Volozhin, like many if not most of his fellow students, he studied much more than Talmud. Like many intellectually aware Russian Jews, he was reaching out to other areas of knowledge. He studied non-Jewish languages,[4] probably including Russian, and was exposed to modern Hebrew and Yiddish literature, like his younger contemporary and fellow alumnus of Volozhin, Chaim Nahman Bialik. Thus the Montreal Yiddish writer, J. I. Segal, in his obituary of Rabbi Cohen, remarked that Rabbi Cohen often discussed Yiddish literature with him. Segal wrote that he was impressed by Cohen's knowledge of that literature, especially the works of Mendele Mokher Seforim.[5]

Rabbi Cohen came to Canada, in a classic case of chain migration, in the wake of his elder brothers, Lazarus and Fishel Cohen, in 1889[6] or 1890.[7] Lazarus Cohen, in particular, was an important figure in the Montreal community. He had achieved great wealth in business and was a leader and a pillar of traditionalist Congregation Shaar Hashomayim. Hirsh first attempted to become a grocer in Montreal but, despite his older brothers' mercantile connections, he was unsuccessful. For a time, he lived in Chicago, learning the art and the politics of the kosher meat industry in the very place that his teacher in Europe, Rabbi David Wilowsky, the "Slutzker Rov," would attempt to establish himself as chief rabbi.[8] He returned to Montreal by about 1896 or 1897 and commenced a career of religious leadership. He would eventually be proclaimed and recognized by many people as the "chief rabbi" of Montreal, and even, by some, as the "chief rabbi of Canada,"[9] though neither of those offices existed in any official way. We will see how these positions became his. But until 1901, it is important to note that we do not hear of him as a rabbi. He practised as a *shohet* [kosher slaughterer] for some time.[10] We also know that from 1896 to 1897 he taught Talmud on a daily basis and preached on Sabbaths and holidays to a group[11] which eventually, in 1902, coalesced as Congregation Chevra Shas.[12] Nonetheless, all these activities do not mean that Rabbi Cohen had as yet achieved a generally recognized rabbinical position in Montreal from which he made his main living. In fact, during these years, Cohen lived in the shadow of a prominent Eastern European immigrant rabbi who, if he had remained in Montreal for his entire career, might well have become known as its "chief rabbi."

This rabbi's name was Aaron Mordecai Ashinsky.[13] He was born in 1866[14] in Poland and was thus slightly younger than Cohen. He received his rabbinical ordination [*semikha*] at age nineteen. A year later, in 1886, he came to America where he became rabbi of an Eastern European congregation in Syracuse, New York. In 1889 a consortium of immigrant synagogues in Detroit invited him to be their rabbi, and he moved there. He was, however, dissatisfied with his rabbinical position and considered a career change. One of the signs of his dissatisfaction is that he enrolled in a medical school in Detroit.[15] During this time, he was becoming fluent in English and more used to the ways of North America. The major issue which caused him to leave Detroit was the opposition there to his plan to modernize Jewish education by founding a modern Talmud Torah to replace the traditional *heder*.

From Detroit, Ashinsky was invited to came to Montreal to be the rabbi of Congregation Bnai Jacob, then the most prominent Eastern European congregation in Montreal, in 1896.[16] It is likely that one of the factors leading Rabbi Ashinsky to accept this offer and to come to Montreal was his new congregation's support for the founding of an up-to-date Talmud Torah there. Thus as soon as he came to Montreal, Rabbi Ashinsky founded Montreal's Talmud Torah and served as its first director, giving his time and labour gratis.[17] He was also a committed Zionist, serving as one of the organizers of the Canadian Zionist Federation,[18] as well as being a founder of the *Mizrahi* [religious Zionist] movement in Canada.

All of these activities brought Rabbi Ashinsky's name before the public, and he began to get a wider recognition of his position as the pre-eminent Eastern European rabbi of Montreal beyond the confines of his synagogue. Thus in 1899 he was appointed Jewish chaplain for the provincial prison. While the office itself was fairly minor, it was symbolically important because the position of prison chaplain for the Dominion prison system had been held by Rabbi Bernard Kaplan of the Shaar Hashomayim Congregation.[19] Thus Ashinsky's appointment could be read as a recognition of the growing presence of Eastern European Jews in the Montreal community. It seems likely that someone in the Montreal Jewish "establishment" had interceded on his behalf with the authorities. It is further likely that this post was deemed appropriate for an Eastern European rabbi on the grounds that most of the Jewish prisoners in his care were likely to have been recent Eastern European immigrants.[20]

Other signs of Ashinsky's growing prominence included demands that he speak publicly outside of Montreal. Thus in 1900, during the Boer War, he preached in Winnipeg on the greatness and supremacy of the British Empire.[21] In June 1901, he spoke in Ottawa in both English and Yiddish.[22] The clearest sign of Ashinsky's having "made it" as the representative Eastern European rabbi in Montreal came in 1901 through the role he played at the cornerstone laying of the new building of the Baron de Hirsch Institute, a very important symbolic event in the life of the Jewish community of Montreal as a whole. At that ceremony, he appeared along with Rabbis Meldola de Sola of Shearith Israel, Bernard Kaplan of Shaar

Hashomayim, and Elias Friedlaender of Temple Emanu-El. He recited an original Hebrew prayer he had composed for the occasion.[23] His participation in this ceremony meant, in effect, that the Montreal Jewish community establishment had declared that there were now four "official" rabbis in Montreal, and that Rabbi Ashinsky was one of their number. However, despite all these promising developments, Rabbi Ashinsky left for another congregation in Pittsburgh in 1901. Why did he quit Montreal at this time? A contemporary observer, Nachman Heller, had observed some of Rabbi Ashinsky's troubles, which may have contributed to his leaving:

Ashinsky ... is officiating as minister of a small congregation in Montreal, in whose interests he has got to work day and night, never having a chance to get his meals on time, never being able to go to sleep at the proper hour, for a salary that is not sufficient to cover his expenditures.[24]

In leaving, Rabbi Ashinsky left a vacuum in the rabbinical leadership of the immigrant Jewish community that Hirsh Cohen would ultimately fill.

In 1901, Rabbi Cohen succeeded Rabbi Ashinsky as the superintendent of the Montreal Talmud Torah. This may at least be partially explained by the fact that Cohen's brother, Lazarus, was a major supporter of the school who largely financed the institution's chronic deficit.[25] In 1904, he was appointed chaplain of the Montreal jail, again replacing Ashinsky. Montreal's English-language Jewish community newspaper, the *Jewish Times*, approvingly commented on his appointment:

Rabbi Cohen is eminently qualified for the office as he is a thorough Hebrew scholar, speaks several languages, and has an intimate knowledge of the circumstances in which his co-religionists are placed, in this and other countries.[26]

In this case, we have Cohen's personal reaction to this event in a letter to his family:

An important [piece] of good news. I have at last received my long-awaited government position as chaplain for the Montreal jail with a monthly salary of $25.00. This means more than the few dollars.[27]

Indeed the appointment gave Rabbi Cohen a key symbolic victory though he did not yet have a clear field before him to become the recognized preeminent Eastern European rabbi in Montreal. A possible rival for this position was Rabbi Ashinsky's successor as rabbi of Bnai Jacob, Rabbi Solomon Beir Sprince.[28] Rabbi Sprince was, however, new to North America and, as the *Jewish Times* commented, "labor[ed] under the disadvantage of not speaking English."[29] Rabbi Sprince had succeeded to one of Rabbi Ashinsky's key positions, that of supervisor of kosher slaughtering in Montreal. There is some evidence of Sprince and Cohen cooperating in an appeal for the Jews of Jerusalem who were stricken with the cholera.[30] However, by 1905, Rabbi Cohen had succeeded in supplanting Rabbi Sprince in the position of *kashrut* supervision. As Rabbi Cohen stated in a letter:

Also the Butcher's Association decided that the five dollars weekly that Rabbi Sprince had taken for the slaughtering, which they added to voluntarily, will belong to me. There is a chance that soon I will have entire [control] of the slaughterhouse.[31]

In 1906, a threat to Rabbi Cohen's hard-earned supremacy at the Talmud Torah, the jail and the slaughterhouse surfaced: reports spread that Rabbi Ashinsky was coming back to Montreal, having been invited to be the "chief rabbi" of a consortium of Eastern European congregations. We do not know directly whether Rabbi Cohen felt apprehensive about this development. We do know, however, that the Montreal Jewish establishment had reservations concerning Rabbi Ashinsky's return. The *Jewish Times*, which may be understood to voice the opinions of the community's elite, reacted coolly to the news, to say the least. It stated: "He [Ashinsky] will not be chief rabbi of Montreal, as the secular press has erroneously stated, there being no such official." The article made the point that the congregations Ashinsky was to head were "of recent growth," as opposed to the older congregations: Shaar Hashomayim, Shearith Israel, Temple Emanu-El, Beth Israel and Beth David,[32] the latter two having Rabbi Hirsh Cohen as their spiritual leader. It is noteworthy in this connection to remark that Bnai Jacob, Rabbi Ashinsky's old congregation, which, as we have seen, had pretensions to be the "flagship" Eastern European congregation in

Montreal, is not mentioned. The *Jewish Times* article continued: "It would be quite wrong to give him such a title ... as it is not a fact in the first place, and to make such a statement would be an injustice to the other elder rabbis of the city."[33]

Rabbi Ashinsky did not come in the end. In later years, he related to another ex-Montrealer, Dr. A. Roback, that he had met opposition from a certain party and was "unwilling to provoke dissension or unpleasantness in the community."[34] Whatever the reason for Ashinsky's not coming, this did not end Rabbi Cohen's troubles. In Ashinsky's place, the consortium of synagogues, calling itself the "United Orthodox Congregations," chose as its head Rabbi Simon Glazer, then residing in Toledo, Ohio.[35] Rabbi Glazer came to Montreal in 1907. His claim to leadership of the Montreal Jewish community was proclaimed in an article that appeared in the *Montreal Star* of August 28, 1907. It was immediately contradicted by Montreal's Jewish "establishment." Glazer's opposition also included, importantly, Hirsh Wolofsky, publisher of Montreal's newly founded Yiddish daily, the *Keneder Odler*, who would remain one of Rabbi Cohen's primary allies throughout his career.[36] The opposition's candidate for the post of Eastern European rabbi of record was Rabbi Cohen, who, along with establishment and press backing, had the rabbinic credentials to fill the job.[37] Thus would begin a ten-year struggle for leadership of the Eastern European rabbinate in Montreal between Rabbis Cohen and Glazer, and a further struggle between Rabbi Cohen and Rabbi Glazer's successor as rabbi of the consortium, Rabbi Yudel Rosenberg.[38]

A signal event in Cohen's campaign for acceptance came in 1907, when he wrote:

On *shabbat ha-gadol* I spoke in the great Bnai Jacob Shul which was reckoned among my opponents for the past ten years since Ashinsky was their rabbi. In the end they chose to invite me.[39]

He became head of the Montreal Board of Kashruth in 1908,[40] which was set up to oppose Rabbi Glazer's efforts in that field, and in the same year he was elected rabbi of the Adath Yeshurun Congregation, though not without a dispute.[41] In the end, as we will see in the following chapters, Rabbi Cohen persevered and by the 1920s became widely recognized by Montreal Jewry as its "chief rabbi," a post he filled until his death, though he spent the last years of his life cared for by his daughter and son-in-law in Mt. Vernon, New York, where he died in 1950.⁴² In the subsequent chapters of this book, the main protagonist may indeed be one of Cohen's colleagues or rivals, but Rabbi Cohen will remain a constant presence as that rabbi's ally or enemy. That importance makes an evaluation of his character imperative.

Often, historians attempting to evaluate such a person's life and works are limited to "public" documents, such as newspaper accounts, which deal with public actions and statements.⁴³ In this manner we are able, for example, to follow Rabbi Cohen's fight for separate Jewish schools in Montreal in the 1920s.⁴⁴ In Rabbi Cohen's case, however, we are fortunate to be able to go beyond his public face. That is because a cache consisting of literally hundreds of letters from Rabbi Cohen to his son-in-law and daughter from 1904 to 1940 was donated to the Canadian Jewish Congress National Archives in 1997. This collection of personal letters gives an intimate portrait of Rabbi Cohen the person behind the facade of office that was his public persona.

Rabbi Cohen was largely known for his public speaking,⁴⁵ which was often characterized by a sharp and biting wit. However, in private he was often unable express his inner feelings openly, other than in these letters. As he himself admitted, this affected his family life. He stated in a letter of 1911:

I have the defect [*hissaron*] that I do not outwardly demonstrate to the children the love I feel for them inside. It is true that the children suffer because of it. It is also true, however, that I suffer more from it than they do.⁴⁶

He felt that he had no one to talk to. Thus he continued:

You are the only ones to whom I can express myself, for in truth I live, like the English say, a double life.

A major reason for this seeming emotional frigidity stemmed from the year 1906, in which personal tragedy struck. In that year his beloved wife, Sarah Kreindel, died from a lingering illness, as well as, in fairly quick succession, three of his seven children. He only remarried in 1914.⁴⁷ In 1907, after his wife's death, he expressed his feelings in this way:

Regarding myself, as you know I am very busy from early morning until late at night. However, this is the main thing, my spirit is completely broken. As long as I am with people, [I am all right] but when I am alone....

I sit in an office with three large rooms with all the improvements which would be a bargain for a lawyer or a doctor – twenty-five dollars a month. I see, as it appears how the world glows coming in, that one should lie down in a dark basement and be sorrowful.... For my real sickness there is no cure[48]

One reason Rabbi Cohen was able to continue under such emotional pressure is that he was always, as he put it, "busy." As he stated in 1933:

... rabbis, slaughterers, emissaries, widows, divorcees, agunot ... nudniks of all sorts, local and national troubles, general and specific, family and strangers keep me busy, and that is also for the good.[49]

On the same subject he wrote in 1910:

Why haven't you written for such a long time? Why are you so busy? Your lulavim have not been lost. You don't have to make a sukkah. You have no sermons to deliver; no weddings to officiate; ... no divorces ... no halakhic questions to answer; no slaughterers to examine; no butchers to warn; no poor people to supply; no Talmud Torah to build; no agunot to permit; no articles to write; no prisons to travel to; no hospitals to visit; no din torahs to preside over; no hard luck stories to hear; no marital harmony to remake ... no mourners to comfort; no sick to visit; no dreams to interpret; no advice to give; no certificates to write; no petitions to sign; no meetings to address; no positions of *sandek* to accept; no correspondence with the entire world; no difficult *meharshos*[50] to elucidate ... no six glasses of tea a day to drink; no Glazer's mockery and accusations to swallow; no judges to see; no Governor General to meet; no school question to settle; no missionaries to answer; no immigrants to facilitate; no Sunday Laws to fight; no immigration officers to write; no classes to lead; no charitable emissaries to allow to leave pushkes; no money to send to yeshivas; no bills to pay; no checks to write ... and more and more.[51]

Rabbi Cohen's house was the scene of many meetings, in which his personality was dominant. He recalled his daughter's comment on one of these meetings in 1932: "They come for meetings in the house. Ania says to Leizer, 'Pa is a Mussolini.' I agree but [I dominate] without soldiers, only with intelligence [sekhel]."[52]

As far as he was concerned, his colleagues were often less than helpful to him in these tasks. As he stated in 1913:

Especially in the last years when the Jewish community has increased, simply everything is upon me because my colleagues are either idlers [batlanim] or half or completely "German."[53]

Modern communications had established new ways in which Rabbi Cohen could communicate with those who needed his halakhic advice, which happened especially often in the period before Passover, which he defined as his "busy season"[54]: "My telephone is already a complete *Yoreh De'ah* with 'meat and milk' and mourning and even a portion of the *hoshen mishpat*."[55]

In this pre-Passover "busy season," he was also responsible for the distribution of a great deal of charity for the poor. In a letter from the Depression year of 1931, he particularly noted that he had to worry about the newly impoverished [*yordim*] who had nothing for Passover.[56]

Preparing sermons and other addresses to be delivered at synagogues and other venues was a large part of Rabbi Cohen's public duties. Beyond being delivered orally, they were often published in the pages of the *Keneder Odler*. Thus, though he never wrote a book, his words were often in print.

He spoke at a number of different synagogues. On Rosh ha-Shana of 1904, he stated: "On the second day of Rosh ha-Shana I spoke twice. Once before the shofar blowing in the Baron de Hirsch Institute for 1,500 persons. The second time in my shul."[57]

In another, year, prior to 1918, he spoke on the High Holidays at Beth David, the Milton Street Synagogue and at Beth Israel on Dorchester Street.

In a letter of 1906, he describes his sermon preparation:

Normally when I need to speak in a synagogue, I stay up the night before for between three and four hours and compose my speech ... and [though] I am careful not to disturb [my wife's] sleep, she usually wakes and hearing my footsteps she goes in to my room ... when I am finished we drink tea together.[58]

On another occasion, he mentioned that:

I am washing my dishes and in the same time I prepare speeches for a banquet for a silver wedding [anniversary].[59]

Rabbi Cohen was much in demand as a speaker and rabbi in communities outside of Montreal. He recalled that, in 1904, he was called to go to Kingston, Ontario, to officiate at a marriage, "and they kept me there to eulogize Herzl."[60] He travelled as well to such places as Sherbrooke, Ottawa, and Toronto, in which city he testified that he spoke at five different places.[61] He became known throughout Canada, and was asked by the Jews of Alberta in 1906 to recommend someone who could be their rabbi, teacher and *shoḥet*.[62]

One item of importance that emerges from Cohen's letters is the prominence of the selling of the "four species" [*arba' minim*] for Orthodox rabbis of this era. This trade, which satisfied the ritual needs of Jews during the sukkot festival, was both an important seasonal source of income for the rabbi as well as a service to the community. It came, as we can see, with a number of headaches. As he wrote in 1907:

My *etrogim* were sent the day after *yom kippur* and I received them Friday. Time has grown very short and there is much work. However, praised be God, all is sold.[63]

He dealt with a Mr. Weinstock in New York as far back as 1905:

Already today I have telegraphed Mr. Weinstock, 32 Canal Street and have received no answer. Probably they will be here tomorrow morning.[64]

Things did not always go as well. As he wrote the very next year:

At 30 Canal Street [you will find] Boruch Weinstock, agent for *etrogim* of the Land of Israel. I bought from him and paid for fifty sets of etrogim, lulavim and hadassim and he only sent me forty sets which I received yesterday. Today I received a letter from him [stating that] because there are few etrogim there he has not sent me all [the shipment]. I need the ten sets ... moreover this means thirty dollars profit.... The same Weinstock writes me that he has sent me another 30 lulavim and hadassim c.o.d. which I did not order and do not need if he cannot send any etrogim with them.... I am writing to him that he should send me my ten sets or ten etrogim and he should make the lulavim free and if I will be able to sell the extras I will pay him for them and if he will send me twenty etrogim for free I will take his lulavim. I ask that he telegraph me what he will do. It is possible that he will go back [on the bargain] and want more money. And hold on to the money for the fifty ... and do not forget that on the lulavim is a c.o.d. According to my purchase you have for me something more than a dollar a set. However you can give him up to $1.75 if he will send good merchandise.[65]

Another possible hazard of the etrog business is detailed in a letter of 1925:

I have had no trouble with the customs officer with my etrogim. I showed him an etrog and said that in all the bundles is the same. It would appear that my white beard is a passport and guarantee that what I say is the truth.[66]

The Montreal Talmud Torah, as we have seen, was close to Rabbi Cohen's heart. The following letter, which he wrote in 1906, testifies to his concern for that institution:

I need for my Talmud Torah a good teacher, that means a pedagogue who has experience in conducting a school and is able to translate Hebrew into English. Then also he should be an honorable man with an Orthodox appearance. I am even authorized to offer up to $900 as long as he will be the right man.[67]

It is noteworthy here that Rabbi Cohen thought of English, and not Yiddish, as the language to be used in school. He also felt that English could be used in place of Yiddish in synagogue sermons. Thus he stated in 1937:

When I mention speeches in English, I do not mean that [speaking] in English is actually improper [*posul*], only that [the sermon] which is [delivered] in English should be effective. It is a mistake if it is not rich in contents.[68]

He himself could speak English and was able to read books in that language, as demonstrated by his comments, in a letter of 1924, reviewing Maurice Samuel's book, *You Gentiles*.[69] Thus he was able to keep up a good relationship with his brother's synagogue, Shaar ha-Shomayim, which he called *"di daytshe shul,"*[70] and with its spiritual leader, Rabbi Abramowitz.[71]

On the other hand, he was vehemently opposed to changes in synagogue architecture, which seemed to him to portend even more radical change:

> That which is occurring in your synagogue: removing the *bimah*, reversing [the stance of] the cantor with his face to the congregation, [installing] an organ, reminds me of the *Gemara, Shabbat* 105b: "Such is the work of the evil inclination. Today it tells you do thus and tomorrow it says to you do thus until it tells you serve idolatry and you go and do it."
>
> Now when the great majority of the Jewish people live by the *shevarim teruah* [broken notes of the shofar], and a small minority by "blow the great shofar for our freedom," there are also to be found fools and idlers who find time and energy to make a synagogue more like a church [*tifla*] ... the Mount Vernon fools are not the only ones. Such crazies [*meturofim*] are to be found everywhere. If in Judaism one cannot find means to attract people to synagogue other than through female organists and choir members, we are not doing well.[72]

It is thus reasonable to surmise that he was opposed to reform in Judaism. Indeed he used his most pointed satirical barbs, reminiscent of the satire of Mendele Mokher Seforim, when writing of the noted Reform rabbi and Zionist leader, Stephen Wise, in 1925:

> You say that Dr. [Stephen] Wise is a great Jew for the gentiles. I would add that, among them, he is also a great rabbi. As the author of the [Passover] Haggada states:
>> *va-yeḥi* and he was
>> *sham* there, in America
>> *le-goy* for the gentiles
>> *gadol* a great one
>> *aẓum* a strong one – not from fasting
>> *ve-rav* and a rabbi, may the Merciful One save us.[73]

As a matter of course, Rabbi Cohen was in contact with elements within the Jewish community whose level of religious observance was not something he could countenance. He often used imaginative ways to try to influence such people and institutions. Once, when approached for a contribution by the Jewish People's Library, an institution run by "secular" Yiddishists, he gave the Library a cheque for ten dollars, a substantial sum at the time, along with these words:

If your organization will observe the Sabbath, you can keep my donation. If you don't, send me back the check.[74]

Similarly, when the Zionist leader Chaim Weizmann came to Montreal, Cohen refused to attend a banquet in his honour because of his principle "not to go in a gentile hotel where there is no Jewish kitchen." However, he did speak on behalf of Weizmann's cause that Sabbath in his synagogue, and later addressed a mass meeting at the Monument Nationale on behalf of the Keren ha-Yessod.[75]

The Great Depression of the 1930s made a tremendous impact on Rabbi Cohen's life as the needs of the community he headed increased markedly. He commented in a letter of 1931:

As is known the economic situation is very tight and all things are upon me.... Can I create work, give jobs to teachers, slaughterers, inspectors, janitors, lobby the [Jewish] Federation that they should give enough, plead with landlords ... and anything else? One must give to those who do not have anything for the day. Looking at my expenditures last month I found I gave 75 percent away and had 25 percent for myself. Running away [from the poor] is not right.[76]

As Rabbi Cohen pursued his career in the Montreal immigrant Orthodox community, he paid close attention to public issues which impacted on religion, particularly in its relationship with science. Thus, in the mid-1920s, he commented on the Scopes "Monkey Trial":

[Regarding] the Darrow-Bryan dispute, as long as it is in theory, one can agree [with whatever position] one thinks [right] and still remain a believer in the divinity of the Bible. It is the power of the Torah that all theories can be included. When Alexander Von Humboldt and other natural scientists discovered that in the earth there are rock formations which were much much older than our Torah's chronology [allows for], the sages of the Torah were not shocked, and they realized that this way of thinking was long known to the sages of the Talmud and the kabbalists ... that our present world is not the first....[77] However, as I said, this is only in theory. Practically, I am a fundamentalist.... Our great rabbi, Maimonides, philosophized in his *Guide of the Perplexed* in many matters theoretically. But when in his *Yad ha-Hazaka*[78] he dealt with practical things, he was altogether different.[79]

Rabbi Hirsh Cohen, as we have seen, was a complex, multifaceted personality. He would need every bit of his domineering personality, his sharp wit, his prodigious eloquence, and his unceasing efforts to confront the rabbinical challengers who would vie with him for Montreal's "chief rabbinate."

· 3 ·

Rabbi Simon Glazer:
A Rival for the Chief Rabbinate

Should a buzzing noise reach your ear [speaking] against me, know that it is the voice of a snake or snakes, and that it possesses not a grain of truth.... For thirty years I have engaged in holy work in this country, and despite all the troubles, I am at my post. – Rabbi Simon Glazer (1927)[1]

In this chapter, we will be speaking of Rabbi Simon Glazer, a man who wanted to be chief rabbi of Montreal. We will see why he was not allowed to claim the chief rabbinate unopposed.

By 1906, Rabbi Hirsh Cohen had been positioning himself to assume the leadership role among the Eastern European rabbis in Montreal for several years and had come into his own as arguably the most prominent among their number. He was therefore set to claim the mantle of Rabbi Aaron Mordecai Ashinsky, who had left Montreal for a position in Pittsburgh.[2] He had taken over from Rabbi Ashinsky as the head of the Talmud Torah of Montreal. He had also been appointed Jewish chaplain at the Montreal jail. He was, furthermore, poised to be the major rabbi to certify the *kashrut* of meat in Montreal.[3]

However, in 1907, something very important took place in Montreal, and Rabbi Hirsh Cohen's leadership would be sorely and severely challenged by Rabbi Simon Glazer.[4]

What had happened was that a group of Montreal synagogues had decided to come together in a consortium to support a rabbi who would function as their chief rabbi. They needed to do so because no single

Eastern European synagogue in Montreal could afford to pay a rabbi anything remotely resembling a living wage. It was hoped, however, that if a number of congregations got together, then together they would be able to support a rabbi in a decent manner. The first move by the synagogue consortium was to attempt to entice Rabbi Ashinsky back from Pittsburgh. This move would have given the consortium instant credibility within the Montreal Jewish community, given the position that Rabbi Ashinsky had been able to make for himself in Montreal. However, that plan did not come to fruition.

One of the major reasons Rabbi Ashinsky did not come back to Montreal was because his congregation in Pittsburgh was very possessive of him. He tried several times to leave Pittsburgh for another rabbinate. In one of these instances, he had accepted an offer from a congregation in Brooklyn, New York. At that point, his Pittsburgh community took him to a rabbinical court of arbitration [*din Torah*]. The rabbinical arbitrators at this *din Torah* ruled that Rabbi Ashinsky could not legitimately leave his Pittsburgh congregation to go to Brooklyn and had to remain in Pittsburgh. He remained there until the end of his career, greatly honoured by his community.

When the leaders of the Montreal congregational consortium could not get Rabbi Ashinsky, who was both a formidable and familiar figure to Montreal's Eastern European Jews, they continued their search for a rabbi. Eventually they reached an agreement with Rabbi Simon Glazer. Rabbi Glazer was born in Erzwillig, Lithuania, in the Russian Empire on January 21, 1876. At the age of eighteen, in 1896, he left his native land. As you will recall from the discussion in Chapter 1, rabbis did not leave their Eastern European homeland without a reason. His reason was an eminently good one: he left Russia one step ahead of the Russian military draft. In this respect, he was like thousands of other Jewish boys who sought all sorts of means to avoid the threat that several years in the Russian army represented to Jews. When Rabbi Glazer left Russia, he did not go immediately to America. First, he journeyed to the Land of Israel. However, he found it impossible to make a living there, and within a year he found himself arriving in New York City.

In New York, while attempting to chart his course, he happened to meet with the editor of one of the major Yiddish-language newspapers in the city, *Die Yiddishe Gazetten*, which was read largely by Orthodox Jews.

The editor's name was Kasriel Sarasohn. The advice Sarasohn gave Rabbi Glazer changed the course of his life. He advised him not to enter the rabbinate immediately but rather to learn English first. Implementing this advice meant that Glazer would be distinguished from most of the other Eastern European immigrant Orthodox rabbis. The other rabbis tended to be in two categories. In the first category were those rabbis who never learned English well, and who perforce remained within the boundaries of the immigrant community. Within that community, communicating in Yiddish sufficed. Others did master English, to a greater or lesser extent, but most of them never achieved real fluency in it. When these rabbis needed to step out of the immigrant community and make themselves known to a broader constituency, lack of fluent English often hampered them, and the Eastern European Orthodox rabbinate's ability to communicate with North American Jews beyond the immigrant generation was severely limited in many cases.

Rabbi Glazer took Sarasohn's advice to heart. For fully four years, he studied English and other secular subjects intensively, while earning a living as a cantor and Hebrew teacher. Thus by 1902 he had mastered the English language to the extent that he was able to write entire books and to deliver sermons in English. He was able to interact with government officials without need for a translator. As may be imagined, this was a very important plus for him.

His first rabbinical position was in Des Moines, Iowa, starting in 1902, just after his marriage. By 1904, he had published his first book, a history of the Jews of Iowa.[5] One must consider that this book, whatever its deficiencies, was the product of a man who had been in America for less than a decade. Moreover, he also began editing an English-language Jewish newspaper in Iowa, *The Jewish Herald*.

In 1905, he moved from Des Moines to Toledo, Ohio. There as well he began to edit an English-language Jewish newspaper, *The Jewish Compromiser*. In Toledo, he also published, once again in English, *The Sabbath School Guide*,[6] a textbook for Jewish children's Sunday schools. Sunday school may not have been Rabbi Glazer's preference in terms of Jewish education in America, but it did constitute the reality he encountered, and he was determined that if Jewish children would be exposed to Jewish education only in Sunday schools, and in the English language, that they make the best possible use of this educational experience. What he could readily see was that rabbis within the Reform movement had been writing the textbooks for Jewish Sunday schools for some time and that they had a virtual lock on the market. Rabbi Glazer was determined to break into this market and expose Sunday school children to the teachings of Orthodox Judaism. He remained in Toledo until 1907 when he moved to Montreal.[7]

However, he had made a sort of appearance in Montreal previously, in the columns of Montreal's English-language Jewish newspaper, *The Jewish Times*. He had written an apologia for the Talmud entitled "The Talmud: Fundamental Principles," which appeared in October 1903.[8] The publication of this essay, which in most respects is a fairly conventional defence of Talmudic literature against its detractors, apparently played a part in a dispute that took place within the Montreal Jewish community, as elsewhere in North America, over the propriety of teaching Talmud to North American Jewish children. Whereas in Eastern Europe, Talmudic literature constituted the mainstay of any educational experience that passed beyond the elementary level, in North America, the emphasis of the curriculum in the Talmud Torahs, with their relatively limited hours of instruction, was almost wholly on the Hebrew Bible. What about Talmud? In some Talmud Torahs, the subject was given a grudging hour or two a week. On the other hand, there were schools that, on principle, did not want Talmud in their curriculum at all. It had a very bad reputation in many circles as a symbol of the obscurantism and benightedness of Orthodox Judaism, in general, and of Eastern European Orthodox Judaism, in particular. Thus, whereas there existed adult Talmud classes in Montreal, pioneered by Rabbi Hirsh Cohen, and whereas Rabbi Cohen also advocated teaching Talmud in the upper grades of his Talmud Torah,[9] there apparently existed in Montreal an organized group of Jews who objected to Jewish children in Montreal studying Talmud.[10] Thus Rabbi Glazer's article in praise of the Talmud appeared in *The Jewish Times*, not for the sake of refuting anti-Semites objecting to the Talmud, but rather to refute those Montreal Jews who opposed Talmud study on principle.

When Rabbi Glazer came to Montreal in 1907, he became chief rabbi of a consortium known variously as the "United Orthodox Congregations," the "United Orthodox Synagogues," or the "United Synagogue." In this connection it must be remembered that, for Canada, as part of the British Empire, the terms "chief rabbi" and "united synagogue" had a specific resonance. Constitutionally speaking, the Jews of England were under the religious authority of a chief rabbi and a synagogue federation known as the United Synagogue. In England, the chief rabbi was in charge of the supervision of kosher meat. No purveyor of kosher meat in England could do so without a licence from the chief rabbi. No divorces were to be issued without the consent of the chief rabbi and his *Bet Din*.[11]

Thus when Rabbi Glazer came to Montreal and was advertised as being the "chief rabbi" of a "United Synagogue," it must have sounded to many ears as though he was claiming supreme rabbinical power in the community. Moreover, when Rabbi Glazer asserted that he possessed the authority to license kosher butchers or authorize Jewish divorces in Montreal, this was perceived by many Montreal Jews as a threat to the community's status quo.[12] The established Jewish community in Montreal was worried that if this newcomer, who had been living in North America for barely a decade, were to be recognized by non-Jewish individuals and governmental agencies as chief rabbi of Montreal, there would be a number of important implications. Would it mean that Rabbi Meldola de Sola of the Spanish and Portuguese Congregation would be in an inferior position to him? What about Rabbi Abramowitz of Shaar Hashomayim?

Therefore, from the moment that Rabbi Glazer arrived in Montreal, all his initiatives met with strong opposition. For example, he claimed that, as chief rabbi, he had the right to license kosher butchers. What did he do in order to establish this claim? He approached Montreal's City Council with a petition. The Council referred this petition to its Committee on Markets. At the meeting of that Committee, Rabbis Abramowitz and Meldola de Sola appeared and stated that *Mr.*[13] Glazer was not recognized by Montreal Jews as chief rabbi, and therefore should not be granted the authority he desired. Alderman Levy, representing a "Jewish" constituency, suggested that the Committee table the matter and let the rabbis settle things among themselves.[14] This particular confrontation foreshadowed the course events would take in the succeeding decades. Questions of *kashrut* supervision would more than once be placed before the Montreal City Council as well as before the justices of the Quebec Superior Court. Judges and aldermen, possessing absolutely no expertise in the intricacies of rabbinic law, were called upon to decide what were for any non-rabbi extremely arcane issues because the rabbis themselves and their community were unable to arrive at a consensus.

At this point, having failed to carry his point at City Hall, Rabbi Glazer published a list of butcher shops authorized by him as kosher. He advised the public to patronize these stores. Thereupon all the butchers who were not licensed by Rabbi Glazer brought a libel suit against him on the grounds that he had impugned the *kashrut* of the meat they sold to the public.[15] While the details of this particular case are not presently available, it is likely that it is similar to a suit that was brought in Toronto in 1913 by a slaughterer against Rabbis Jacob Gordon and Joseph Weinreb of that city. In that case:

The plaintiff [the slaughterer who claimed defamation on the part of the rabbi] explains and justifies his legal proceedings on the following grounds.

1. He was on examination as aforesaid found and is a shochet of learning and ability and has never been found guilty of or charged with any ignorance either in theory or in practice.
2. That the said rules did not bind the plaintiff as (he alleges) they were made without his privity or consent.
3. No rabbis have as of right any control or authority over shochetim and in particular the defendants had no control or authority over the plaintiff.
4. The defendants had no right to make a close corporation out of the shechita business.
5. The defendants had no certificates or diplomas giving them the right to practice as Rabonim [rabbis] and in any event they are incompetent.[16]

Concerning the libel suit brought by the butchers against Rabbi Glazer, *The Jewish Times* editorialized:

The position he has arrogated to himself as chief rabbi gives him no standing. His pretentions have been repudiated by the older and more well-informed rabbis of the city, and before he gets through with the trouble he has raised he may learn his place.[17]

Another establishment voice was raised against Glazer without, however, naming him specifically. This time the denunciation was not in the local,

Montreal Jewish newspaper, but rather in the *Jewish Chronicle* of London. On July 16, 1909, Maxwell Goldstein wrote:

The newcomers have not only founded congregations of their own, but they have even appointed a foreign Chief Rabbi for themselves. At one time he styled himself the Chief Rabbi of Canada, but now he is recognized by the foreign section as the Chief Rabbi of the United Hebrew Orthodox Congregations. The difficulty with us is how to cooperate with these people. They must not be ignored. The only thing to do is to take them by the hand, and lead them by persuasive methods to recognize their duties to the community.[18]

The Montreal community had taken sides. Rabbi Glazer, his rabbinical court,[19] and his congregations were on one side, the Montreal Jewish establishment and its three major synagogues, plus Rabbi Hirsh Cohen and his followers, were on the other side.

The communal dispute over Rabbi Glazer's claims did not stop with lawsuits. It also got physical. In 1907, Rabbi Glazer was assaulted in his office. This is how it was reported by *The Montreal Herald*, which was sensationalist in its presentation:

Because they assaulted their rabbi, Rev. Simon Glazer, in his study, on 29 Gilbault Street, warrents were sworn out for the arrest of Abraham Neanton, B. Blumenthal and a man named Macaroffsky. Neanton is under arrest and the police are looking for the other two. Macaroffsky is the one who is accused of striking Rabbi Glazer, but the other two tried, the rabbi alleges, to spoil his features. The trouble arose over the refusal of Rabbi Glazer, who has sole control of the Kosher meat business here, to grant a license as "killer"[20] to Wolf Goldsman, a friend of Neanton. Neanton wanted to establish a "kosher" shop, and wanted Rabbi Glazer to allow him to have Goldsman as his killer. The rabbi refused to accede to Neanton's request as his predecessors had refused to grant Goldsman a license, on the ground that Goldsman had a rather unsavory reputation. He said though that he would give Neanton a "kosher" license if he would buy his meats from other duly licensed Kosher butchers. This did not suit Neanton.

Rabbi Glazer heard that on Friday of last week and Monday of this week Goldsman had been acting as killer and sent his steward to Goldsman to tell him that he would have to discontinue and that he would take every measure to advertise Goldsman as an impostor even if he had to effect his arrest. It was this ultimatum, it is alleged, that caused Neanton and Goldsman's sons-in-law to assault the rabbi.

Today to *The Herald* Rabbi Glazer gave the following account of the affair: "The three came to my house and asked me if it was true that I would not grant Goldsman a license. I told them that I certainly would not, and they began to curse me fluently and made a rush at me. I jumped for the rear door and got through but Macaroffsky went around the back way and punched me. Meanwhile, my servant had run downstairs and out on the street yelling 'Murder, police,' and her screams alarmed the trio who scampered downstairs, still swearing at me. They told me that I was not the 'Czar of Russia,' and I told them that they were in an enlightened country, and that I would have the law on them."

The article went on to state that:

The kosher business of Montreal amounts to nearly $3,000,000 a year[21] and Rabbi Glazer has the making of the appointments. He has eleven men to kill cattle and nine to inspect, sixteen to kill poultry, and forty-one retail dealers. When he pronounces meat unfit it is thrown away. In fact he is absolute master of the Jewish meat trade in Montreal. There is a great demand for the various licenses but the recipient has to be of unimpeachable character and reputation.[22]

Whatever the real value of the kosher meat industry of Montreal, which supplied a community experiencing tremendous growth,[23] it was clearly important and worth fighting for.[24] Religiously inclined or not, members of the Montreal Jewish community in this era overwhelmingly bought meat from Jewish butchers who were or claimed to be selling kosher meat, though it must also be said that not every consumer was necessarily particular to verify the claims of *kashrut*. Rabbi Hirsh Cohen reported in 1933 the kosher butchers' estimate that 80 per cent of Jewish homes in Montreal purchased kosher meat.[25]

By the teens or the twenties of the twentieth century, there had arisen a network of between sixty and ninety retail butcher shops catering to the Jewish trade. Each shop was relatively small and served an average of some five hundred Jews. Incidentally, this proportion of Jewish butcher shops to total Jewish population seems to be relatively constant, whether we are speaking of large communities like Montreal or smaller communities like Bangor, Maine and Johnstown, Pennsylvania, where, in the 1920s, there were approximately 1,000 to 1,200 Jews respectively, or Madison, Wisconsin, which had a community of somewhat under 1,000; each of these smaller communities possessed two kosher butcher shops.[26]

The kosher butcher shops in Montreal, whatever their exact number at any given time, were more than simple retail establishments. They constituted centres where Jews, and especially Jewish women, gathered. Given the lack of reliable refrigeration facilities in homes, trips to the butcher constituted a fairly frequent activity for housewives, especially since Jews in North America tended to rely heavily on meat in their diet.[27]

Rabbi Glazer's battle with his opponents was often discouraging. Thus, in November 1908, he wrote the following to the leadership of the Beth David [Roumanian] Congregation:

The entire city of Montreal today eats meat that has no supervision. At many of the local butchers today, the meat [sold] is "meat which has been hidden from sight."[28] The butchers, not you as a community, control the *shehita* and the *shohtim*. A year's work has been completely nullified because the butchers did not wish to pay *shehita* fees.

All the Orthodox congregations of this city have united. They have established a rabbinical court, and made a contract concerning the *shohtim* and the *shehita*. Now only the butchers have [control over] the *shohtim*, not the congregations.

Since I, as rabbi of your congregation, am obligated to see that you have kosher meat to eat, I have literally put myself on the line [*moser nefesh*] for it. And now, unfortunately, I must request that you give your attention to the *shohtim* and butchers. As it is now, I can in no way be responsible for the *kashrut* of the *shehita* and of the butchers.

I ask that you hold a meeting as soon as possible to see how to help reestablish *kashrut* in such a manner that I could be able to testify, according to the laws of the holy Torah, concerning [the *kashrut* of] meat that such a mother city in Israel should be able to eat.[29]

Rabbi Glazer was also at work in other areas. He was numbered among the co-founders of the Montreal Yiddish-language newspaper, the *Keneder Odler*. In fact, he is credited by its publisher, Hirsh Wolofsky, who was to become his inveterate enemy, with having suggested the newspaper's name.[30] When he was frozen out of the newspaper's leadership, he tried several times to found a rival newspaper, entitled *Der Stern*, with but little success. This failure certainly worked to his detriment.[31] Since he was opposed by Wolofsky, who controlled the *Keneder Odler* as well as (from 1914) the community's English-language newspaper, *The Canadian Jewish Chronicle*, Rabbi Glazer became, in the Montreal Jewish community, a media "non-person," while his arch-rival, Rabbi Hirsh Cohen, regularly appeared in the *Odler*'s and *Chronicle*'s columns. Thus Rabbi Glazer was forced to reply to the accusations and denunciations against him published in the *Keneder Odler* with handbills and libel suits,[32] not a very effective method.

Rabbi Glazer was an activist in the area of labour relations. He was, apparently, a supporter of the organization of the Jewish Butcher's Employees Association of Montreal in 1909 and instrumental in getting this association recognized by other Jewish labour organizations.[33] He also intervened in other labour disputes involving Jewish workers, in one of which he incurred the wrath of one of the manufacturers for having denounced him in a sermon.[34]

We are in possession of a number of interesting documents by Rabbi Glazer. By far the most interesting is a diary he wrote concerning his activities in the year 1909. His diary told what he was doing and how much he got for it. He recorded an annual income of $1905.00, though we cannot know with any certainty whether this constituted his total income for that period. His monthly income ranged from a low of $122.00 in January to a pre-Passover high of $211.50 for March (which included $95.00 for selling the *ḥamets*[35]). In 1909, he earned $189.50 for marriages, $122.00 for divorces, and $205.00 for what he described as "cases."

I will give you an example of one of the "cases" that Rabbi Glazer was called upon to solve:

Montreal, October 11, 1909.

We the undersigned, having been appointed as arbitrators and umpire respectively do render our final decision anent the differences of *A* vs. *B*,[36] which originated at the Austria-Hungarian synagogue during services of Simchath Torah last.... In consideration of the fact that the said *B*, during sacred services, when the Torah was out of the Ark ... has willfully slapped the face of the said *A*, and causing him pain by knocking a tooth out of his mouth, and in consideration of the fact that the synagogue is sacred to us and our children, it is our decision that the said *B* shall pay as an indemnity the following sums: to the synagogue he disgraced by causing a row ... $50.00 ... to the Talmud Torah Anshei S'fard ... $25.00; to the Montreal Home and Orphan Asylum ... $25.00.... And, in consideration that he caused a tooth with bridge work to fall out of the mouth of the said *A* by slapping him, the said *B* shall pay the said *A* the sum of ... $15.00.

Besides these, the said *B*, before being a good-standing member again in the said synagogue he disgraced, he shall have a letter of apology written to the said Austria-Hungarian congregation, and also an apology to the said *A*.

In consideration of the fact that the said *A*, without any due cause, in the synagogue while the Parnass[37] was attending his sacred duty, he, *A*, insulted the said Parnass.... *A* shall receive no ha-Kapha[38] for two years, and no Aliyah[39] for six months, unless the said *A* will, at a public meeting, offer a due apology to the Parnass, Mr. *C*,[40] and it shall serve as a warning so that the officers elected by the people shall be respected.[41]

Rabbi Glazer, therefore, was in the business of having his title of chief rabbi recognized and respected by his community. As he stated in 1910:

Am I the Chief Rabbi of the United Orthodox Congregations? Yes. And I would be misrepresenting my office, to which I was elected by ten congregations here and in Quebec, if I should renounce the title.[42]

The difficulty was that whatever he did was countered by his opposition. Thus, for example, in 1909, there was a great dispute concerning matza. There was a matza factory in Toronto, run by a man named Weinstock. Weinstock attempted to get the Canadian Customs to levy a duty on imported matza so that American matza companies, like Manischewitz, would operate at a price disadvantage in Canada. Weinstock wanted Rabbi Glazer to issue a certification of the *kashrut* of his product. Rabbi Glazer refused, but, as it happened, his rabbinical arch-rival, Rabbi Cohen, was willing to do so. Rabbi Glazer, in response, issued a poster denouncing the Weinstock matza factory, giving reasons why he would not certify its *kashrut*. Among the reasons he gave was that "there are witnesses from Toronto who have testified that this factory is not merely manufacturing Matzas, it also bakes leavened bread. On Saturday nights there is hot, fresh bread[43] coming out of its ovens."[44]

Rabbi Glazer did not merely issue the poster; he also travelled to Ottawa to meet with William Paterson, the minister in charge of Canada Customs. He made sure that no duty was imposed upon imported matza. His success meant that the Toronto matza factory failed. In one very biting article written by Rabbi Glazer against his rival, whom he called *Mr. Cohen*,[45] he stated "there is a lot of unused matza baking machinery in Toronto." The rivalry between Rabbis Glazer and Cohen and their followers was very personal, and, as they were living in the same city and circulating in much the same circles, they could not avoid bumping into one another frequently. At one point in his 1909 diary, Rabbi Glazer recorded that he spoke at a public meeting at the Baron de Hirsch Institute. He wrote, "speaking at the same podium was my great enemy, Lyon Cohen [nephew of Hirsh], but I got the best of it."[46]

One of the incidents which was measurably affected by the rivalry between Rabbis Glazer and Cohen was the case of Solomon Lamdan, a poultry *shoḥet* who had been arrested for illegally slaughtering chickens near the St. Lawrence Market.[47] Rabbi Glazer attempted to get Lamdan kosher food and facilities for daily prayer but was constrained to work through Rabbi Cohen who had earlier been appointed Jewish chaplain at the jail.[48] Rabbi Glazer's actions on behalf of Lamdan included contacting not merely the administration of the jail, but also the mayor of Montreal and the premier of Quebec. His actions were so consistently opposed by the Jewish establishment, represented by S. W. Jacobs, that it was observed by Keinosuke Oiwa, in his study of the Montreal Jewish community in this era, that "Uptowners seem to have been more concerned with the involvement of Rabbi Glazer than with Lamdan's imprisonment itself."[49]

As we have seen, Rabbi Glazer was an activist by inclination and would not allow his reputation or the Jewish name in general to be impugned without attempting to intervene with responsible politicians.[50] Thus in 1910, when a French Canadian named Plamondon published a grave denunciation of the Talmud, as a book which was anti-Christian and taught inhumane doctrines, Montreal Jewry reacted. We know quite well what transpired from the point of view of the Montreal Jewish establishment, which sought redress in court and employed Rabbi Abramowitz of Shaar Hashomayim for this purpose.[51] What is less well known is that it was Rabbi Glazer who intervened first, writing letters to the Quebec

City newspaper, *Le Soleil*, attempting to refute the anti-Semitic charges against the Talmud.

In 1913 a very sensational court case in Halifax, Nova Scotia, also drew the attention of Montreal Jews. The *shoḥet* of Halifax, a man by the name of Leavitt, had been arrested on a complaint by the Society for the Prevention of Cruelty to Animals. The complaint specified that the traditional Jewish method of slaughtering animals was inhumane and cruel and in contravention of Nova Scotia's Cruelty to Animals Act. Thus confronted with a challenge not dissimilar to that of Plamondon, Rabbi Glazer went to Halifax, at his own expense, because he felt it was his duty as chief rabbi. He was the rabbinical expert witness for the defence in the case of Rex vs. Leavitt. The case was finally won by the Jewish side on the basis of the testimony of Rabbi Glazer and of other expert witnesses, especially a professor of physiology who testified that the kosher method of slaughtering was indeed a very humane one. Thus Rabbi Glazer's appreciation of his duty as chief rabbi of his congregations extended to other Canadian Jewish problems.[52]

Rabbi Glazer was appreciated by his supporters, who, in 1912, contributed to a fund to build him a house. Who, exactly, were his supporters? Which congregations sided with Rabbi Glazer? Four lists of his congregations are extant. The first stems from 1909,[53] the second from 1912,[54] and the third from 1918.[55] The final one stems from 1927, long after Rabbi Glazer had left Montreal. It consists of those congregations in Montreal that supported the publication of his translation of Maimonides and may be taken as indicative of support for Rabbi Glazer during his tenure in Montreal[56]:

1909	*1912*	*1918*	*1927*
Galician	Galician Kehal Yeshurun	Kehal Yeshurun	
Chevra Kadisha	Chevra Kadisha		Chevra Kadisha
Austrian Hungarian	Austrian Hungarian	Shaarei Tefillah	Shaare Tephilah Austria-Hungarian Congregation

1909	1912	1918	1927
Rumanian	Rumanian	Beth David	Beth David Rumanian Congregation
Beth Judah	Beth Judah	Beth Judah	Beth Judah
Beth Israel (Quebec)	Beth Israel (Quebec)		Beth Israel (Quebec)
	Kol Yisrael Haverim (Papineau)	Haverim Kol Yisrael	
	Tifereth Israel (Mile End)		Tifereth Israel
		Kerem Israel	Kerem Israel
	Shomrim Laboker		
	Beth Solomon	Beth Solomon	Beth Solomon

Some synagogues appear on all three lists, though sometimes under slightly different names. Thus the Galician synagogue, Kehal Yeshurun, appeared on all three lists. Others appear but once, and it is evident that congregational loyalties shifted over time. The most prominent Eastern European synagogue not affiliated with Rabbi Glazer was Bnai Jacob. Chevra Shas, which had been founded by Rabbi Cohen, also remained in opposition.

Rabbi Glazer lectured widely outside of Montreal, including in his journeys Ottawa and Toronto. He spoke publicly in English as well as in Yiddish. Thus in 1911, to celebrate the coronation of King George V and Queen Mary, a special thanksgiving service was held in the Chevra Kadisha synagogue in which Rabbi Glazer was advertised as speaking in English.[57] Rabbi Glazer was interested in looking beyond the immediate controversies within the Montreal Jewish community in which he was constantly engaged. He had begun an attempt to chart the future of North American Jewry and to influence what American Orthodox Judaism was going to look like. To this end, he wrote a very interesting book during his years in Montreal, publishing it in 1917.[58] Its title was *The Guide of Judaism*. The Hebrew subtitle, much to the same effect, was *Moreh ha-*

Yahadut.⁵⁹ Glazer designed the book to be a systematic work for the study and instruction of Judaism in its entirety. It takes its general structure from Maimonides' *Mishneh Torah*, which was designed as an all-inclusive work on Judaism.⁶⁰ Rabbi Glazer's guide to Judaism is completed in approximately 180 pages. From his preface, it is possible to understand not merely that he wrote in English, but also the high level of his English writing. He stated:

… the *vis vitae* of Judaism in the New World, its renaissance and its progress is possible only in this generation of patriotism and consciousness of self. The bricks of the great edifice of European Jewishness are being carried over the Atlantic. One Jewish center was always built upon the ruins of another. Such is our history and its philosophy.

The problems confronting Israel to-day are: How shall, or rather, how can Judaism be perpetuated in the face of Western civilization? Is Judaism really in danger because of its Oriental origin?

Eliminating Reform as a factor in solving these problems, the question arises: What alternative have the spiritual leaders in Israel to offer to the growing generation which is both free and cultured?

Judaism, since the last quarter of the eighteenth century, continued to develop among the great masses of European Jewries along three distinct lines: the Mendessohnian school, the Israel Baal-Shem school, and the Elijah Gaon school. Frankfurt, Warsaw and Wilna fairly illustrate the characteristics of the intentions of those schools. Will it be possible, or, facing conditions as they are, is it desirable to perpetuate the divisions and create a *Hassidic* Chicago, an *Ashkenazic* Philadelphia, or a *Pilpulistic* New York?

By means of observation during two decades among various types of communities, and alongside Reform colleagues and radical agitators, it is my firm conviction that the problems of Judaism in the New World can, and will be solved by only one means – by means of EDUCATION.

And, as an *avant propos*, I dedicate this work to American Israel, to the growing and grown generation.⁶¹

Glazer was thus a man who did not merely know English (and at least a smattering of Latin and French); he was also able to write a powerful essay, which expressed some very interesting ideas, and, indeed, a unique vision of Judaism's future in North America. One of the things he was saying here is that the elements of European Jewishness were being carried over the Atlantic; however, the structure of Judaism that was going to be built would not have the same appearance. Though a "pilpulistic" Vilna existed, and was going to be a building block of the future North American Judaism, we will, nonetheless, not witness a "pilpulistic" New York. What will we have, then? Glazer's vision was of a Judaism that is not Reform, and not radical, which were the two major rival structures of Jewish meaning offered to the immigrant Jews. It will be, therefore, a traditional Judaism. This traditional Judaism, however, will be studied – at least by the masses – not in Hebrew, and not in Yiddish, but in English. Nonetheless, Rabbi Glazer hoped that this Judaism would be true to its roots. At the beginning of the book, therefore, Rabbi Glazer presented, in Hebrew, the sources in Rabbinic literature and in Maimonides from which he derived his material.

Glazer's book, in accordance with his Maimonidean model, begins with the existence of God and ends with the coming of the Messiah. Here is what he says concerning the messianic era:

When the Messianic era will dawn, the throne will be restored to the House of David, and all laws of Judaism will be in force again. But let no man think that the world will change in its physical appearance, or that the laws of nature will be changed. The Messianic era will be an era of peace among all nations, and between all nations and Israel, which will be permitted to enjoy its own undisturbed. But before such era will be inaugurated, great wars, the greatest in history, will come to pass, and thereafter all men will live in brotherly peace. May it come to pass in our days, Amen.[62]

That last part, concerning the great wars before the coming of Messiah, is certainly part of the Jewish tradition, but it is emphatically not part of Maimonides' description in his *Mishneh Torah*, which greatly deemphasized the apocalyptic elements of medieval Jewish messianic thought. It is important, therefore, to bear in mind that Rabbi Glazer published this book in 1917, in the middle of an event contemporaries called "The Great War." Did he possibly think that the Great War would inaugurate the messianic era? My educated guess says that likely he did, along with numerous other Orthodox Jews of his era.

In order to get a further idea of who Rabbi Glazer was and what he stood for, we will examine some selections from a book of sermons he published, in English, in 1930. Even though it is likely that these sermons were written after he left Montreal, they can still be said to represent his thinking in his Montreal period as well.

One concept that stands out in his collection of sermons is his conviction that the situation of North American Judaism and rabbis had undergone a dramatic change. Thus he wrote:

As Israel advances in years on this hemisphere, the gradual departure from the Old Country customs becomes more conspicuous every year. No longer is the Rabbi the actual head, the real teacher, the spiritual father of his community. Every congregation is a community by itself.[63]

Some of the tensions found in North American Judaism by Rabbi Glazer can be illustrated in two sermons he preached on the festival of Hanukkah. In the first, he commented on the claim to the festival being made by the Zionists:

This festival which we celebrate to-day is universally known as Hanukah – dedication – in commemoration of the miracle of the cruse of ointment. True, it is historically called also Maccabean festival – Hag ha-Machbim – ; but it is, in a like measure, also known as the festival of lights – Hag-ha-Neroth. Perhaps this very fact, this inability to worship heroes, did not contribute to the well-being of Israel; perhaps, too, if this characteristic could have been claimed, Israel, as a nation, would have been a greater success. And, there are many today who unconsciously advocate such radical departure to cease worshipping the miraculous and commence worshipping the natural. Even this very festival, its very base, is being diverted to support another prop. Nationalism struggles hardest when it encounters a situation similar to that of Hanukah. The bit of ointment with the seal of the high priest was played up long enough, say they; it is high time that the military genius of the Maccabees be given the front page in the history of Hanukah. And, some well-intentioned zealots are sincerely angry, particularly at the Rabbis of old for having emphasized the miracle-end of Hanukah. The delightful misinformation which is distributed about the ancient Rabbis leads one to believe that they purposely ignored the heroic efforts of the Maccabees, and stressed emphasis upon the miracle of the oil-cruse. "What benediction does one deliver when lighting the Hanukah-lights?"

Who sanctified us with His commandments and commanded us. Where can one find such commandment? Rabbi Eviya said: "Thou shalt not turn aside from the decision which they will declare unto thee, to the right hand, nor to the left." Rabbi Nehemiah said: "Ask thy father and he will declare unto thee, thine elders, and they will tell thee" (Tractate Sabbath, 23a). Both, Rabbi Eviya and Rabbi Nehemiah, made an analysis of the religious character of Hanukah and found it a sound doctrine. There must be constituted authority in Israel. The question, "Where can one find such commandment?" covers a lot of ground; perhaps as much as the ground covered by all modern critics of the religiosity of the festival. Rabbi Eviya's commentary that it is based upon the edict of constituted authority amply satisfies the religiously inclined wing. But it fails to convince the national element, which was led to believe that the Rabbis were antagonistically inclined toward the Maccabees. This was the task of Rabbi Nehemiah; he supplied the necessary material to refute the charge. "Ask thy father and he will declare unto thee, Thine elders, and they will tell thee." The whole people of Israel, throughout the generations, in all countries, centuries after there was no more a Synhedrion, or any other constituted authority to dominate the entire Jewry, accepted the religious rather than the national, the miraculous rather than the rational view concerning Hanukah. The philosophy of the History of Israel, if it means anything at all to the student of Jewish life, teaches that neither the triumphs nor the defeats of our nation can be attributed to natural causes, to the normal march of events, to either the plans of diplomatists or the strategy of generals. The uninitiated might be lead to believe that the Jewish people was merely drifting through the ages. But that is not the truth. Every recorded event refutes such notion. Verily, when it comes to the events in Jerusalem, "be silent, all flesh, before the Lord; for He is aroused out of His holy habitation."

In the second Hanukkah sermon, we witness the ways in which the holiday was being swallowed up by all sorts of extraneous factors, while Rabbi Glazer was gently pointing out that there was yet an intrinsically Jewish part of Hanukkah in danger of being lost:

"The Hanukah-light which is set up above twenty ells is disqualified." (Tractate Sabbath, 22a). The Hanukah-minded people try to find a symbol in everything connected with the festival. The joy of the celebration, both physical and spiritual, particularly on the American continent, is oftentimes misplaced and dislocated. The true lesson of the festival is to be found in its mystic fascination, in its almost perplexing many-sidedness. The boy and girl have presents; the baby of the home, the charm of the lights; the mother, her special delicacies; the father, his favorite game; the young man and the young woman, the ball; the preacher, the special theme; the Rabbi, extra sermon; the Hazan, the extra concert; the actor, the new play. Everybody is so busy about Hanukah, that Hanukah itself remains lonely, somewhere on a high pedestal, which no one can see. The lights are holy; they must not be used for week-day purposes; they must not be utilized for work, for ordinary light, heat, or power; they must be left burning, glittering, to be looked at and admired, to be seen as a work of the ages, more ancient than the works of the greatest masters in the world's leading museums. Seeing the lights, looking at them, one must also look for an answer to the question, What is Hanukah? And every one finds it. But not in the game he plays, not in the ball he attends, not in the special delicacies his wife gives him at the supper-table, even not in the Ze'dakah he gives. For the Hanukah lights have a meaning all removed from the senses, from the things pleasurable, earthly. The Hanukah light is the last defense of Israel; in gross darkness its small flame shows a path; in time of danger, an avenue of escape; in time of despair a ray of hope. One must see, must observe and take note of the light itself. Verily, "the Hanukah light which is set up above twenty ells is disqualified." No one can see it in passing. Its significance is lost. Its light must attract; its flame is holy.[64]

Finally, like Rabbi Cohen, his rival, Glazer was an Orthodox rabbi who was, for all his faith in the Bible and its revelation, not a fundamentalist:

There are some denominations who take every word in the Bible literally; they are called Fundamentalists; and their errors are a mess of stupidity, because they do not understand the spirit of the Torah, and because they study it in languages other than Hebrew, so that they cannot see it in its true light. The Talmud has given us a clear conception of the Torah. The beginning of recorded history has nothing to do with the creation of the world. The formation of the universe, perhaps, took millions of years. God created the sun and the moon and the stars; each planetary system, according to the Talmud, received its own atmosphere, peculiar to its own region. For example, the atmosphere on our earth is altogether different than the atmosphere on the moon, or on Mars, or on Saturn, or on any other planet. There are countless solar systems; no human mind has ever been able to calculate their number. Since creation scientists have come and gone, many things have happened, and no one has yet discovered that this statement of the Talmudists is erroneous. No one has as yet been able to master the secret of time and space, save only to learn that both are infinite. And, because of that, it is immaterial whether it has taken millions of years before the earth was created in its present form, whether it is the result of evolution, or whether it is the result of the great long process of creation. The Torah tells us the simple story that God created everything. It was the masterful hand of God which has made possible all of this to be. That belief is fundamental with us, not the length of time it took to form this massive universe in its present state. Now, as to the question of the flood: the fundamentalists maintain that the flood covered the globe; consequently, they ought to arrive at the conclusion that the earth is flat, and, if that should be considered a Biblical doctrine it is a contradiction to a scientific fact. On such premise science and the Bible can never be united; and there will always have to be people to believe that the earth is flat in order to respect the Bible. Nothing is further from the truth than such doctrine in Judaism. In the Talmud it is stated that the flood did not cover Palestine, but that it did cover Mesopotamia, because Palestine is higher, and the flood could not reach it. Abraham "ascended" to Palestine, and Jacob "descended" from Palestine into Egypt. Thus it is obvious that fundamentalism is not a necessary doctrine in order to believe in and revere the Torah, or that Judaism fears the light of science.[65]

Rabbi Glazer stayed and struggled in Montreal for about a decade. He came to Montreal at the age of twenty-nine. Similarly, when Rabbi Ashinsky came to Montreal he had been barely thirty. In 1918, worn down by over a decade of relentless opposition and strife, he left Montreal for greener pastures. He first went to Seattle, about as far in North America as he could go, staying there for a couple of years. Then he went to Kansas City, where he reconstituted the idea of being a chief rabbi of a consortium of immigrant Orthodox congregations. Only in Kansas City he did not have the same sort of Jewish opposition to his projects as he had in Montreal. In Kansas City, however, he remained a fighter. One of the things he fought was the Ku Klux Klan, which was very powerful in the United States as a whole (and not merely in the southern states) in the twenties. He challenged the Imperial Grand Dragon of the KKK to a public debate, though that person refused to appear on the same platform with Rabbi Glazer.[66] In 1922, Rabbi Glazer played an important part in the Jewish lobbying effort to get the United States government to endorse the Balfour Declaration and support the nascent Jewish national home in Palestine. Ultimately, Rabbi Glazer moved from Kansas City to New York, first to a congregation in Harlem, then to one further downtown in Manhattan, and finally to one in Brooklyn. He died in 1938.

When Rabbi Glazer left Montreal, his United Congregations sought to engage another chief rabbi who was equally strong and militant to inherit his responsibilities and troubles. Rabbi Glazer's successor, however, was a very different sort of man. Whereas Rabbi Glazer was a Lithuanian Jew, a *mitnaged*, his successor was a Polish *Ḥasid*. Whereas Rabbi Glazer wrote fluently in English, his successor was never comfortable in English, and the few letters written in his name in English are a far cry from Rabbi Glazer's elevated prose. His name was Rabbi Yudel Rosenberg, and we will speak of him and his tribulations in the next chapter.

· 4 ·

Rabbi Yudel Rosenberg: Kabbalist and Communal Leader[1]

The one and only excuse which answers almost all the [halakhic] problems of America is: "All right. It's America, isn't it?" – Rabbi Yudel Rosenberg (1916)[2]

In this chapter, we will discuss the life and works of Judah [Yudel] Rosenberg (1859–1935).[3] Through an examination of his extant writings, and other archival sources, we will obtain a fuller idea of the challenges facing an immigrant Orthodox rabbi in Canada in the first third of the twentieth century. We will also begin to understand the difficulties he had in making a place for himself in the New World as well as the intellectual daring of the solution he proposed for the spiritual regeneration of Orthodoxy in that seemingly most unpromising setting.

Rabbi Rosenberg was born in Poland in the town of Skaryszew, near Radom. He received a traditional *ḥasidic* education in rabbinic literature and in kabbalistic and *ḥasidic* texts. He was also, like Rabbi Hirsh Cohen, who was to be his arch-rival for leadership of the Montreal rabbinate,[4] exposed to secular learning both through the Hebrew works of the nineteenth-century Jewish modernist movement known as "Enlightenment" [*haskala*], as well as through his mastery of the Russian language, which he studied in order to obtain governmental permission to function as a rabbi.[5] It is noteworthy that, though many Eastern European Jews with a similar background who were exposed to secular thought chose to abandon the Orthodox tradition, Rosenberg, like his rival Hirsh Cohen, remained loyal. Despite his lack of rebellion against the rabbinic tradition, however, Rosenberg's exposure to secular thought was in many respects decisive in determining his ultimate stance within that tradition. Throughout his life, he retained an abiding interest in subjects such as science, politics, and economics and, more importantly, internalized many of these interests into his Judaic thought.[6]

Rosenberg received rabbinic ordination as a young man. However, it was not until after a couple of failed attempts at business that he went into the rabbinate, functioning as a rabbi in the town of Tarlow, and in the Polish cities of Lublin, Warsaw, and Lodz. He emigrated to Canada in 1913, at the invitation of a congregation of Polish Jews in Toronto because, as he wrote at the time, he was utterly unable to make ends meet as a rabbi in Poland. In 1919, he moved from Toronto to Montreal, where he believed he would have greater opportunities, and served as rabbi in Montreal until his death in 1935.

During the last thirty years of his life, Rosenberg wrote prolifically, in both Hebrew and Yiddish, on a wide variety of subjects.[7] For a scholarly audience, he wrote a supercommentary on the talmudic tractate, *Nedarim*,[8] a number of responsa [answers to legal questions],[9] several volumes of homilies on the Pentateuch,[10] and a short-lived rabbinic journal.[11] As well, he wrote or edited a number of liturgical and halakhic works meant to be read by a popular audience.[12] A book he wrote on Jewish folk medicine went through numerous editions.[13] He wrote several hagiographical works, including biographies of King Solomon,[14] the Prophet Elijah,[15] two Hasidic leaders, the "Grandfather" of Shpole[16] and Elijah Guttmacher of Graetz[17] and, perhaps most notably, a series of stories concerning Rabbi Judah Loewe of Prague, most prominent of which was his account of Rabbi Loewe and the Golem.[18] Joseph Dan wrote that this story:

... seems to be the best known contribution of twentieth century Hebrew literature to world literature. There is but one source for almost all the stories on this subject – the small book of Rabbi Judah Yudl Rosenberg.... The vast majority of this book is the fruit of the author's creative imagination.[19]

Rosenberg's major literary project, in which he engaged for some twenty-five years, was a translation and reworking of the classic work of Jewish mysticism, the *Zohar*. He re-edited the work to form a true commentary on the Bible and translated it from an often obscure Aramaic to a clear and simple Hebrew. He also added his own commentary.[20] As I will argue later on, this project was of the utmost importance for Rosenberg's vision of the regeneration of Judaism.

Within the Canadian Jewish community, Rosenberg elicited both respect and controversy. He had considerable influence in Orthodox circles in the two major centres of Jewish population in Canada: Toronto and Montreal. As well, his reputation spread throughout the Jewish world.[21] In particular, his influence was felt in the Canadian Jewish community in the field of *kashrut*, the regulation of the Jewish dietary laws.

In the pre-World War I era, the provision of kosher meat in North American Jewish communities was utterly anarchic. Unscrupulous butchers would sell non-kosher meat as kosher and defied most rabbinic attempts to regulate their industry. The situation inspired a major European rabbinic figure, Rabbi Jacob Willowsky, to declare that in America even the stones are impure. This anarchic situation spawned several attempts to create a powerful and respected Orthodox rabbinate in New York and elsewhere.[22]

Rosenberg, who had been heavily involved in controversies surrounding *kashrut* during his tenure in Toronto,[23] was brought to Montreal by the same issue. Rosenberg's daughter records in her memoir:

Father had originally come to Montreal for a Din Torah [rabbinical trial] ... between a powerful rabbi and a group of shoychtim [ritual slaughterers]. The upshot was that the shoychtim were divided into two camps.... After the Din Torah, father became rabbi of those shoychtim he thought had been maligned.[24]

What Leah Rosenberg did not specify is that Rabbi Rosenberg came to Montreal to succeed Rabbi Glazer in the leadership of his coalition of congregations.[25] This is clear from Rabbi Rosenberg's Montreal letterhead. In a letter of 1920 to Rabbi Glazer, he refers to himself as "Rabbi of the United Hebrew Community of Montreal, Canada."[26] He inherited as well from Rabbi Glazer the enmity of Rabbi Cohen and his supporters.[27] Thus, soon after he had arrived in Montreal, Rabbi Cohen published an attack on Rabbi Rosenberg in the *Keneder Odler*, in which he called him an ignoramus, whose rabbinic learning did not measure up to that of a student [*yeshiva bohur*].[28]

Whereas in Toronto, Rosenberg's scanty income had come primarily from fees paid to him for performing rabbinic functions such as marriages, divorces, and circumcisions, in Montreal the bulk of his income was derived from the regulation of *kashrut* and most of his time was spent in the supervision of kosher slaughtering.[29] Efforts to regulate *kashrut* in Montreal led, in 1922, to the formation of the Jewish Community Council of Montreal [*Va'ad ha-'Ir*]. The *Va'ad* was organized largely to regulate the kosher meat industry in the city. Whereas hitherto payment of those supervising the slaughter and preparation of kosher meat came from the butchers themselves – creating an obvious conflict of interest – now the salaries of those officials would come from a disinterested communal organization, the Council. The Council would receive its funds from a levy placed upon the slaughter of kosher animals and distribute this income not merely for the salaries of rabbinic supervisors and slaughterers but also to support local Jewish education.[30]

The institution of this new system involved the cooperation of the rabbinic supervisors, the slaughterers and the butchers. Such cooperation was by no means easy to obtain in an industry that suffered from nearly constant strife. Rosenberg, in particular, was initially quite ambivalent concerning cooperation with the *Va'ad*, which was under the leadership of his rival, Rabbi Hirsh Cohen. After an initial period of affiliation, Rosenberg and a group of rabbis and slaughterers broke with the *Va'ad* and formed a rump organization that they named *Va'ad ha-Kashrut* of Montreal. This breach caused considerable ill-feeling within the Montreal Jewish community as each side declared the meat produced by the other group to be non-kosher. The fight between the two warring parties involved mass meetings, some violence and a suit brought before the Quebec Superior Court.[31] Only in 1925 was the impasse between the two factions resolved when Rosenberg and his group were co-opted into the *Va'ad* organization with Rosenberg serving as vice-chairman of the rabbinical council, a post he retained until his death.

In examining Rosenberg's writings from his Canadian period, it is possible to discern many reflections of the problems and struggles faced by the Orthodox rabbi. The following is typical:

We see with our own eyes ... that pious scholars are despised by the people. Their life [is one of] penury and shame. Similarly the religious schools are in a lowly state, for the rich men among the people do not wish to support and strengthen them. On the contrary, they ... give for the support of those schools where they make Jewish children into gentiles through the teachers ... who educate the holy flock in an alien education opposed to the Torah and [Jewish] faith as well as through their directors who are called by the name of "rabbi" – that is to say, "there is evil in him" [*ra' bei*].... For these leaders and shepherds there is no financial want.[32]

Rosenberg refers here not to the Protestant school system, which educated the vast majority of Jewish children in Montreal, but rather to non-Orthodox Jewish schools, which he felt were detrimental to the preservation of Judaism. Another reference to non-Orthodox Judaism has to do with the phenomenon, well-attested elsewhere in North America, of immigrants attending services in the Reform temples in order to hear the polished English sermons of their rabbis. Thus Rosenberg warned:

Hear not the poisoned speeches of the Reform "rabbis," who possess the selfsame sinful souls of the prophets of Baal, who caused ... the destruction of the First Temple, or else the selfsame sinful souls of the Hellenistic leaders who brought upon the Jewish people the destruction of the Second Temple.[33]

The observance of the Jewish Sabbath and holidays has classically been considered the hallmark of Orthodox Judaism.[34] Thus the non-observance of the Sabbath and festivals by vast numbers of Jews was roundly condemned by Rosenberg. He did not, however, merely condemn; he also attempted an analysis of the situation and offered some solutions. Many Jews excused their non-observance by blaming economic conditions that made it difficult, if not impossible, to obtain the sort of job that allowed for Sabbath observance. Rosenberg acknowledged this argument and stated that the solution to this problem was to be found in the five-day, forty-hour week, then advocated by labour.[35] He further stated, in an argument addressed to the increasing number of Jews who viewed their Judaism as being primarily ethnic rather than religious, that one could justify the observance of the Sabbath not merely on religious, but also on nationalistic grounds. Jewish national pride dictated that the Jews should observe their day of rest as the Muslims did theirs and the Christians theirs.[36] Owners of stores and factories that employed Jews on the Sabbath and festivals were warned of divine punishment awaiting them in the next world.[37]

Beyond the wilful desecration of the Sabbath by many Jews, over whom Rosenberg could exercise no control since they had consciously abandoned the halakha, there was also widespread ignorance of the details of Sabbath observance even by those who considered themselves observant. Such people thought nothing of performing such actions on the Sabbath as pushing baby carriages on the street,[38] turning electric lights on and off,[39] or purchasing bread (after the Sabbath) that had been baked on the Sabbath day.[40]

Even worse than ignorance was the fact that public desecrators of the Sabbath, when they did choose to attend synagogue services, whether on the High Holy Days or else to commemorate the anniversary of a relative's death [*yohrzeit*] could and did receive all possible synagogal honours.[41]

Despite this, however, Rosenberg recognized that the support of the non-observant was essential for the continuation of Orthodox institutions. This somewhat ambivalent relationship was discussed by Rosenberg in terms of the birds sent out of the ark by Noah:

The raven which fled from Noah symbolizes those merchants who do not observe the Sabbath properly and flee from it in order to earn money.... Yet they obtain some merit if they support the Torah and bring bread and livelihood to those who occupy themselves in the Torah. The dove which did not flee ... designates those who observe the Torah ... [who] say it is better [to obtain] a bitter livelihood from the hand of the Holy One – blessed be He – ... and to avoid desecration of the Sabbath than [to obtain] a sweet, bountiful [livelihood] from flesh and blood [in which] he is forced to desecrate the Sabbath.[42]

Another area of Jewish law that was widely ignored, even by the ostensibly "observant," was the *mikveh*, the ritual immersion marking the end of the period of forbidden sexual intercourse connected with the woman's menstrual cycle. Even in those places where ritual baths were established, many women refused to immerse themselves out of modesty or because of fears of unsanitary conditions in those baths. Rosenberg attempted to rectify this situation through the publication of a pamphlet, entitled *Mikveh Yehuda*, giving detailed instructions on how to set up, at minimal cost and effort, a *mikveh* in one's own home.[43]

Other areas of lax observance attacked by Rosenberg included *sha'atnez*, the mixing of linen and wool in cloth. Because of new manufacturing techniques, thousands of Jews were now guilty of this sin unbeknownst to them.[44] *Kashrut*, of course, was a primary concern of Rosenberg. He expressed this concern in one of his homilies in this fashion:

Our sages – their memory be a blessing – stated, "The most proper among butchers is a partner of Amalek." ... For the war of Amalek in every generation is the impure power which seeks to defile the mouths of Israel with forbidden foods. This is a very grave sin. For a sin [committed] outside the body can be erased through repentance and disappear. However if the body has been fattened with forbidden foods ... even if he does repent, the body remains with the sickness of impurity.... Thus ... the butcher who boasts that he is kosher and yet does not wish to place himself under the supervision of the local rabbi ... signifies that he feeds [the public] non-kosher food.[45]

Moreover, according to Rosenberg, other Jews felt that *kashrut* in general was not worth the trouble, since, as they asked:

... what did it matter whatever was eaten. Does not everything become dung in the intestines? What holiness is attached to the intestines?[46]

In general, the impression given by a perusal of Rosenberg's writings is that the life of the Orthodox rabbi in Canada was a ceaseless struggle. As Rosenberg put it, somewhat apocalyptically, it was a fight:

... between the pious remnants of Israel and the helpers of Satan ... in the end of days. At that time, Jacob, the spirit of Ancient Israel [*yisrael sabba*] will remain almost alone with no help or support. For the people will go in darkness and will not wish to go in the spirit of Ancient Israel. Only the tiny minority will be the remnant which God calls. Then Jacob will remain limping on his hip because of the coldness of those who support the Torah. "until the dawn breaks" – that is, until the light of messiah glimmers.[47]

The religious outlook of Rabbi Yudel Rosenberg, as gleaned from his writings, was quite pessimistic. In this, he was similar to many of his contemporary Orthodox rabbinical colleagues, though he was, perhaps, more articulate than most. It would be wrong, however, to assume that Rosenberg felt that the cause was lost by any means. In fact, he believed that he possessed the key to the salvation of Orthodox Judaism and its reconciliation with the modern world. This key was – kabbala.

By the early twentieth century, kabbala – the Jewish mystical tradition – had been thoroughly discredited among westernized Jews and, while it was formally honoured by Eastern European Jewry, particularly by the *hasidim*, it was little studied per se by the masses.[48] Nonetheless kabbala, to kabbalists, held the promise of nothing less than the salvation of the Jewish people, should its study become sufficiently widespread.[49] Rosenberg, in particular, was convinced that "the raising of the fortune of the community of Israel in its holy faith" rested upon the popularization of kabbala.[50] It is to this popularization that he devoted the greatest portion of his literary effort for some twenty-five years.

What Rosenberg hoped to do in his *magnum opus*, the translation and re-edition of the *Zohar* was to make this classic of kabbalistic literature available to the masses – something impossible to do in its original Aramaic. As he stated:

I know that my book ... is not needed by the great men who are comparable to divine angels.... However they too will rejoice ... when they see the awakening of ordinary men to study and understand the statements of the holy *Zohar*. For that is a sign that salvation will be soon revealed.... The good of the community of Israel will arise through the study of the *Zohar*. We cannot say that that [salvation] depends upon [the study of the *Zohar*] by the great ones of the generation alone.... For there will yet come a new revelation [of the *Zohar*] to the masses of Israel ... who will taste of the Tree of Life.[51]

In order to bring about this new revelation of the *Zohar* to ordinary Jews, Rosenberg laid aside his hesitations at translating the *Zohar*.[52] He felt that the translation would serve to help stem the tide of secularism that was engulfing the Jewish people. Secular literature was popular among Jews, he felt, because the authors took pains to beautify their works and to write them in a pure and simple style, whereas holy books – and the *Zohar* in particular – were written obscurely and looked upon as basically incomprehensible. In such conditions, obviously, no new revelation could come about.[53]

For these reasons, Rosenberg engaged in what he felt to be a war against secularism. His weapon was the pen. Addressing the Jewish masses, he declared:

Why must you bring into your houses impure books and stories full of poison, whether the poison of heresy or the poison of immodesty, and read them? They sully the mind and deaden the heart.... Would it not be better for you to bring into your homes books of ethics and wisdom which are not against the Torah for your sons and daughters to read especially in these times of the "footsteps of the messiah"? For heresy is strengthened every day as our sages – their memory be a blessing – foresaw in the period prior to the revelation of king messiah.

Therefore there is a holy obligation upon everyone who possesses the fear of God to fight with all his strength against heresy.... The strongest weapon to fight against it is the pen, to distribute to the people books like these from which the heart will be able to understand without going into the "counsel of the wicked."[54]

Once again, the sentiments expressed by Rosenberg, and particularly his belief that the Jewish people were experiencing the events of the generation immediately preceding the messianic advent, were common to many rabbis of his time. They constituted a response to the onslaught of modernity and the breakup of the universal halakhic consensus within the Jewish community.[55] What serves to differentiate him from his peers – beyond his belief in the efficacy of the popularization of kabbala – was his belief that kabbala was also the key to the reconciliation of Torah and science.

Rosenberg always prided himself on his knowledge of secular affairs and science[56] and always rejected the notion that Torah and science, properly understood, were antagonistic. Taking aim at those Jews who had abandoned the tradition in favour of what they considered to be a modern lifestyle, Rosenberg stated:

Possibly you believe that civilization is connected to the profanation of the Sabbath. However you must know that among the Jewish people there have always been found great sages, researchers, philosophers, doctors, astronomers who were quite Orthodox and strictly observed the Sabbath.... Now you understand very well [from the example of] Maimonides that the holy Jewish Torah does not compare with civilization as fire [does with] water.[57]

In accordance with his program of presenting kabbala as the key to the salvation of Judaism, he took pains to describe kabbala as "the source of all spiritual sciences and also the source of the highest and noblest morality."[58] His goal was to present his material in such a way that it be in accordance with both kabbala and science "so that all the nations of the world and their sages should see that everything is implicit in the holy Torah."[59]

Woven in among his commentaries and homilies are a number of instances in which he combined kabbala and science. In dealing with the creation account in Genesis, Rosenberg connected the sun and the six planets [Mercury, Venus, Earth, Mars, Jupiter, and Saturn] to the seven lower *sefirot* [kabbalistic term for the emanation of God's power]. He continued:

And if recently the astronomers have discovered other planets greater and farther away whose orbit is connected with the sun, it must be said that they are symbolized by the three first *sefirot* of the World of Formation. [the third, in descending order, of the four supernal "worlds" in Lurianic kabbala]. Thus kabbala and science do not contradict each other.[60]

The fact that scientists believed the world was considerably older than the few thousand years provided for by the Jewish calendar was not a matter of concern for Rosenberg. He did not consider this a contradiction because the kabbalistic book, *Sefer ha-Temuna*, had stated that the world had passed through a number of aeons [*shemitot*] prior to the commencement of the present one.[61]

Indeed, Rosenberg was not content to claim that kabbala did not contradict the scientists. He also declared that the *Zohar* had anticipated the scientists in a number of discoveries:

The holy *Zohar* is not merely a book for the pious.... It also contains many matters of natural science.... It is known that the *Zohar* appeared in the world a hundred [*sic*] years before the discovery of the portion of the earth [which includes] America.... Yet there is found in it the science of geography just as was later discovered by the two scientists, Columbus and Copernicus. That is that the earth is round like a ball, that it is inhabited on all sides and that it possesses two types of motion, one motion spherical ... like a wheel on its axle and the other motion elliptical around the sun....

Everyone who understands will be able to see that almost the same things were hinted at [in the *Zohar*] as were discovered by the scientist Copernicus about three hundred years after the *Zohar* appeared in the world.[62]

Similarly the "tower which floated in the air," which Jewish legend ascribed to King Solomon, was considered by Rosenberg to be a machine, similar to the modern airplane, which worked in accordance with natural properties such as electricity and magnetism.[63]

Even evolution, that most threatening of nineteenth-century scientific theories for traditional religious belief, had its connection with kabbala:

It must be seen that the science called … "evolution" which was established by the mad scientist Darwin has something stolen from the words of the *Zohar* which speaks here of the creatures and types of men found in the other portions of the earth. Darwin, however, wrote that all men are descended from the apes. And it certainly seems that he is like an ape which is accustomed to imitate men in their movements. Thus he desired to imitate and say [things] similar to the words of the *Zohar* only in a spirit of madness…. On the contrary, in several places in the *Zohar* the opposite is stated that the apes are the descendents of sinful men. Something similar is agreed upon by the honest scientists of the nations of the world.[64]

In general, Rosenberg wished to leave the impression that the *Zohar* was respected by the scholars of the gentiles, who had even translated it into their own languages. How much more so, then, should the Jews honour and study this book "which is ours and which [contains] our soul and the length of our lives."[65]

Rosenberg's mission to save Judaism through the study of kabbala might well have seemed quixotic to his contemporaries. His ideas concerning the accommodation of science to kabbala – and vice versa – may seem naive. Yet they constituted the opening phase of a process which, perhaps in a more sophisticated way, marks the intellectual history of Judaism to the present.

Rosenberg published his edition and translation of the *Zohar* in the 1920s – the same period that Gershom Scholem began his masterful life-work of rescuing kabbala from neglect in the academic world. Both Rosenberg and Scholem, then, had much the same mission. Each was to take a subject that was neglected and misunderstood in the context of contemporary Judaism and to make it the key element in the regeneration of Judaism in the modern era. The difference, of course, is in the audiences they addressed. Scholem and his works found popularity in academe. Similarly Rosenberg's translation found a considerable readership among Orthodox Jews, judging from the numerous reprints of the work.[66] Moreover both Scholem and Rosenberg seem – in their respective spheres – to have anticipated that kabbala was to become a prime factor in Judaic thought. Rosenberg must, then, be considered a predecessor of present-day popularizers of kabbala among Orthodox Jews such as Adin Steinsaltz and Aryeh Kaplan.[67]

Rosenberg was no scientist, though he absorbed a good deal of scientific information available to him in either Hebrew or Yiddish. Nonetheless, here, too, he anticipated some of the major strategies of contemporary Orthodox Judaism in dealing with scientific theories and discoveries. These include the notion that all valid science is to be found in the Torah in some form, that there is no basic contradiction between Torah and true science, and that science is the handmaiden of Torah.[68]

In short, we have been dealing with a man whose life and works, though they have been obscured by the passage of time, will amply reward further study. Through him, we may come to understand not merely the pressures of the modern world upon Orthodox Judaism in the late nineteenth and early twentieth centuries, but also the beginnings of the sort of creative response to these pressures that ultimately enabled Orthodoxy to emerge as a viable force within Judaism of the late twentieth century.

· 5 ·

Rabbis and Shoḥtim: The Cases of Getsel Laxer and Hyman Meir Crestohl

In the countries of the United States and Canada, the rabbinate is based only upon an oral Torah. The rabbinical position is suspended in the air and [depends] upon the breath of the members much more than does [the position] of the cantor.
– Leibush Herzig (1916)[1]

In this chapter, we will be talking about two men who did not quite achieve the status of Rabbis Cohen, Glazer and Rosenberg. They both were and were not "rabbis." They certainly were rabbis in terms of their education. They possessed certificates of rabbinic ordination [*semikha*], which were certainly as valid as anyone else's.[2] They also acted as rabbis in Quebec cities outside Montreal, delivering sermons in their synagogues on Sabbaths and holidays, presiding at weddings and doing all the other things that pertained to rabbinical posts in North American Orthodox synagogues. However, when they moved to Montreal, they were unable to make their living as rabbis alone, though congregational work was at least a part of their activity in the city. They were, therefore, forced to supplement their rabbinical activities, from which they may have derived a certain prestige, with the kosher slaughter [*sheḥita*] of animals, from which they could earn a living, but which was physically demanding and could not have been pleasant for some.[3]

These men are of great importance in the story we are trying to tell in this book. Insofar as anyone of the relatively neglected group of Eastern European rabbinic intellectuals in North America has gotten scholarly attention, it has been the rabbis at or near the top of the heap, men like

Rabbis Eliezer Silver in Cincinnati[4] and Yudel Rosenberg in Montreal,[5] who were relatively well known both in their home communities and beyond.

The reality for most rabbis, however, was quite different. Practically without exception, no North American Orthodox rabbi of the early twentieth century was able to make a living solely from being a congregational rabbi, because few congregations could afford to pay their rabbi a decent salary. As we have seen, consortia of Eastern European immigrant congregations coalesced in order to support a rabbi collectively. Moreover, the very concept of a "congregational rabbi" was one that had little resonance in the Eastern Europe of the late nineteenth and early twentieth centuries, where rabbis led entire communities and not individual congregations. Its adoption in Western Europe and North America marked a phase in the process of Judaism's modernization.[6] Thus numerous Eastern European immigrant Orthodox rabbis, in an attempt to make ends meet, vied for the honourable (if often controversial) and remunerative position of supervisor of kosher slaughtering. Such jobs, however, were few in number compared to the number of immigrant rabbis, and rivalry between rabbis for these supervisory posts often led to ferocious conflict in city after city. Those men with rabbinical educations who did not achieve such positions had to turn to the difficult and exacting physical labour of slaughtering animals in order to earn a decent living. If we know much too little about these relative successes among Yiddish-speaking immigrant Orthodox rabbis, we have not yet begun to explore the dimensions of the lower levels of the Orthodox religious establishment in the New World.

Probably the best way to understand them is to think of them as the sort of people the progressive Hutchins Hapgood, in his pioneering 1902 study of New York's Jewish ghetto, called "submerged intellectuals."[7]

These were people of significant intellectual attainments who, in the atmosphere and economic climate of the Jewish immigrant community were not able to function full-time in an intellectual capacity. Under conditions of great privation, they continued to engage in their intellectual activities, but received little or no credit for doing so. We are speaking in this chapter about just such men. They never completely made it into the North American rabbinate, but nonetheless wished to use their often considerable store of rabbinical learning in order to make a living. These men, not quite able to achieve one of the very few Orthodox rabbinical positions with some degree of economic security, were forced to take lower status positions as ritual slaughterers [*shohtim*] in the only industry in North America that required rabbinic expertise – kosher meat.[8]

The story is told that when Rabbi Moses Feinstein, one of the most famous Orthodox rabbis of the twentieth century first emigrated from Russia to the United States in the 1930s, and his supporters were attempting to find him employment, it was proposed to make him a ritual slaughterer. That he avoided this fate and became the premier halakhic authority of his generation was a tribute to his persistence in seeking another sort of work, but it is a telling illustration of the basic lack of opportunity that faced such men.[9]

In this chapter we are dealing with men who never came close to achieving Moses Feinstein's renown, who did not escape the slaughterhouse, but whose literary remains can serve to instruct us. The group they represented was not a small one. In 1931, Louis Rosenberg, the statistician of Canadian Jewry, noted that there were 291 Jews engaged in "Jewish religious services" in Canada, up from 117 in 1921. Of them, 33 were rabbis. Thus for every rabbi, there were almost nine other "Jewish religious workers." Of the 33 rabbis, 14 were in Montreal. In Montreal, therefore, there were likely over a hundred Jews occupied in some area of "Jewish religious services."[10]

The particular area of "Jewish religious services" that likely employed the majority of these workers was the kosher meat industry. The slaughterhouse work in which they engaged required not merely scholarly knowledge of the subject, but also physical strength and endurance in a factory "assembly line" slaughtering atmosphere in which speed had to be maintained. Insofar as the *shohtim* were conscientious, and desired to take the time to do things in the right way, they were thereby in conflict with the constant demand for speed.

When considering the circle of *shohtim* in Montreal in this era, one of the most interesting things is the number of men who were writers, whether they managed to publish their works in their lifetime, or else left them in manuscript. Thus, among the slaughterers in the Montreal slaughterhouses in the 1920s and 1930s, no less than five: Getsel Laxer,

Hyman Crestohl,[11] Ḥayyim Kruger, Aaron Rosenberg, and Abraham Stern wrote manuscripts and published books in Hebrew and Yiddish on Judaic subjects.[12]

Kruger was a Hebraic scholar who moonlighted as a journalist for the *Keneder Odler*. Beyond that, he published numerous articles in Yiddish[13] on medieval Jewish philosophy, especially on Rav Saadia Gaon and on Maimonides.[14] Rosenberg, son of Rabbi Yudel Rosenberg, published a volume of Biblical commentary.[15] Stern published a volume of Talmudic essays [ḥiddushim],[16] and another of Hasidic tales.[17]

Getsel Laxer[18]

We will speak first about Getsel Laxer (1878–1942).[19] Who was Eliakim Getsel ben Yehiel Mikhl Laxer[20]? Biographical details are few. He referred to himself as "Austrian" in one document, which signifies that he was born in the Austro-Hungarian Empire.[21] Family tradition gives his birthplace as Totris in the province of Bukovina.[22] I have seen no reference to his life in Europe in his papers other than his 1898 marriage document [ketuba]. He came to Canada in 1900. According to the family tradition, he first tried living in New York but soon left it. The first documentary evidence we have from him is a draft of a letter dated 1904, written from Sherbrooke, Quebec,[23] where, from approximately 1900 to 1913, he served the Jewish community as rabbi, cantor, Hebrew teacher and *shoḥet*.[24]

Laxer, apparently, had a somewhat interesting time in Sherbrooke. According to his family's account, he arranged with a local Catholic bishop of Irish extraction to exchange lessons. He gave the bishop lessons in Hebrew, and, in return, the bishop taught him English. It is from this experience that, according to the family, Rabbi Laxer gained facility in speaking the English language.

However pleasant the conditions for Rabbi Laxer and his family in Sherbrooke, he faced the problem faced by all rabbis of small communities, in his day and in ours; the Jewish educational and social facilities of small towns could not compare to those of big cities. He did not want his family to suffer because of staying in a town like Sherbrooke, whose Jewish population peaked at 265 in the 1921 Dominion of Canada Census.[25]

Thus, in 1913, Rabbi Laxer and his family moved to Montreal. According to the family account, the reason was to gain greater social and educational opportunities for the children. The other reason for the move was, ironically, that Rabbi Laxer really did not like being a *shohet*, which was an expected part of his job in Sherbrooke. He had hopes that he and his family would be able to make a living in Montreal producing and selling cottage cheese. Certainly, this was as far away from the slaughtering of animals as one can get. However, this attempt failed, and thus Rabbi Laxer became a rabbi and a *shohet* in Montreal.

In his papers, there is an undated document in which Rabbi Laxer describes himself as having a congregational affiliation: "Getsel Laxer, rabbi of the Hevrah Tiferet Yisrael, Montreal."[26] That position, however, did not last long. An undated copy of his letterhead indicates that he lived at 7 Esplanade Avenue, and it bears no congregational affiliation. Family tradition informs us that for many years he led high holiday services in Chatham, New Brunswick, a town of barely four thousand, whose Jewish population peaked at 75 in 1911.[27] Had he managed to make a go of it in a Montreal congregation, he would likely not have had to travel as far afield as Chatham. One clue which perhaps sheds light on his failure to make a go in the rabbinate is contained in the notes for a high holiday sermon he preached on Yom Kippur of 5696 [1935], in which he sharply criticized those who "desecrated the Sabbaths and festivals all year and on Yom Kippur alone they 'correct' all of those Sabbaths." He went on to say that the prophetic reading [*haftarah*] of Yom Kippur morning, in which the prophet condemns those who fast hypocritically,[28] refers to such people. If the congregation which heard this sermon was typical, it was full of people who regularly transgressed the Sabbath and would likely not have appreciated the preacher's barbs.[29] In other words, he may have been considered too undiplomatic to last long as a congregational rabbi.

The best possible illustration of the ambivalence he felt about his rabbinical identity is the title, or rather titles, he gave himself in his letterhead. His name and title are printed in both Hebrew and English. In English, he gave himself the title of "Rabbi," whereas in Hebrew he styled himself "Reverend", a title adopted by many Orthodox para-rabbinical functionaries in North America.[30] Thus, for the readers of English, he could be a "rabbi," whereas the readers of Hebrew would understand that he made no such claim.

The last dated letter in the collection of documents in Laxer's hand dated from 1940 and was a letter of greetings from the *shohtim* of the East

End Slaughterhouse of Montreal on the occasion of Rabbi Hirsh Cohen's eightieth birthday. The papers Getsel Laxer left behind[31] tell basically two stories that will enable us to better understand who he was and what he stood for. They concern his life as scholar and would-be author, on the one hand, and his life as a *shoḥet*, on the other. Both stories are worthy of our attention.

Getsel Laxer was by no means an original scholar, one who desired to dazzle the reader with his brilliant and original insights. He was rather an anthologizer, someone who took what others had written and rearranged them for the benefit of his audience. The best example of this is Laxer's lengthiest and most finished manuscript, entitled *Gal Likkutim mi-Ba'alei Tosafot* [A Heap of Excerpts from the Tosafistic Masters]. It consists of an alphabetically arranged anthology of citations from the twelfth- and thirteenth-century Tosafistic commentary on the Talmud.[32] The reader of this work would thus be in a position to find out readily and quickly what these important medieval scholars had to say about various personalities, objects, prayers, and concepts. Similar to that is his commentary on *Pirkei Avot*, which, at least in its manuscript form, consists of an extensive system of references to sources, from throughout rabbinic literature, bearing upon each and every word or phrase of the Mishnaic tractate. Whether he ever intended to flesh out this commentary further is a moot point. However, even in its "fleshed out" form, it would have surely consisted of an anthology rather than a vehicle for his own thoughts, as often happens in commentaries. Other major works of the same general nature, in greater or lesser states of preparation, were written by Laxer on the Pentateuch, the Prayerbook, the minor Tractate *Kallah Rabbati*, and the Laws of Ritual Slaughtering.[33]

Even in his introduction[34] to these works, he scrupulously refrains from revealing anything directly about himself. Instead, the introduction consists of yet another anthology of rabbinical comments on the Biblical saying "Is Saul also among the prophets?"[35] Laxer was likely anticipating, though only by implication, surprise among his readers that such a man as he would engage in a literary enterprise. While it is true that rabbinic authors often expressed some diffidence in their introductions concerning their worthiness to write their works, Getsel Laxer's introduction is an extreme case. In all the commentary material I reviewed, only one comment I found reveals Laxer's own personal outlook. In speaking about the wicked Esau and the righteous Jacob, he noted that the prophecy that "the elder will serve the younger"[36] has been fulfilled through the gentile's serving the Jew as *"shabbes goy":*

For without Esau, how would Israel observe the Sabbath in the time of cold to kindle fire on the Sabbath day.... Our eyes see that we are now in exile a mockery and a scorn [to the gentiles]. Nonetheless Esau the elder serves the younger.[37]

In any event, it is most eminently clear that Getsel Laxer controlled and was able to organize in his mind an impressive range of works of Biblical and rabbinic literature and that he was recognized as a scholar of rabbinics by Montreal rabbis such as Joshua Halevi Herschorn.[38]

What can Laxer's works in manuscript tell us about Judaism in Montreal in the early twentieth century? The most important thing, and the major reason why, in my opinion, this material is worth such detailed study, is its very existence. These works, lovingly handed down to his descendants, testify to a compelling need on Laxer's part to assert his expertise in the world of rabbinic learning. In this he was not alone among Montreal's slaughterers of this era, as we have seen. Their literary productions need to be considered in some ways parallel with the works of many of Montreal's Yiddishist educators of that era, who are seen by David Roskies as attempting to create a new Jewish civilization in the New World to replace the old one which was no more.[39]

Though his writings are, as we said, of some significance for our understanding of who Getsel Laxer was and what he stood for, they were never published and hence never came to wide public attention. His significance in the public affairs of the Montreal Jewish community stemmed from his role as a dissident in many of the disputes concerning *shehita* in Montreal in the 1920s and 1930s. In the battle for the dominance of the Montreal rabbinate that was fought out between Rabbi Hirsh Cohen and Rabbis Simon Glazer and Yudel Rosenberg, Rabbi Laxer was a staunch partisan of Rabbis Glazer and Rosenberg, and thus often in bitter and violent opposition to Rabbi Cohen and his supporters. In the end, he turned on Rabbi Rosenberg as well, as we shall see.

Laxer became one of the most militant members of the guild of Montreal *shohtim* known as *Agudat ha-shohtim*. It is important to note that the profession of *shohet* required not only expert knowledge of the halakha of *shehita*, as well as the physical strength and prowess to carry out the act properly. Most importantly, to function as a slaughterer in the kosher meat industry of Montreal, one needed membership in the guild, which eventually registered as a union under the labour laws of Quebec. Gaining such a membership was not an altogether easy thing to do. Each member of the union had what was known as a *hazaka*, which signified that one had the right to practise the kosher slaughtering of cattle and sheep in the four abattoirs of Montreal in which kosher slaughtering was undertaken.[40] Like a seat on the stock exchange, a *hazaka* was worth money. Thus a newcomer could not merely show his credentials to the supervising rabbi to gain access to the profession. He also had to arrange to purchase a *hazaka*, e.g., from the widow of a deceased member. In the absence of a social safety net, the purchase of the *hazaka* meant some financial help for the widow at a difficult time in her life.

In the 1920s, a member of the *Agudat ha-Shohtim* of Montreal earned approximately $40.00 per week. This was not a munificent sum, but in that period, it was a living wage for a family, especially considering that certain "perks" came with the job. These included taking home quantities of "organ meat" like liver and lung. According to the Laxer family tradition, Rabbi Laxer would regularly give packages of this meat to poor people. The supervising rabbis, whose job was considerably less disagreeable, got as much or more.

As one of the activist members of the *Agudat ha-Shohtim*, it was Laxer who was the principal plaintiff in the 1923 suit in Quebec Superior Court "Getzel [sic] Laxer et al., vs. The Jewish Butchers Society of Montreal et al.," which was of great significance in the solution to the dispute over the supervision of kosher meat in Montreal in the period 1923–25.[41]

His leadership in this and other dissident movements within the Montreal kosher meat industry is sharply illustrated by two documents preserved in his papers, both of which add significantly to our available information on this subject. The first of these is a reply to a column in the *Keneder Odler* criticizing the rabbis and slaughterers of Montreal[42] and was probably designed to be published as a handbill, since Montreal's Yiddish daily sided decisively with the communal *kashrut* "establishment" and did not give its columns to dissidents.[43] It is undated but can be dated to the Spring of 1922.[44] In the letter, whose authorship is uncertain, we find the following description of tensions within Montreal *kashrut*:

We ask you householders: Do you wish to know what is happening among the rabbis and slaughterers? Do you wish to know whether the rabbis and slaughterers make a living? Do you invite rabbis to your weddings and circumcisions to give them a benefit? Do you send the rabbis holiday and Purim gifts as European householders do? Do you make the least effort to help the slaughterers in their cursed lot? ... One slaughterer seceded from the Association of Slaughterers ... which caused a disturbance in *kashrut* in the opinion of all the local rabbis.[45] This slaughterer sought out some other slaughterers who were never recognized by the local rabbis as kosher slaughterers. They have also adopted a new rabbi.... All the local rabbis have certainly declared more than once that the[ir] meat is forbidden. Well, let's ask the question. Do you the householders heed what the rabbis declare to you according to the Torah? Do you therefore refrain from buying the meat from their forbidden slaughtering? You say rather that the revolution is a lucky stroke for Montreal, without which a pound of kosher meat might cost fifty cents.

Now there is a new trouble. Do you householders wish to hear about the dispute between the rabbis from which the city suffers in matters of *kashrut*? ... That the Borden Milk Company this year has asked Rabbi Rosenberg to give the certification for Passover milk.[46] However Rabbi Cohen says that since he once had given such a certification, no other rabbi can give the certification. Because Rabbi Cohen is a person of influence since he usurped the right to have the agreements with the meat companies in his name, the check for *shehita* money is in his name. He has demanded from Rabbi Rosenberg $1,500 for the $100 left him from Borden's certification and he has withheld Rabbi Rosenberg's wages from slaughtering. Until this week, *Parshat Naso* [June 10, 1922], Rabbi Cohen has seized $400 from Rabbi Rosenberg's wages. However we the slaughterers cannot allow Rabbi Rosenberg to remain without bread, God forbid. You understand very well that all this leaves you cold.

Now we ask you householders whether you wish to interest yourselves in the cursed lot of the rabbis and the slaughterers and to make an end to the chaos and lawlessness which passes for calm in Montreal?

This document is of prime importance because it helps explain the underlying tensions between Rabbis Cohen and Rosenberg, at a period in which they were formally cooperating.[47] It sets the stage for Montreal's "Kosher Meat War" (1923–25), to be discussed in Chapter 7, which was precipitated by a rift between those two rabbis.

The second document brings us closer to an understanding of Getsel Laxer the *shoḥet* and his often stormy relationships with other slaughterers and rabbis. Whereas the previous document shows him to have been allied to Rabbi Rosenberg, this one will place them in an adversarial relationship. It is a draft of a letter presumably sent in 1930 to Rabbi Meir Shapira of Lublin, Poland, one of the most famous rabbis of the era.[48] There is no evidence that this query, if it was ever sent, was answered. In it, Laxer pours forth his frustrations and gives us a tremendously interesting portrait of the development of the kosher slaughtering industry in Montreal in the mid- to late 1920s:

May our rabbi teach us in the matter I will explain.... Now it is about five years since peace was made between all the slaughterers and the sides and we became slaughterers from all the sides. Then all of the [parties] came to a compromise that the slaughterers here would gain two-thirds of the money for *sheḥita*. This compromise lasted until *Parshat Nizzavim* of 5688 [September 8, 1928]. After that the verse was fulfilled "slaves have ruled over us"[49] and our rights were taken away. We, the slaughterers were given a weekly salary for slaughtering and not the two-thirds as previously. The slaughterers submitted to them, and all the workers of evil boasted, saying "our hand has prevailed and we will do with the slaughterers what we wish." Thus was their rule for thirteen months. After that we three slaughterers, Getsel Laxer, Jonah Aspler and Leibush Herzig, all born in Austria,[50] placed our souls in our hands and went out to battle with them. That is, we found a wholesale company which came to us, the three slaughterers, to slaughter its cattle and sheep (from *parshat berakha* to *parshat tizave*, 5690 [October 27, 1929–March 15, 1930]), and [after that] the war was forgotten. We came to a compromise also at this time on the principle of two-thirds of the slaughtering money to the slaughterers as a whole. All of us now as then are free agents. All the city rested and was quiet. However we, the aforementioned three demand from the [other] thirteen slaughterers who remained subject to the Community Council [*Va'ad ha-'Ir*] and during the strife (from *parshat berakha to tizave*) lay "on ivory couches,"[51] the [monetary] loss that we have lost each and every week of the strife. It is our claim that they – the thirteen – not merely did not lose their weekly wage (which when the Community Council was in charge [consisted of] $37 apiece for each slaughterer per week) whereas we, the three aforementioned slaughterers got only $22 per week during the strife. Moreover we have improved the lot of the thirteen slaughterers who stayed with the Community Council while we were fighting and we got them a percentage of the slaughtering money which gave them more than $40 per week.... There is no doubt that we have improved the entire situation.... Therefore we the aforementioned three demand from the thirteen that they go back and divide the loss we have lost, approximately $900, among all the slaughterers equally for those who went to war and those who stayed in peace.... We said to them several times previously that we were going out to save [the situation] and also on the first day we went out we said to the thirteen slaughterers that we were going out for all [of them].... They claim that they did not send us. Therefore we claim that since we went, even without [their] permission, to improve the situation ... our expenses and losses are due us.... Therefore we ask from your excellency that you will answer with your opinion of this, not as a practical decision [*halakha le-ma'aseh*] ... only with the legal discussion [*shakla ve-tarya*] for we have no justice on earth, here among the local rabbis, and we have no one upon whom to depend except upon our Father in Heaven.[52]

As it happens, we have the other side of this story preserved in a responsum of Rabbi Yudel Rosenberg.[53] Laxer's reference to his inability to get justice from the Montreal rabbinate is probably the result of the hearing he received from Rabbi Rosenberg. Here is Rosenberg's version:

There came before me a *din torah* [hearing based upon Torah law] from the local Slaughterers' Association.... Some years ago there was founded in this city a [Jewish] communal [organization] called the [Jewish] Community Council. All the Association of Slaughterers, nineteen in number, stood under the Community Council which paid them a weekly salary for about three years. The Community Council also paid the rabbis. Then three slaughterers seceded from the Association and the Community Council to stand as independents to slaughter. They also established for themselves a rabbi to say that they are under his supervision even though the Community Council banned their slaughtering. This situation lasted for approximately three years.... After that another three slaughterers seceded from the Association of Slaughterers on the grounds that they wanted to increase their salary by two or three dollars. They went out to slaughter by themselves without any [supervising] rabbi. Though the Community Council banned their slaughtering they remained thus for four months fighting the Community Council and the Rabbinical Council. They caused the remaining slaughterers a loss by reducing the revenue of the Community Council ... so that the Community Council was forced to cut the salaries of the rabbis by ten dollars a week.

In the first month the Community Council as well as the thirteen slaughterers asked them to come back under the authority of the Community Council and the Rabbinical Council, promising to raise their wages. However they remained at war and refused by any means to make peace with the Community Council. They proposed ... that they would unite with the three slaughterers who had previously seceded from the Community Council and that the six slaughterers would stand alone in the slaughterhouse and not mix at all with the thirteen [remaining] slaughterers and that they would not receive any salary from the Community Council but rather [one] from the manufacturers [zovhei ha-zevah] of sixty dollars a week. However since the Rabbinical Council announced and publicized that their slaughtering was forbidden, revenues for slaughtering of the secessionists kept getting smaller until they submitted and agreed to make peace with the Community Council. When the thirteen [remaining] slaughterers heard that the secessionists submitted and wanted peace and also heard that famine ruled in their households, they had mercy on the three slaughterers and sent them a sum of money for sustenance in order to propitiate them ... to make the peace easier. Thus the matter was ended. When all the sides saw that the dispute caused loss to everyone, all of them sought to make peace. Since the manufacturers did not wish to add to the price of slaughtering unless the Community Council would add to the Association of Slaughterers also the three slaughterers who originally went out, the Community Council was forced, in making peace, to have them also enter under their auspices. The revenue from slaughtering was increased and the Community Council was enabled to add a small amount to the wages of all the slaughterers.

Rabbi Rosenberg's decision in this case went decisively against Getsel Laxer and his colleagues and in favour of the thirteen, and this served to strain relations between the two men who, as we saw in our 1922 document, were erstwhile allies.[54] Though they lived in close proximity to one another on Esplanade Avenue, they refused to speak to each other. In analyzing the claims of the three, Rosenberg noted that the three claimed that they were in fact tacitly supported by the thirteen slaughterers who remained, who were called by them "idlers and cowards, fearful of conflict with the Community Council."

Getsel Laxer's motivations in this incident are reasonably clear and straightforward. He knew himself to be a *shohet* expert in the laws of ritual slaughtering. He felt himself to be equal, if not superior in this respect, to the greatest rabbis of his generation.[55] Thus he vented his frustration over the fact that the Jewish Community Council's rabbis were "slaves ruling over us" who, moreover, took one-third of the money earned by slaughtering for their salaries and overhead. If that "overhead" were eliminated and the one-third added to the slaughterer's wages, they would surely increase by the same amount from approximately $40 to $60 per week. It needn't be said that the tensions shown by these documents, both within the Slaughterers' Association and between the Association and the Community Council, shed considerable light on the conditions of the kosher meat industry of Montreal and on the role of Getsel Laxer and his colleagues in the development of both the material and the intellectual life of the Montreal rabbinate.

Hyman Meyer Crestohl

Hyman [Haim] Meyer Crestohl, rabbi and *shohet* in Quebec City and Montreal, was born in Russian Poland in 1865.[56] He married Rose Weitzman and had three sons.[57] He died in Montreal on May 5, 1928.[58] Crestohl received an extensive education in the literary sources of Orthodox Judaism in his native Poland and obtained his rabbinical ordination from eminent rabbinical authorities there.[59] He also was deeply exposed in his youth to an informal education in European literature and thought in a manner which was not uncommon among contemporary rabbinical students.[60] After his ordination, he served as rabbi of the Polish town of Siedlice.[61] He was a Zionist by conviction and became an early member of *Mizrahi*, the religious faction of the Zionist movement. He became an activist and a propagandist for that movement. As such, he was in contact with many of the leaders of political Zionism in Europe, such as Chaim Weizmann, Nahum Sokolow, and Rabbis Samuel Mohilever and Isaac Reines.[62]

In 1904 he went from Warsaw to New York as an emissary of *Mizrahi*[63] and stayed in New York until 1911.[64] Among the Crestohl papers we have a letter of recommendation on his behalf, written by Rabbi Reines to *Mizrahi* activists in America. In that letter, Reines praised his public-speaking ability as well his rabbinical qualifications. Reines asked those who would read the letter to make an effort to help Rabbi Crestohl gain his livelihood. It is interesting to see the sort of thing that Rabbi Reines recommended. The recipients of his letter were not asked to find him a rabbinical position. Rather they were given the following possibilities: a position as a *shohet*, or, possibly as a fundraising emissary for *Mizrahi* or for the Yeshiva of Lida, or, possibly, a vendor of lottery tickets. The choices for a man like Rabbi Crestohl in New York in 1904 were thus not all that promising. He evidently stayed in New York State for several years, including a period as rabbi in the town of Gloversville.[65] We find him living in Brooklyn in 1910.

In 1911, he emigrated to Canada, serving first as rabbi of a congregation in Quebec City from 1911 to 1919.[66] In Quebec City, Rabbi Crestohl was the rabbi of the second, breakaway congregation, Ohabei Shalom.[67] Whatever the original reason for the split in this small Jewish community in the year 1907,[68] the dispute between Rabbis Simon Glazer and Hirsh Cohen, both then vying for the leadership of the immigrant Orthodox community in Montreal, which had split the community there, played itself out also in Quebec. The loyalties of the established congregation in Quebec City, Beth Israel, went to Rabbi Glazer in 1909.[69] Thus, apparently, Rabbi Cohen's supporters coalesced around the new congregation. That there was bad blood between the two communities will be seen presently but can be also illustrated by the fact that one of the more prominent Jewish residents of Quebec, Mr. Montefiore Joseph, could inform Montreal's *Jewish Times* in 1910 that, "we have one synagogue," pointedly ignoring the existence of the other.[70]

One piece of evidence supporting this tie between Ohabei Sholom and Rabbi Cohen is a series of three letters from Rabbi Cohen to Crestohl in 1916–18, in one of which he spoke of supplying Crestohl with two sets of *arba' minim*.[71] Significantly, Rabbi Cohen did not address Rabbi Crestohl as "Rabbi," in these letters, but as "*shohet* in Quebec." There was a subtle but distinct line of hierarchy between the two. Much more to the point, however, is a draft of a letter Rabbi Crestohl wrote to Rabbi Glazer, in his role as editor of a short-lived Montreal Yiddish newspaper entitled *Di Idishe Velt*.[72] Rabbi Glazer had, apparently, published an attack on both Crestohl personally and on the community he led under the title "*Skandal in Kvebek*" shortly after Crestohl's arrival. In response, Crestohl wrote a long and detailed refutation.

He began this refutation by expressing his surprise and shock that the attack on him should come from a fellow rabbi. Using the strong and pointed words of the Babylonian Talmud, he rhetorically stated: "Prostitutes do makeup for one another. How much more so should disciples of the sages [help each other]?"[73]

The first charge in the article was that his position as *shohet* in the community was illegitimate, since he was trespassing on the territory of another slaughterer, authorized by Rabbi Glazer in his role as chief rabbi of the Beth Israel community, which he considered the only legitimate one in the city. Thus the meat emanating from the animals Crestohl had slaughtered was not to be considered kosher. The second charge was that Crestohl was a man who would issue Jewish divorces to anyone for a few dollars, strongly implying that financial, and not halakhic, questions determined the results.[74]

The third charge involved an incident that reveals the tensions inherent in the relations between members of the two Quebec synagogues. On a cold winter Friday afternoon, January 5, 1912, a woman of the Ohabei Sholom community died. Though Quebec City had two synagogues, it had only one Jewish cemetery, controlled by Beth Israel. Thus the chief officer of the Beth Israel Cemetery was called and indicated that he would make all arrangements for the burial. The article charged or implied that Crestohl had instructed the gentile caretaker of the cemetery to dig the grave on Saturday afternoon, which would have been a violation of the Sabbath laws. Not so, replied Crestohl. The cemetery watchman had been informed that he should be ready to dig the grave after dark on Saturday night, because that Saturday, January 6, was the Catholic holiday of the "Three Kings" [Epiphany] and it was feared that, if not suitably informed, he might get drunk and not be there at the right time. Because it was terribly cold, and the watchman did not want to dig the grave at night, he took it upon himself to dig the grave on the Saturday afternoon. As to the article attributing consternation on the part of the officers of the Beth Israel Cemetery at this violation of the Sabbath, Crestohl sarcastically responded, "whoever knows the officers ... including the chief officer, knows how much they are aggravated by Sabbath desecration."

Crestohl further stated that the Beth Israel Cemetery official told the husband of the deceased woman, who was himself bedridden with three children in the house, that they would not touch the body until they were paid $15.00, and that, finally, they would not bury her in the plot of the family's choice, but in another one.

At this point in the feud, Rabbi Crestohl was asked and gave permission for the body to be transported for burial out of Quebec City. Rabbi Glazer criticized Rabbi Crestohl for this and cited the authoritative Code of Judaic law, the *Shulḥan 'Arukh*, which stated that one was not to transport a deceased's body from a city that possessed a Jewish burial ground. In his justification for his permission, which contained several learned references, Crestohl also indicated some of the ambivalence of the authority of an Orthodox rabbi in a community like Quebec. He had initially hesitated to respond to the halakhic query because he had determined not to answer halakhic questions in Quebec on the grounds that he had once issued an opinion in a matter of importance that was not obeyed. What swayed him, ultimately, was the plea of the deceased's bedridden husband that if she were buried in Quebec, he would die.

During his time in Quebec, Rabbi Crestohl maintained his ties with the Zionist movement in Canada, founding the Dorshei Zion Society of Quebec City and serving on the council of the Federation of Zionist Societies of Canada.[75] During World War I, he was also active in ministering to the religious needs of Jewish soldiers training at Valcartier.[76]

In 1920 he moved to Montreal. As is the case with more than one small-town rabbi, including Getsel Laxer, the move was prompted by the desire to have the social and intellectual resources of a large Jewish community, such as Montreal, especially for the education and marriage prospects of his children. As early as 1918, he had inquired about the possibility of moving to Montreal and becoming a *shoḥet*, for which he understood that he would be obliged to purchase a *ḥazaka* [membership right] in the *Agudat ha-Shoḥtim* of Montreal.[77] Unfortunately for him, negotiations lasted a frustrating two years, including numerous trips to Montreal to confer with his potential colleagues. During this period, despairing of getting the position in Montreal, he actively considered another opportunity to become the rabbi of the Jewish community of Halifax. In one letter, Crestohl poured forth his frustrations and disgust in a letter to Meyer Cohen, a Montreal *shoḥet*. He began by saying that he was writing this letter in Yiddish, instead of his usual Hebrew, so that he will be better understood, and so that he will not desecrate the Holy tongue by talking about such vile things. He had heard accusations against him that he did not put on *tefilin*, or that, alternatively, the *tefilin* he did put on were invalid and he was completely fed up with the hypocrisy of men who hide "a large mound of dirt with the mantle of piety." He spoke of one of the *shohtim* who was well known to be incompetent at his job, of another whose brother, also working as a *shohet* in Montreal and Quebec, was a bigamist, having one wife in Romania and another in Montreal.

Ultimately the dispute was settled, though 'amicably' is probably not a just description, and he moved to Montreal in 1920. By the late 1920s he was elected secretary of the slaughterers' organization. He also was appointed as rabbi of the Russian-Polish Hadrath Kodesh Congregation (1920–28).[78] Even at this point, he hesitated to unequivocally identify himself as a rabbi. On his business card, the Hebrew side identifies him as "*ha-rov*" [rabbi], whereas on the English part he calls himself "Rev.," a title more suitable to a lesser religious functionary than a rabbi.[79] Since it was not possible for him to make ends meet as a congregational rabbi, even with the additional income he derived as a *shohet*,[80] he also advertised himself on his card as a circumciser and performer of weddings. On the flip side of his business card, he also advertised that: "You can also get Chickens cleaned and fixed Retail to Wholesale Prices."[81] In 1920, he also became first president of the Mizrahi Organization of Canada.[82]

As we have seen, Crestohl had plenty of opposition getting into Montreal. This did not completely cease when he arrived there to settle. As a partisan of Rabbi Cohen from his years in Quebec City, he was a target for Cohen's opponents, chief among them Rabbi Yudel Rosenberg, who had taken over Rabbi Glazer's rabbinical post in 1919. In a circular, Rabbi Rosenberg declared that Rabbi Crestohl's slaughtering was invalid and not kosher. Rabbi Crestohl was called in this circular "an old former country *shohet*" [*an alter gevezener kontri shohet*].[83] True to his style of previous years, Rabbi Crestohl countered with a circular of his own in which Rabbi Rosenberg was charged with, among other things, acquiescing in the false testimony of one of the *shohtim* under his supervision, which was given in front of the Holy Ark of the Papineau Synagogue.

Crestohl, like many of his fellow *shohtim*, was well known as a scholar of rabbinic literature and wrote many works on that subject.[84] However, the fact that his works remained in manuscript served to limit his influence to the Montreal Jewish community. Only one of his treatises was published, posthumously, by his children.[85]

Both Getsel Laxer and Hyman Crestohl illustrate the tensions, resentments, and conflicts that were inherent in the kosher meat industry of

Montreal and in its rabbinical functionaries, to the frequent consternation of the Montreal Jewish community. The situation cried out for reform. In the next chapter, we will consider one such attempt at ameliorating the situation through the founding of a body that would take over the regulatory apparatus of the kosher meat industry – the Jewish Community Council [*Va'ad ha-'Ir*] of Montreal.

· 6 ·

The Founding of the Jewish Community Council of Montreal (Va'ad ha-'Ir)[1]

I place these suggestions before the public merely with the desire to show that our local communal affairs can be honorably adjusted and conducted under the supervision of a Kehillah, to the credit of every Jew in the city and to the advantage of all our necessary institutions. – Hirsh Wolofsky (1922)[2]

In this chapter, we will be looking at something slightly different. In the previous chapters, we have largely been concentrating on rabbinic personalities. Now we are shifting our focus from rabbis and their controversies to something broader. Just as one cannot understand the Montreal Jewish community and its development without understanding who the rabbis were and what they stood for, it is similarly impossible to understand the rabbis without knowing something about the broader communal situation they faced. That broader picture will be depicted in this chapter, which will culminate in the founding of the Jewish Community Council of Montreal, known in Hebrew as the *Va'ad ha-'Ir*.[3]

Before we get to the *Va'ad ha-'Ir*, however, there are some broader questions that need to be discussed. The broadest of them all is how does one organize a Jewish community in North America, or, indeed, anywhere in the world in the twentieth century? In small communities, the process may be relatively easy. If there are few synagogues in town, if Jewish organizations are also few, then the process of establishing a Jewish community and Jewish leadership is relatively simple to comprehend. If, however, we are speaking of the larger communities in the early twentieth century, of the magnitude of Montreal, Chicago, New York, or Warsaw, the question becomes how does one deal with a complex array of Jewish opinions, ideologies, and organizations? How does one construct a community containing the very stringently Orthodox, the militantly anti-religious, as well as all those in between? All call themselves Jews; all have cogent claims to membership in the Jewish community. Another question to be answered is who takes the lead in organizing such a community, since certainly, as in all organizational endeavours, someone must take the lead? Thus when we talk about the Eastern European Jewish immigrant community of Montreal, getting together in 1922/3 in order to found an organization known as the *Va'ad ha-'Ir*, it is important to know what sort of models they had at their disposal to inform their decisions.

The man who stood behind the creation of the *Va'ad ha-'Ir*, and who will soon be introduced, as well as his co-workers, understood that there were several possible models for the creation of an organized Jewish community in North America from which to choose. The first question that needed to be answered was: who takes the lead? In the United States, the first group to attempt to organize the large Jewish communities of New York, Philadelphia, and elsewhere in the twentieth century consisted of the people who coalesced around an organization called the American Jewish Committee.[4] The American Jewish Committee was made up largely, though not totally, of Jews stemming from the older, mid-nineteenth-century immigration of Jews to the United States. The immigrants in this group had largely come from Germany and not from Eastern Europe, and there were as well a significant number of native-born Americans among them. They therefore had an extra generation to acculturate themselves in North America – an extra experience at being "American." In the first decade of the twentieth century, Russian anti-Jewish pogroms, particularly the Kishinev Pogrom of 1903, created a mass outrage within the American Jewish community. That outrage fostered a feeling that the American Jewish community needed to create an effective leadership group that would be able to lobby the American government on issues relevant to the Jewish community. The founders of the American Jewish Committee understood that "organization was in the air," and that if they, the acculturated and the affluent, did not come to the fore and lead, others, less "Americanized" surely would come to fill that need and carry the community in possibly irresponsible directions. In their view, the Eastern European Jews had, first of all, not sufficiently assimilated American values, and thus were not to be considered worthy representatives of the American Jewish community.[5] In asserting their leadership of the American Jewish community, the founders of the American Jewish Committee co-opted certain Eastern European Jews to their body. Nonetheless, the model offered by the American Jewish Committee was one of an elite choosing its own organizational structure and people, while asserting that its structure and people represented the American Jewish community as a whole.

While the American Jewish Committee was, and remains to this day, an important factor in the organizational life of American Jewry, there were yet other models from which to choose. Another model available was that of Federations of Jewish Charities. Starting in Boston in the 1890s, cities containing large numbers of Jewish organizations decided to federate in order to more efficiently raise funds. Jews in cities with federations would not have to give separately to each individual institution. Rather they would give once a year to a federated Jewish charitable appeal, which took upon itself the task of a fair and just allocation of Jewish charitable funds. The federations thus achieved, through the power of allocation of funds, considerable power and influence within the Jewish community.[6]

There was yet another model of communal leadership that originated within the Eastern European Jewish community itself, starting in the first decade of the twentieth century. By that time, the mass immigration of Jews from Eastern Europe to the United States had been ongoing for more than two decades. That meant that the immigrants who had arrived in the 1880s had been in America for sufficient time to begin to feel "at home." Many of them had by then gone beyond the hand-to-mouth existence of their first years in the New World. They were on their feet financially and had largely assimilated what being a Jew in America meant. While retaining a respect for the German-Jewish leadership that claimed to speak on their behalf, they began to insist that their voices be heard in the councils of American Jewry. They claimed, as Americans, their right to representation in these councils. They felt that, in a democratic society, the Jewish masses had to have their say, not only the upper classes. Out of the struggle of the newer Eastern European immigrant Jewish community to find its authentic leadership voice, arose one of the most interesting political movements in American Jewish history. It was called the "Kehilla" movement.[7]

"Kehilla" is the classical Hebrew word for community. European Jewish communities were often called *"Kehilla Kedosha,"* or "Holy Community."[8] Perhaps it is because the people behind the American Kehilla experiment were not necessarily "holy" people, that the adjective "Holy" was dropped from the title. What the leaders of the American Kehilla movement wanted to do was to make sure that all Jews and all Jewish organizations would be represented in the communal leadership, not merely the German-Jewish elite and its institutions. This especially applied to the organizations created by the Eastern European immigrants: their synagogues, *landsmanschaften,*[9] and loan societies. These were organizations that were not typically represented in the Federations of Jewish Charities, which were dominated by the Jewish monied classes, overwhelmingly of German-Jewish descent. In their totality, however, these Eastern European organizations were important in the lives of thousands of Jews. Jewish trade unions, in the garment industry and beyond, also demanded representation. The idea of the Kehilla movement was to make use of all of these organizations and their potentials and to make sure that all their constituencies were represented. Furthermore, the Kehilla movement wanted to do things that the established American Jewish leadership groups had tended to neglect. A good example is Jewish education. Federations of Jewish Charities in North American cities (Montreal Jews founded a Federation of Jewish Charities in 1917 as part of this trend) were founded mainly to support the areas of social welfare and immigrant aid. They did not, however, significantly support Jewish education. For the elite, Jewish education was not a pressing issue. There was not much worry about how to make Jewish children Jewish in these circles at this time. It was fairly well assumed that living in Jewish neighbourhoods and being exposed to the services of the synagogue would take care of the Jewishness of the children, as though it could be absorbed by a sort of osmosis. Jewish education, moreover, was felt to be the domain of the individual congregations, rather than the community as a whole. In any event, these elite organizations did not want to touch Jewish education, though they did agree that education aimed at the Americanization (or, in the case of Montreal, the Canadianization) of the immigrant population was highly desirable. Insofar as Jewish education was controlled either by Orthodox Jews, or by Jews of radical political and social inclinations, it was not really attractive to them. Indeed, by and large, the Jewish federations would not seriously support Jewish education until the 1960s, when the process of acculturation to North America had fully run its course, and there began to be a generally perceived need to educate children Jewishly. On the other hand, for the Eastern European immigrant community, Jewish education for its children was considered of vital importance from the very beginning. Thus it is significant that the Kehilla movement, from its inception, supported important initiatives in the field of Jewish education.

The Kehilla movement started in New York in 1908. From there, it spread to Philadelphia,[10] St. Louis, Denver, and other cities throughout the United States. In all these places, there was a coming together of the German-Jewish elites and the Eastern European emergent leadership to create an organization that would be, as much as possible, inclusive of all Jewish organizations in the city and address community needs that the federations were not addressing.

One of these needs was *kashrut*. The conflictual situation found in Montreal with respect to *kashrut* certification was to be replicated throughout North America. Another need, already mentioned, was support for Jewish education. Still another feature of the Kehilla system was an attempt to create a mechanism whereby labour disputes between Jewish workers and Jewish bosses could and should be settled within the community without recourse to strikes. This might be done either through facilitation of negotiations, or else through a more formal arbitration board, which could create a just situation for both labour and management within the Jewish community.

The Kehilla movement was a wonderful dream. Certain parts of it came into reality. Thus, for example, the highly influential New York Board of Jewish Education began as a bureau of the New York Kehilla. However, the Kehilla ultimately foundered during World War I. First of all, the movement split over the Balfour Declaration of 1917, which promised the establishment of a Jewish national home in Palestine. In the aftermath of the Balfour Declaration, the Eastern European Jewish community in North America, whose sympathies, save for a small radical fringe, were fairly solidly on the side of the Zionists, split off from the German-Jewish elite, which was fairly solidly non- or anti-Zionist. The Eastern Europeans demanded that their Kehilla lobby the United States government to support the Balfour Declaration, and, by extension, the creation of a Jewish homeland in Palestine after the war. They did so with the battle cry of American democracy. Their side had the majority of the votes, though the German-Jewish elite had in fact provided most of the financing. In general the elite groups were afraid of the possibility of accusations of "dual loyalty" against the Jews and opposed this move.

Ultimately, the Eastern European and Zionist leadership pushed for the creation of an American Jewish Congress, which was to demand that Jewish rights in Palestine be established and formally recognized in whatever international order would come into being after the war. The German-Jewish elite, which disliked Jewish nationalism and even objected to the widespread knowledge that a "Jewish vote" existed, was horrified. The split between the elite and the masses ultimately destroyed the Kehilla movement's viability. By 1922, the New York Kehilla had dissolved; the Philadelphia Kehilla had gone out of existence several years before this. The Kehilla movement, however important it is for our story, was thus ultimately a failure.

Within the Montreal Jewish community, the largest and most influential Jewish community in the Dominion of Canada, there existed the same sort of split between an acculturated, Canadianized and fairly well-to-do minority, which was in charge of Montreal's Federation of Jewish Charities, and the Eastern European immigrant majority. However, relatively speaking, the former group were less numerous and generally less influential relative to the totality of the Jewish community than was the case in the United States. The question confronting the Montreal community was the same as that posed in the United States: who would organize the Canadian Jewish community? Starting in the first decades of the twentieth century, there were a number of attempts to do so.[11] Thus the Canadian Zionist Federation sought to create a Dominion-wide communal representation on the basis of its cross-Canada network of societies. B'nai B'rith, for its part, claimed that Zionism was unable to unite all elements in the Canadian Jewish community and put forth its own counterclaim to leadership in the creation of an organization to represent Canadian Jewry. Ultimately, neither the Zionists nor B'nai B'rith were able to create by themselves a Canadian Jewish representative organization.

Nonetheless, as in the United States, World War I was crucial as a catalyst in the organizational development of Canadian Jewry.[12] In the same way as an American Jewish Congress was organized to articulate the political positions of the Jews of the United States, so there was a movement to create a Canadian Jewish Congress to be the voice of Canadian Jewry, expressing its demands for the postwar world. Of course, beyond expressing its support for a Jewish homeland in Palestine, the Canadian Jewish Congress also sought to address other issues relevant to the Canadian Jewish community, such as anti-semitism. The Canadian Jewish Congress thus promised to be the democratically elected, organized voice of Canadian Jewry. However, like the Kehilla movement, as well as the American Jewish Congress movement, the Canadian Jewish Congress movement did not take hold immediately.

To be sure, the Canadian Jewish Congress had a successful inaugural meeting in Montreal in 1919, which has a well-deserved place in the annals of Canadian Jewry. However, what is less well known, and of extreme importance for our subject, is that, after its initial meeting, the Canadian Jewish Congress petered out. The next time the Canadian Jewish Congress held a plenary meeting was in 1934. Between 1919 and the thirties, there were certainly efforts, especially by H. M. Caiserman,[13] to keep the organization going, but lack of money and lack of interest caused these efforts to ultimately fail.

Thus the people who were engaged in creating the *Va'ad ha-'Ir* in 1922 were doing so in the year the last of the American Kehilla organizations ceased existing. They were not unaware of this event, for they were keen observers of the North American Jewish scene. From the perspective of 1922, moreover, the Canadian Jewish Congress movement had likewise more or less petered out. How were they to proceed?

One factor that they surely had to take into account was the existence of the elite-sponsored Federation of Jewish Charities, which dealt largely with health and social welfare issues. A second factor to be dealt with was the school issue. The position of Jewish children within the constitutionally mandated denominational school system in the province of Quebec had raised questions as early as 1903.[14] Now, in the 1920s, the question returned with added political force and divided the community between those acculturated elements, largely those who constituted the leadership of the Federation, who saw in the Protestant school system a major Canadianizing force for Jewish children, and those, largely among the immigrant population, who advocated Jewish schools for Jewish children. Then, too, there was the chaos in the religious community. Since 1907, there had been two warring factions within the Montreal Jewish community – one led by Rabbi Hirsh Cohen,[15] and the other led first by Rabbi

Simon Glazer,[16] and, after him, by Rabbi Yudel Rosenberg.[17] Between the two factions there were continual charges and countercharges, with particular reference to the certification of kosher meat.

By 1921, Rabbis Cohen and Rosenberg and their followers came to the decision that it was better to unite Montreal's Orthodox rabbinate. They thus began to jointly advertise butchers under their supervision. They co-opted Rabbis Garber and Zalmanovitz and, together, began calling themselves *"di hige shtot rabbonim"* [rabbis of the city]. There was also an attempt to create a lay leadership that would support this united rabbinate. This was known as the *Va'ad ha-'Ir ha-Dati* (the Religious Community Council).[18] However, there was a man in Montreal who observed these developments and who had a much broader vision. This man's name was Hirsh Wolofsky.[19] Wolofsky was the Jewish media baron of Montreal. He was the publisher of Montreal's Yiddish-language daily, the *Keneder Odler*, which had been published since 1907. By 1922, it was a fairly well-established voice in the community. He also published Montreal's English-language Jewish weekly, *The Canadian Jewish Chronicle*. He thus possessed a "bully pulpit," in the two languages that then counted within the Montreal Jewish community.

Wolofsky was a man of considerable and broad vision. He had to be because the Montreal Jewish community had barely sufficient room for one viable Yiddish daily. In New York, in the era of the 1920s, the Yiddish reader had the luxury of choosing a Yiddish newspaper according to his or her ideology. Communists would read the *Freiheit*; Socialists the *Forverts*. If you were Orthodox, you would read the *Tog* or the *Morgen Journal*. Each of these newspapers spoke for part of the community only. The *Freiheit* could thus damn the capitalists, and if the capitalists did not like it – *tant pis!* The *Tog* could support Orthodoxy, and if the Communists didn't like it – so much the better! However, a publisher in Wolofsky's situation could not afford to alienate anybody. To make his *Keneder Odler* a success, he needed to think on a whole-community basis. Thus Wolofsky's newspaper attempted to be respectful of both religion and non-religion; of labour and management alike. Wolofsky charted a course to keep his publications afloat and was successful in so doing.

This situation was likely the source of his insight that the uniting of the rabbinate of 1921 could lead to even bigger things. He saw beyond the religiously oriented *Va'ad ha-'Ir ha-Dati*. He envisioned what he called a

Kehilla. In both the newspapers he published, and in a separate, bilingual pamphlet issued on September 30, 1922,[20] he put forward his views in an essay entitled in both languages "A Kehilla For/Far Montreal."

His use of the term "Kehilla" is significant, in that this was the same year – 1922 – in which the most prominent example of the American Kehilla movement was going under for the last time. Wolofsky was no fool, and he was certainly well aware of what was going on in the Jewish world. No one, indeed, could have been better positioned than he to find out such things. He had obviously decided that, in Montreal, there were possibilities for a Kehilla-like organization within the Jewish community. Whereas the attempts to unite Jewish communities in the United States through Kehillas had failed, he, Wolofsky, would succeed in Montreal. His prospects for success were good, he felt, because his plan would give each and every Jew in Montreal's Eastern European immigrant community a stake in the success of the venture.

He started his essay by thinking big. As he stated,

When I speak of a Kehilla for Montreal, it must be understood that it will refer not only to Montreal but will represent all of Canada. For while it is true that the Kehilla will function only in this city, it will really be taken as the authority for all Canadian Jewry to follow.

We need to remember that, at this point in history, Canadian Jewry did not have an effective organizational leadership because the Canadian Jewish Congress, which might have created that leadership, was practically moribund. Therefore what Wolofsky was saying was that the "Kehilla for Montreal" was bound to have an influence far beyond Montreal's boundaries.[21]

In analyzing the problems of Montreal's Jewish community, Wolosky saw that it was divided into a number of groups. All of these groups had their individual problems and issues. In the Kehilla he envisioned, all of these groups would benefit. The first thing the Kehilla had to do was to remedy what he termed "the present chaotic condition of affairs" in the community. He continued:

Many will find an excuse for the licentiousness now existing by blaming it on America. In America, they contend, there cannot be that care taken to make

Jewish life as Jewish as possible. It is only when a catastrophe comes upon us such as the recent Kosher butcher scandal that we admit that something must be done the better to regulate our communal life.

The crux of Wolofsky's idea was that the kosher meat crisis, which gave the impetus to organization, could be leveraged. First of all, he wanted to prevent what he called a "Chillul Ha Shem"[22] that the kosher meat accusations, traded back and forth, had caused. But, while he agreed that kosher meat was a valid part of what needed to be fixed, he also emphasized that thinking in a broader perspective was necessary. As he stated:

Taken by itself, the religious group is unable to carry out any of the changes it desires. Let us take for example the terrible meat situation. I have been given to understand that *trefah wurst*[23] is being sold all over the city and that most of the restaurants are using *trefah* meat. The Talmud Torahs are always in financial difficulties.... The Hebrew Schools are constantly before the public begging for money, and such a state of perpetual *schnorring*[24] reacts unfavorably both on pupils and teachers. The children seeing their religious leaders cheapen themselves with all sorts of publicity in their attempt to obtain funds for the schools, seeing the kosher meat business ridiculed by press and public, finding no religious atmosphere in their homes or elsewhere begin to look upon the Jewish religion as more or less of a hoax, as something to get away from as soon as they grow up.

That, then, was the challenge faced by the religious community. The next group Wolofsky discussed were the Jewish workers:

I refer to the unions of Jewish working men, who form a large part of the community. This group, desiring the perpetuation of a Yiddish culture, operate schools of their own, and these schools, too, suffer from the general upheaval. The children in these schools, while not brought up along religious lines, are being taught to be proud of their Jewish heritage. They are being instilled with the true Jewish spirit.

He was, therefore, able to see the merit in all sides. The Yiddish schools may not have been religious, but, because they taught what he termed "the true Jewish spirit," "such schools deserve the support of all sections of the community."

He further stated:

I would even say that the economic situation of the Jewish workingman would be improved under the proper management of a Kehillah. Even strikes, especially when they occur in the shop of a Jewish employer could be more easily adjusted were there a duly-elected Kehillah, a true "Vox Populi" functioning in our midst.

Yet a third factor in Wolofsky's thinking was the existence of the Jewish sick benefit societies and *landsmanschaften*:

There are in Montreal, at present, about 50 Sick Benefit Societies. If all these little societies were to unite in one big organization they would not only increase their usefulness, but they would reduce expenses, while constituting a real power amongst the people.... The same could be said of the local "Loan Syndicates." Were all the local loan syndicates to be united into one strong body, Montreal Jewry could have one strong chartered Jewish bank that would be a credit to the whole community. Under the aegis of a Kehilla organization such a bank – the bank of the whole community, would be patronized by the community and would thus be in a position to help those in need of financial assistance with larger loans.

Once again, Wolofsky was thinking big, going far beyond the kosher meat issue that had started his process of thinking.

What was to be the task of the Kehilla? Its first goal would be to finance a *Beth Din*,[25] so that the religious leaders of Montreal need not be worried by financial difficulties but could devote all their attention to matters of *kashrut*, marriage and divorce, as well as the supervision of Jewish education. There was, as well, to be an economic aspect. Jewish merchants, in the face of Kehilla pressure, would not dare charge exorbitant prices for the necessities of life. In cultural terms, the Kehilla would support the entire spectrum of Jewish schools in Montreal. All of them would be financed in a dignified manner so they would not have to constantly beg the public for funds. The Kehilla would also be in a position to establish new institutions, such as a Jewish hospital.

The Kehilla could also "lay the foundation for a Jewish parochial school" – in other words Wolofsky looked forward to the time when there would be an opportunity to establish a day school that would give secular as well as religious instruction to Montreal's Jewish children."[26] This stance was of some importance, because, in the 1920s, one of the major political issues facing the Jewish community was the "school question." Broadly speaking, the support for separate Jewish schools came from the immigrant community, and support for Jewish childrens' education in Montreal's Protestant schools from the older, acculturated community. Wolofsky's support for the establishment of Jewish parochial schools therefore constituted a stand that would arouse some opposition within the "uptown" community. It was also a stand that gained him the support of Montreal's *Po'alei Zion* [Labour Zionists], a key group in facilitating the organization of the Eastern European Jewish community of Montreal. As David Rome has commented, the *Po'alei Zion* supported the formation of the *Va'ad ha-'Ir* "because they foresaw it could become an important representative instrument, in the absence of a Congress, in the campaign for separate schools."[27]

Wolofsky also wanted the Kehilla to organize the Sick Benefit Societies and the Loan Syndicates "upon a solid foundation of greater usefulness." The Kehilla, finally, would have the task of settling strikes and preventing unnecessary ones.

How was this wonderful scheme to be organized and financed? Organizationally, Wolofsky sought to divide Montreal Jews into "three equal divisions," to be equally represented in the Kehilla council. This division was not to be merely symbolic. There was not to be one Kehilla president; rather, there was to be a three-member presidium, as well as an elected executive of thirty – ten from each division – each representing one of the three groups.[28] In Wolofsky's Kehilla scheme, representatives would thus be chosen in accordance with the threefold division as follows:

a) all religious Jews through their affiliation with the Synagogue [*shul yidn*],
b) all members of local organizations, unions and benefit societies,
c) all private Jewish citizens who are to become individual members of the Kehilla organization.

What Wolofsky could not, and did not, do was to assume that his Kehilla would be representative of the acculturated, affluent Jewish community that was known collectively in Montreal as "uptown." Wolofsky was very careful not to tread on the turf of the people behind the Montreal Federation of Jewish Charities, which certainly did not include any substantial representation of the immigrant community in its leadership. Thus in all that Wolofsky projected for his Kehilla, there is no mention, either by name or function, of the Baron de Hirsch Institute. There was no project to take over the functions of the Jewish Immigrant Aid Society. Wolofsky was therefore not looking at the sort of social welfare issues already covered by the institutions of the Federation. His purview was basically educational and cultural – issues neglected or ignored by the Federation. His Kehilla would be doing things that would be supplementary to, and would not clash with, the things already being covered by the Federation.

A key question Wolofsky addressed was the financing of his projected organization. The Kehilla was going to be financed through kosher meat:

It has been estimated that the local community[29] consumes about 600 heads of cattle per week, but I will make a more conservative estimate and put it down at 500. Up to now, wholesalers have paid $2.25 per head for *Shechita* which covered all points connected with the *shechita*. Let us say that of this money the Kehilla will receive only $1.00 per head, because of the *Rebbonim* [sic] *Shochetim, Mashgechim* will have to be assured of a decent livelihood first. This will bring the income of the Kehilla to about the following: $1.00 per head from the *shechita* money for the year, about $25,000.00.

After listing that figure, for which he had some precedent and justification, Wolofsky continued his estimate using figures that could only, even at the time, been called "highly speculative." He thus envisaged 3,000 members paying individual dues, for a total of $30,000, one hundred organizations, such as synagogues, paying $100 apiece, for a total of $10,000, and, finally, he dared venture into the loosely regulated – if at all – poultry-slaughtering market and estimated that, in the end, it could be made to contribute $20,000 annually to the funds of the Kehilla. He thus estimated that his Kehilla would have $85,000 income per year. As we will see in the next chapter, events proved that he was dreaming in Technicolor.

What was his Kehilla going to do with all that money? Approximately 10 per cent ($8,700) of that money would be going to overhead. Of the rest, $30,000 would go to the Talmud Torahs and the Yeshiva. The Folks Schule and the Peretz Schule would divide approximately $15,000.

That would have constituted a considerable proportion of the annual budget of these institutions. It would have also left a surplus of approximately $30,000, which he would allocate to such things as a Jewish hospital "and others for which the need will surely rise." This, then, is Wolofsky's vision.

His pamphlet was written in September of 1922. On October 29, a preliminary meeting was held to begin the practical organization of this body. It convened 164 delegates representing seventy-three different organizations. At that meeting, Wolofsky's idea was adopted almost in its entirety. There were, however, several important exceptions. The first of these exceptions concerned the name of the organization. He wanted it to be called a "Kehilla," but it ultimately saw the light of day as the *Va'ad ha-'Ir*. The name was changed partially at least because the demise of the Kehilla movement in the United States may have discredited the name. With respect to the name ultimately adopted, *Va'ad*, it seems at least possible that they were looking at the example of the new, halutzic Jewish community of Palestine – the *Yishuv*. Indeed, as Wolofsky states in his memoirs, it was his trip to Palestine, in 1921, that gave him the name.[30] The Jewish community of Palestine had just established its own representative organization called the *Va'ad Leumi*.[31] It was the *Va'ad Leumi* that ultimately emerged, in 1948, as the Provisional Government of the State of Israel. Another indication that the Jewish community of Palestine was the inspiration of the founders of the *Va'ad ha-'Ir* was the name the organizers of the *Va'ad ha-'Ir* chose for the Jewish court of arbitration they set up: *Mishpat ha-Shalom* [the Justice of Peace]. It was likely inspired by the contemporary attempt by Jews in Palestine to set up an internal judiciary system, independent of either traditional rabbinical courts on the one hand or the court system of the Mandatory government on the other. This system was called *Mishpat ha-Shalom ha-'Ivri* [Hebrew Justice of Peace].[32]

The new *Va'ad ha-'Ir*'s basic governance structure remained basically true to Wolofsky's vision, especially in its division of representation into three equal parts. The three divisions, however, were somewhat different. Instead of one of the divisions consisting of unaffiliated, private members, the three divisions now consisted of: a) synagogues, b) labour organizations, and c) loan syndicates and sick benefit societies. Efforts were to be made by the founders of the *Va'ad ha-'Ir* to make sure that there were women as well as men elected as representatives.

The October 29 meeting determined that there would be elections for representatives to the first *Va'ad ha-'Ir* on December 17, 1922. In these elections, there were seventy-five candidates for the thirty-three council positions. Approximately ten thousand Jews voted in these elections, or approximately 25 per cent of the total Jewish population of Greater Montreal. This voluntary turnout demonstrates the degree to which the idea had stirred the Jewish community.

The main contribution Wolofsky made to the founding of the *Va'ad ha-'Ir* of Montreal was his idea that organization of the Eastern European immigrant Jewish community would not succeed unless it went beyond the religiously observant community. He therefore made sure that all segments of the community had a stake in the organization's success. The financial engine of the *Va'ad ha-'Ir* was kosher meat. Religious Jews certainly patronized kosher butchers out of conviction. However, the non-religious elements of the community, who purchased their meat from Jewish butcher shops out of habit and not out of conviction, needed incentives to continue their kosher meat purchases. For them, the knowledge that the dollars they spent at the meat market would help their own schools – the Peretz and Folks Shules – and not just the Talmud Torahs made a discernible difference.

Wolofsky's idea took form fairly quickly. The supervising rabbis, slaughterers, and *mashgihim* [supervisors], instead of being paid directly by the slaughterhouses or the butchers, a situation prone to conflict of interest, were now paid by the *Va'ad ha-'Ir*. Slaughterers were to receive approximately forty dollars per week. Rabbi Hirsh Cohen, as head of the Rabbinical Council attached to the *Va'ad ha-'Ir* received sixty dollars per week from the *Va'ad*, along with his other sources of income. Rabbi Yudel Rosenberg started out at forty dollars per week, immediately asked for a raise, and then received forty-five dollars per week. The *Va'ad* also immediately began making payments to the Jewish schools of Montreal. In the first three months of its operation, the *Va'ad* paid over $2,000 to the Talmud Torahs and a somewhat lesser sum to the Yiddishist schools. A good beginning had been made.[33]

Unfortunately the good fortune that had accompanied Wolofsky's idea so far did not last. Within three months of the beginning of the *Va'ad*'s operations, the organization nearly self-destructed.[34] It was blown apart because Rabbis Rosenberg and Herschorn and their supporters among the slaughterers, prominent among whom was Getsel Laxer,[35] seceded from the *Va'ad ha-'Ir*. Why did they do it? To begin with, there were many hard words and feelings in the past few years between the different factions of rabbis and slaughterers, as we have seen in previous chapters. These could not be, and were not, forgotten so quickly. Secondly, there was the issue, which Rabbi Rosenberg brought up in his propaganda, of how far an organization that had taken upon itself to supervise the supply of kosher meat should be in the power of Jews who had no religious commitment. Whatever the reasons, the result was a kosher meat war that began in 1923 and lasted until 1925. It was not literally called a "war" by those who participated in it. They preferred to call it the "Kosher Meat Question" [*di bosor kosher frage*]. On the other hand, when it was finished, the parties involved made a "peace" [*sholom*]. One does not make "peace" unless there has first been a "war." This kosher meat war will be described in the next chapter.

· 7 ·

The Kosher Meat Wars of the 1920s and their Aftermath[1]

It is now clear to everyone that if Rabbi Cohen knew his prohibition to be substantial ... he would come to a din torah and prove that the shoḥtim are forbidden. Why has he not done so? This is the best demonstration that his prohibitions are false ... and that the [prohibited] shoḥtim are really kosher. – Circular in the name of "The Rabbis and Shoḥtim of the Va'ad ha-Kashrut" (1924)[2]

In this chapter, we will be talking about something I have dubbed the "Kosher Meat War." The people involved, did not call it a "war," but rather "the Kosher Meat Question." However, when they finished it, they spoke of "making peace [*sholom*]," and so I feel justified in this title. One does not make "peace" unless there has been a "war." The Jewish people of Montreal, and especially the rabbis, *shoḥtim*, and butchers must have felt as though they had gone through a war by the time they were done.

At the very end of 1922, and the beginning of the year 1923, the Jewish Community Council [*Va'ad ha-'Ir*] had just been inaugurated. The organizational meeting of the *Va'ad ha-'Ir* took place on October 29, 1922. The first election for the *Va'ad* took place on December 17. For about three months, more or less, the coalition that Hirsh Wolofsky and others had brought together to create this new institution held.[3] However, even while the coalition was holding itself together, it was held by a thread. There were a number of fault lines in the *Va'ad ha-'Ir*. One of them was between the rabbis. The rabbis involved in the leadership of the *Va'ad*, particularly Hirsh Cohen and Yudel Rosenberg, had to have retained vivid memories of the insults, accusations, and hurt feelings of the previous few years, in which they had acted as sworn enemies. Another fault line was between the other rabbis and Rabbi Herschorn, who, in 1921, had acted as an interloper in the kosher meat supervision scene in Montreal. There were further fault lines among the *shohtim*. There were militant *shohtim*, whose leader was Rabbi Getsel Laxer,[4] who were loath to take orders from other people. This was particularly so because Rabbi Laxer felt himself to be the equal in intellect and halakhic learning with the supervising rabbis. Why should these rabbis have the "easy" jobs, which paid more money than the *shohtim*'s hard physical labour on the killing floor. These *shohtim*, therefore, did not particularly like the hierarchy that was being imposed upon them by the *Va'ad ha-'Ir*.

The butchers themselves also had their reservations about the *Va'ad*. Most of the Jewish butchers of Montreal in the early 1920 ran small, marginal businesses. In order to be a Jewish butcher, one did not have to invest all that much money. One also did not have to know all that much English, since almost all of the clientele would be able to, and would even prefer to, communicate in Yiddish. For many new immigrants, Jewish butcher shops marked their first step in their new country. The businesses were marginal, firstly, because there was plenty of competition. In the 1920s, there were over eighty butchers serving the Jewish community. This meant one butcher shop for every five hundred Jews. Some of them were quite successful, which meant that they sold approximately four thousand pounds of meat per week. If the markup was one cent, or even one-half cent per pound, this would enable to butcher to make a decent living. There were other butchers, however, who sold as little as five hundred pounds per week, and who obviously were eking out a marginal living.

They were organized in a group known as the "Association of Jewish Butchers of Montreal"[5] in order to advance their own interests. From the point of view of the consumers they served, the Association was nothing less than a monopolistic "cartel." The muckraking journalists of the *Keneder Odler* called it the "Butcher Trust."[6] In an era of widespread support for antitrust legislation to curb the likes of John D. Rockefeller's Standard Oil Trust, branding an organization as a "trust" was a certain method of creating tension and even hostility within the community.

Thus it is clear that the public distrusted them and rightly assumed that the butchers wanted to get out from under the supervision of the *Va'ad* because they were afraid that the *Va'ad ha-'Ir* was going to be too strict with them. They were in fact correct. At one session of the Finance Committee of the *Va'ad ha-'Ir*, one of the members stated that the Jewish butchers of Montreal cannot take close supervision because, if one looked closely at the halakhic observance of these men, many of them would not pass muster. In January of 1923, there was a mass protest meeting because there was a rumour in the community that the "Butcher Trust" wanted to raise the price of meat by two cents per pound.

Finally, as a result of all of these inherent fault lines, in February 1923, Rabbis Yudel Rosenberg and Sheea Herschorn, and seven *shohtim*, led by Getsel Laxer, left the *Va'ad ha-'Ir*. Having seceded from the *Va'ad*, they proceeded to reform the United Synagogue organization which had been founded and presided over by Rabbi Glazer,[7] and after him by Rabbi Rosenberg until the Montreal rabbinate united in 1921.[8] Thus the *kashrut* supervision in Montreal was divided. On the one side stood the *Va'ad ha-'Ir*, and on the other stood the United Synagogue.

Why did Rabbi Rosenberg and the others secede? Beyond the fault lines previously described, we would do well to pay attention to the reasons articulated by Rabbi Rosenberg. We do not have a direct statement of his, but a great deal can be discerned from the rebuttal to his arguments published in the *Keneder Odler*, which enjoyed a media monopoly within the Montreal Jewish community and which remained consistently on the *Va'ad*'s side. For the *Keneder Odler*, Rabbi Rosenberg and his partisans among the *shohtim* and butchers were traitors [*fareter*], and the paper also took upon itself the right to defrock Rabbis Rosenberg and Herschorn, consistently calling them "the former rabbis." To all of this, Rabbi Rosenberg and his group could only reply by means of handbills or circulars, few of which have been preserved. Nonetheless we are able to understand at least some of Rabbi Rosenberg's articulated positions on this issue.

His first objection was technical in nature, such as the inadequate number of inspectors [*mashgihim*], errors in slaughtering, etc. Secondly, he was dissatisfied with his salary. Rabbi Cohen was getting $60.00 a week, whereas Rabbi Rosenberg was getting only $45.00 a week. He obviously did not relish playing second fiddle in a financial sense. Finally, as we remember, Hirsh Wolofsky had built the coalition that founded the *Va'ad ha-'Ir* on the premise that both religious and non-religious Jews had to cooperate to make the organization a success. This meant that the educational institutions to be supported by the *Va'ad* included not only the Talmud Torah and yeshiva, but also the Yiddishist Folks Shule, Peretz Shule, and Arbeiter Ring Shule. Rabbi Rosenberg said that he felt uncomfortable with non-religious elements sharing control over the *Va'ad ha-'Ir*, as well as giving money raised through the production and sale of kosher meat to the non- and even anti-religious Yiddishist schools.

The war was not just a propaganda war.[9] It was not merely fought with newspaper editorials and handbills. It was also a physical conflict. There was violence among butchers; there were threats to *sho*ẖ*tim* loyal to the *Va'ad ha-'Ir* to desist from slaughtering or else harm would come to them. Rabbi Cohen accused his opponents of hiring gangsters to enforce the closing of certain butcher shops or to make sure that others remained open. All this is in line with a pattern of violence we have seen previously during Rabbi Glazer's sojourn in Montreal,[10] as well as with Rabbi Rosenberg.[11] Leah Rosenberg, Rabbi Yudel Rosenberg's daughter recalls violence directed against her father because of the kosher meat controversy:

We became victims. Just before Yom Kippur a crowd gathered outside our home and threw stones. Father finally went out and faced the people. He told them their behavior was unforgivable and not to be taken lightly a day before Yom Kippur. The people were petrified and left.[12]

The scene described by Leah Rosenberg, though undated, presumably dates from the "Kosher Meat War." Newspaper reports from that period indicate that Rabbi Rosenberg was attacked on the street and that, moreover, any bearded Jew, who by his attire might have been suspected as belonging to Rabbi Rosenberg's group, could not show his face on the street with impunity.[13]

On March 8, 1923, the *Keneder Odler*, reported that a Mr. H. Cohen, who managed the butcher shop of the Consumers' League on 25 Roy St., loyal to Rabbi Cohen and Jewish Community Council [*Va'ad ha-'Ir*],[14] had been assaulted on Main Street [St. Laurence Boulevard] near Pine Avenue. Witnesses said that the assault was perpetrated by a butcher, whose name was given to the police.[15] The *Montreal Star* reported that the victim was hit on the head from behind and left unconscious and was still confined to bed several days later. Three of the officers of the Jewish Butchers' Association were arraigned in this case on a charge of attempted murder.[16]

Just a week later, the *Keneder Odler* reported that there were also threats received by *shoḥtim* loyal to the *Va'ad ha-'Ir*, warning them to desist from slaughtering or else harm would come to them. All the *shoḥtim* received the following letter, delivered to their home addresses:

Mr.——————
If you will go and slaughter for the Canadian Packing Company, you will be shorter by a head.
Signature Unclear

The slaughterers who received the threat were reported to be certain that this was the work of Getsel Laxer, one of the prominent *shoḥtim* on the opposing side, who had threatened them in the slaughterhouse.[17]

The charged nature of the situation can be ascertained from the minutes of the *Va'ad ha-'Ir* conference held in Prince Arthur Hall on April 5, 1923. During that meeting, the leaders of the Consumers' League offered to picket the opposition's butcher shops. A Mr. Lachavitsky felt impelled to specify that the picketing should be peaceful in nature and that "anyone bringing in violence shall be held personally responsible."[18]

On April 29 of that year, a headline in the *Keneder Odler* proclaimed that the opponents of the *Va'ad ha-'Ir* had hired gangsters to get their opponents out of the way.[19] More threatening letters, similar to those that had been sent to the *shoḥtim* in previous weeks, had been received by several members of the *Va'ad ha-'Ir*. They had been handed to a private investigation agency for further action. In an open letter from the *Va'ad ha-Rabbonim*[20] to the *Va'ad ha-'Ir*, Rabbi Hirsh Cohen accused his opponents of hiring gangsters to enforce closing of certain butcher shops or to make sure that others remained open. In that letter he stated:

Horrible things [concerning] those who call themselves butchers have reached our ears, which no fantasy could eclipse. Hear and be amazed:

A group of butchers and *shoḥtim*, with the approval of rabbis have hired gangsters. They have given them a $100.00 deposit and have promised a further $200.00 so that the gangsters should clear away the other *shoḥtim*. They have justified[21] [their action] with a permission [*heter*] since "blood has a double meaning"[22] and since they [their opponents] cause them loss of money, they could spill blood. [It is] only through a miracle that other *shohtim* threatened to reveal [the plot] and that they watched out at night that this should not take place, [otherwise] the murder would have come to pass.²³

At the outbreak of this kosher meat war, the *Va'ad ha-'Ir*, in its public statements, asserted that from 60 to 70 per cent of the kosher meat trade in Montreal was in its hands. Presumably the rest was going to the other side. While it had every reason to minimize the damage it had suffered, its statements of income from late 1922 and early 1923 show that the *Va'ad's* public statements were more or less accurate. I am going to present to you income statements from two roughly comparable periods.²⁴

TABLE 1

Length of Period	November 8, 1922– March 2, 1923	May 31– September 30, 1923
Total revenue of *Va'ad*	$23,485.62	$16,460.02
Income from kosher slaughtering	$21,911.02	Not specified
Payments to *shohtim*	$13,220	$8,400
Payments to rabbis	$3,228	$2,295
Payments to *mashgihim*	$1,280	$1,608.50²⁵
Subsidy to United Talmud Torahs	$2,200	$250
Subsidy to Jewish Peoples' School	$580	$75
Subsidy to Peretz Shule	$550	$60
Subsidy to Arbeiter Ring Shule	$115	$15

We should recall, when reading these figures, that Hirsh Wolofsky, when he projected the income of the *Va'ad*, had predicted that the United Talmud Torahs would receive some $20,000 yearly.²⁶ While the initial reality was considerably less than the dream, nonetheless, assuming the first income statement (which roughly corresponded to the period in which the *Va'ad* held together) to constitute one-third of a year, the school system would have benefited from an infusion of nearly $7,000, which would have constituted a considerable part of its budget. When the *Va'ad* began losing income, roughly one-third between the two income statements, the first thing that went was the educational subsidy. After that, they began cutting salaries. Rabbi Cohen's salary went from sixty to forty-eight dollars per week. They fired the secretary, who was getting fifteen dollars per week and replaced her with a "girl" to simply answer the telephone at three dollars a week, so that the office would remain "open." They had to get a bank loan for $800.00, which they renewed every three months. As the kosher meat war was prolonged, the interest-free loans they had received from various synagogues and benefit societies were an important factor in keeping the enterprise afloat, and when the benefit societies demanded their loans back, it was a serious blow to the *Va'ad*, which was in no position to pay them back. As well, other people were suing the *Va'ad* for unpaid rent. Thus we read in the finance committee's minutes for February 21, 1924:

Madame Boucher has taken action to recover rent for January to May 1, 1924 amounting to $240.00. It was decided in order to gain time that we hand this to our lawyer. Carried.

At the next meeting, February 28, 1924, there was a follow-up to this item:

Mr Nadler[27] reports having given the case of Madame Boucher to Mr. Louis Fitch[28] who promised to try to drag the case for about two weeks.

If the *Va'ad ha-'Ir* was reduced to having to tell its lawyer to muddy the waters for a couple of weeks, then the cash-flow situation had decidedly gone from bad to worse. Ultimately the *Va'ad* succeeded in compromising on the rent with Madame Boucher for the sum of $150.00, of which $50.00 was to have been paid in cash, and then two further monthly payments of the same amount. The *Va'ad ha-'Ir* had clearly been seriously challenged.

As for the Jewish butchers of Montreal, most sided with the secessionists. They obviously saw an advantage for themselves in freedom from the *Va'ad ha-'Ir*'s control. At the beginning, very few butchers sided with the *Va'ad*. The first butcher shop adhering to the *Va'ad ha-'Ir* only opened its doors on March 2, 1923. Nonetheless, though the butchers themselves were initially with Rabbi Rosenberg and his colleagues, the public and the media (*Keneder Odler*) were wholeheartedly on the side of the *Va'ad ha-'Ir*. Thus the *Va'ad* possessed a built-in advantage. The *Va'ad ha-'Ir*, pressing that advantage, declared a boycott against butchers selling meat other than that which it certified as kosher. It declared that the meat certified by Rabbis Rosenberg and Herschorn was not kosher.

In response to this move, the other side began a price war. Kosher meat was then selling in *Va'ad ha-'Ir* butcher shops at 14 cents per pound. The Association of Jewish Butchers began selling their meat at 8–10 cents per pound. In the meantime, there was a war of headlines. The *Va'ad ha-'Ir*, on March 20, claimed to control fourteen butcher shops (of approximately eighty). On March 22, it claimed twenty-four. On March 25, it claimed twenty-seven. It was advertising in the *Keneder Odler* practically on a daily basis, giving the names and locations of *Va'ad ha-'Ir*-affiliated butcher shops. The public was clearly coming in on the *Va'ad*'s side and apparently not buying meat from the other butchers, even at bargain-basement prices, because it was their goal to break the "Butcher Trust." Even though "Butcher Trust" prices were currently low, the public sensed that the "Butcher Trust" could not be trusted not to jack up prices if the issue were decided in its favour. Many butchers concluded that the right side of this issue was the side the customers were on.

By this time, it was obvious that the conflict was going nowhere. Thus the Association of Jewish Butchers began sending out peace feelers to the *Va'ad ha-'Ir*. But at this point the *Va'ad* was extremely angry and felt it had achieved the upper hand in the struggle. In the *Va'ad ha-'Ir*'s minutes there are very harsh words, particularly against the opposing *shoḥtim*. They were referred to as "Laxer and his gang." There were calls for negotiations, but by April of 1923, the *Keneder Odler* was reporting that hopes for peace between the two sides were in vain.

In the months and years that followed, there were numerous attempts to mediate between the two sides. A number of Jewish mutual-benefit societies attempted to mediate. There were attempts to get eminent rabbis from outside Montreal to mediate the dispute. For this purpose, they tried to get Rabbi Bernard Levinthal of Philadelphia, acknowledged by many as the dean of the immigrant Orthodox rabbinate in North America. He did not come. In his place, he sent Rabbi Ḥayyim Fishel Epstein of St. Louis. When Rabbi Abraham Isaac Kook, chief Ashkenazic rabbi of Palestine came to North America in 1924, he went to Montreal to attempt mediation. He, too, failed.[29] All attempts of this nature were to no avail.

There was, however, a certain tide in this conflict. The *Va'ad ha-'Ir* claimed the loyalty of more and more butchers. On June 20, 1923, the

Va'ad ha-'Ir listed seventy-two butchers on its side. On July 25, it was able to produce a list of *holdout* butcher shops that were still affiliated with the other side, which contained only eleven names. It is thus clear that the *Va'ad ha-'Ir* had an advantage in the conflict. It was nonetheless hurting very badly. It could not make ends meet on its reduced income. It was in no position to subsidize Jewish education. Moreover, because of the overwhelming nature of the kosher meat war, it had no time or attention to spare for the other issues that were facing the Montreal Jewish community of this era, most particularly the School Question.[30] There were voices within the leadership of the *Va'ad ha-'Ir* advocating abandonment of the kosher meat war entirely. For them, this issue meant the ruination of the organization and its concept. The really important issue for them was not kosher meat, but rather the School Question. Perhaps the answer was for the *Va'ad* to get out of the kosher supervision business entirely. This sentiment was actually expressed as a resolution at a meeting of the *Va'ad*. It was defeated, with fourteen for the resolution, and forty-four opposed. Nonetheless, the fact that this idea was brought to this point in a serious way shows that, even though the *Va'ad ha-'Ir* had an advantage over its opponents, it was seriously hurt.

The other side was obviously hurting much worse, but they carried on with the fight. We know of this in a number of ways. The main front in the kosher meat war was, obviously, kosher meat. However, there were other "fronts." One of them was kosher milk. Every Spring, the three major dairies of Montreal, Guaranteed, Borden's and J. J. Joubert, got together and hired rabbis to certify the *kashrut* of a batch of milk for Passover, which has especially stringent rules with respect to *kashrut*. In one meeting of the Finance Committee of the *Va'ad ha-'Ir*, Mr. Nadler reported that the best deal he was able to reach with the dairies was $600.00, which barely covered the cost of the supervisors' salaries, printing of labels, etc. However, he said, we cannot do any better because Rabbi Rosenberg had approached the companies and offered to do the job gratis.

What saved the other side? First of all, the butchers were a fickle lot. The *Va'ad ha-'Ir* went from zero to seventy affiliated butchers in only a few months. Not all of these butchers were with the *Va'ad* because they particularly wanted to be. As one person in a Finance Committee meeting stated succinctly, "In America, the butchers are for the dollar. The rabbis are for the dollar." Certainly Montreal's Jewish butchers in the 1920s were in business to make a profit. They swayed from side to side with the wind. The *Va'ad* was acutely aware that there were a lot of butchers affiliating with it for opportunistic reasons, who were not religiously or morally "reliable." There was talk of having stricter standards for accepting butchers. Clearly, whatever standards for the certification of *kashrut* were in place, there were butchers who did not pass muster.

Thus, by the Fall of 1923, the number of butchers claimed by the *Va'ad ha-'Ir* fell from a high of seventy-three in midsummer to fifty-eight. This countertide was noticed by the *Keneder Odler*. Through articles and editorials, readers were told that those who bought meat from "traitor" butcher shops were rebelling against God, their city, and the schoolchildren of the Talmud Torahs. Women were warned not to sell their souls to the devil before the High Holidays by buying non-kosher meat from these "traitors."

A good example of the rhetoric of the *Keneder Odler* in this period deals with yet another front of this "war" – kosher chickens. On September 16, the *Keneder Odler* reported that:

The renegades who have sought to destroy all that is holy and dear to Montreal Jews seek now also to help the chicken dealers in their struggle against order. The former rabbis Yudel Rosenberg and Herschorn have sent to the city mayor a protest against the decision that the eight slaughter rooms be under the control of the *Va'ad ha-'Ir*. It is interesting that in Yudel Rosenberg and Herschorn's protest, they say that they represent three-quarters of Montreal Jewry. This was between *Rosh ha-Shana* and *Yom Kippur* when ordinary flesh and blood people guard themselves from telling a lie. However it seems that former rabbis are not plain flesh and blood people, and what others cannot do, they may.[31]

By the Spring of 1924, the war had come to a relative standstill. The *Va'ad* was certainly hurting badly but was still limping along. The other side was almost certainly worse off but continued with the struggle. The butchers wound up roughly evenly divided, with only a slight advantage to the *Va'ad ha-Ir*. The *Keneder Odler* counted the number of butcher shops on the side of the *Va'ad* at this point as between forty-five and fifty. Considering that there were approximately eighty or eighty-five Jewish butcher shops in Montreal, the other side must have claimed the allegiance of some thirty to forty butchers. Ultimately, neither side was strong enough to decisively defeat the other. All sorts of interventions had been tried and failed. What, in the end, succeeded in bringing an end to the kosher meat war? It was the Quebec Superior Court. What the Montreal Jewish community had been unable to decide on its own was decided for it by the secular court system of the province. The court's decision in two important cases brought about the necessary conditions for the final denouement. One of these cases involved kosher meat; the other involved kosher chicken.

First in chronological order is the kosher chicken case. Because the *Va'ad ha-'Ir* controlled the licences for the eight chicken abattoirs in Montreal, Rabbi Rosenberg and his associates went to court. On September 26, 1923, the *Keneder Odler* reacted to this move editorially by stating:

Lately they [the "traitors"] have been seeking through the courts to coerce the butchers away from the *Va'ad ha-'Ir*. The renegades have brought the matter into court. They wish to extract from a lawyer a *hekhsher*[32] for their deeds, something they cannot expect from rabbis. However they will truly obtain from the lawyers the very same *hekhsher* they got from the rabbis.

A suit was brought in Quebec Superior Court before Judge Louis Coderre against the City of Montreal. The suit charged that the City, in limiting the number of kosher chicken abattoirs to eight, while allowing other poultry abattoirs to operate, was discriminating against Jews. The suit was not brought directly by Rabbi Rosenberg, but rather by a chicken dealer. In the archaic language of the law, the case was brought by "Dame Hattie Vineberg, of the City and District of Montreal, wife separate as to property of Julius Friedman, of the same place, and the latter to authorize his wife for the purposes hereof,[33] the same Dame Hattie Vineberg there carrying on business as poultry dealer under the name and style of J. Friedman and Co., and Leib Simon Woloz, of the same place, slaughterer of cattle and poultry." The suit argued that the bylaw provision limiting the amount of Jewish poultry slaughtering establishments while allowing anyone else to set up a chicken abattoir was unconstitutional, "particularly as creating class and religious distinctions to the prejudice of the Jewish citizens," and would result in "great and irreparable injury insofar as it affects the trade of Jewish poultry dealers within the City of Montreal." On April 11, 1924, Judge Coderre found for the plaintiffs, Dame Hattie Vineberg et al., and declared the article limiting the amount of kosher slaughtering establishments for poultry as unconstitutional, awarded them court costs, which amounted to $272.85. The City of Montreal did not appeal this decision. The bylaw was suitably amended in May 1924. That was an important blow against the *Va'ad ha-'Ir*'s control of kosher poultry. Now anyone could set up a kosher poultry abattoir.

The next case was of even more importance. It was a case from the kosher meat front of this war. It involved Rabbi Getsel Laxer and other *shoh̲tim* vs. the Association of Jewish Butchers of Montreal. The Association, most of whose members were now on the *Va'ad*'s side, had reneged on its contract with Laxer and the others to supply them with meat on the grounds that the *Va'ad ha-'Ir* had declared the meat they had slaughtered non-kosher. This case was brought before Mr. Justice Maclennan. In this case as well, the court found for the plaintiffs. Thus the *Va'ad* found itself unable to enforce its control of the kosher meat industry of Montreal in court. This largely negated its relative advantage over the opposing side in terms of number of butcher shops, etc. Finally, on December 2, 1925, the *Keneder Odler* carried an extremely brief notice to the effect that the kosher meat question in Montreal was solved. There was no editorial comment at that time or at a later date. The minutes of the *Va'ad ha-'Ir* from this period have disappeared.[34] The minutes of the *Va'ad*'s Finance Committee, which are extant, simply state: "Mr. Nadler related how *sholom* was achieved." After fully two years of conflict, in the end everything came back together. Starting in December 1925, the *Va'ad* reverted to the *status quo ante bellum*. Rabbis Rosenberg and Herschorn went back on the Rabbinical Council of the *Va'ad ha-'Ir*, with Rabbi Rosenberg resuming his role as vice-chairman. The "renegade" slaughterers went back to work together with their erstwhile foes. The butchers, not particularly happy at this turn of events, resumed their pursuit of the dollar.

A final financial statement will show the situation. We will compare the four-month period at the beginning of the operation of the *Va'ad ha-'Ir* (November, 1922–March, 1923) with the eleven-month period from January 1 to November 30, 1925.[35]

TABLE 2

Time Period	Total Revenue
November, 1922–March, 1923	$23,485
January 1, 1925–November 30, 1925	$29,805

It is quite easy to see from these figures that the opposing sides were bleeding to death financially, so that, in the end, there was no alternative to *sholom*.

Once they got back together again, I think it is fair to say that pretty much everything was as it had been. *Shoh̲tim* were earning approximately $40 per week. Rabbi Cohen got his $60 per week and Rabbi Rosenberg his $45. The tensions that had given rise to the conflict had not gone away, of course.

Thus, in 1927/8, Rabbi Laxer led another secession movement of *shoh̲tim*.[36] The difference between the two secessions was that in the former incident, Rabbis Rosenberg and Herschorn seceded with the slaughterers. In 1927/8, in contrast to 1923–25, only *shoh̲tim* seceded. The rabbis held together and maintained their solidarity. Rabbi Rosenberg's solidarity with the *Va'ad* at this time cost him his relationship with Rabbi Laxer. They had been allies, partners and neighbours. From the late 1920s until Rabbi Rosenberg's death in 1935, however, they did not speak to each other.

The *Va'ad ha-'Ir* was nearly killed almost as soon as it was born. It survived its first couple of years by the skin of its teeth. It was still not completely on firm ground when the Depression hit. At that time, Rabbi Cohen, if you will recall,[37] spoke of people asking him for work, of distributing most of his income in charity. There had been a brief moment of prosperity in the late 1920s, prior to the Depression. During that time, Rabbi Rosenberg, in a very optimistic move, bought plots of land in Palestine,[38] but that moment passed.

The Depression adversely affected Montreal's Jewish community and institutions. Nonetheless the *Va'ad ha-'Ir*, which experienced a further severe crisis and was reorganized in 1933,[39] continued to survive by the skin of its teeth, though particularly among the *shoh̲tim* there was great restiveness.

There was also great restiveness among the chicken slaughterers. At a meeting in 1926, Rabbi Cohen addressed the *Va'ad* concerning the problems of the *shoh̲tei oifes*.[40] As the minutes state:

Rabbi Cohen then spoke about the *shoh̲tei oifes*. He explained that about thirty of them had organized and formed a union, and that they had come to the *Va'ad ha-Rabbonim* asking to be taken under the supervision of the *Va'ad ha-'Ir* and the

Va'ad ha-Rabbonim. In this way they hope to strengthen their union. It is Rabbi Cohen's personal opinion that this is a very difficult matter to undertake. More complex than dealing with the *shohtei gasos*,⁴¹ as the *shohtei gasos* had agreed to divide their salary equally among themselves. And he doesn't see how this could be worked under the same system with the *shohtei oifes* as the amounts of their earnings are varied. Some earn thirty dollars per week. Others only five dollars. He also did not see how the *Va'ad ha-Rabbonim* could promise not to allow any other *shohtim* outside of the union provided they were capable to slaughter chickens in Montreal.

Once again, the confusions, tensions, and fights did not cease. The fault lines were papered over but remained.⁴² The butchers in the 1930s and 1940s were no more amenable to supervision than they had been in previous decades. There are, in fact, numerous reports of individual butchers being caught in flagrant violation of the rules and regulations of the *Va'ad ha-'Ir*.

The consumers themselves were often restive. Jews in Montreal, who for years had witnessed accusations and counter-accusations of the type previously mentioned, were often suspicious of the motives and tactics of rabbis, slaughterers, and butchers. One of the major tactics of the consumers was the boycott of kosher butchers who were still thought to be constantly plotting together to raise the price of meat for consumers.⁴³ An example of violent behaviour in connection with kosher meat in Montreal is a handbill from one of the recurring kosher meat boycotts, this one in the year 1933. Following is the full text of the handbill:

DO NOT EAT ANY MEAT!
THE MEAT IS DRIPPING WITH HUMAN BLOOD!

On Saturday night, the butchers struck and wounded several women and men who had peacefully crowded into the butcher shops. One woman and two men lie wounded in hospital. One of them, Mr. Klein, received a [blow from a] butcher's file in the head and is in critical condition.

JEWISH WOMEN AND MEN: DO NOT PURCHASE ANY MEAT
DRIPPING WITH HUMAN BLOOD, WITH THE BLOOD OF THOSE
WHO ARE FIGHTING FOR CHEAPER MEAT.

DO NOT SCAB, AND DO NOT BETRAY [EITHER] YOURSELVES OR
THE JEWISH MASSES OF MONTREAL.

Strike for cheap meat. Do not buy any meat until the strike will have been won.

Come in masses to a protest

MASS MEETING

MONDAY, NOVEMBER 20

8:30 P.M.

IN CARMEN SILVA HALL

Protest against the gangster methods of the butchers and of those who stand behind them.[44]

In examining the text of the handbill, it is worth noting that the language is suffused throughout with the rhetoric of the militant labour movement, which was a potent force within the immigrant Jewish community of Montreal.[45]

Nonetheless, despite all these crises, the *Va'ad* persevered and soldiered on, providing a means whereby the rabbis of Montreal and their community could attempt to form a solid, working relationship. The ultimate success of the organization is that it continues its work to this day, though it has changed structurally and ideologically in some important ways which are part and parcel of the "turn to the right" of North American Orthodox Judaism in recent decades.[46]

· 8 ·

New Thoughts from an Ancient Source: Hirsh Wolofsky's Commentary on the Torah[1]

The North American Yiddish press in the early twentieth century has long been recognized by scholars of American Jewish history as a force for Americanization and modernization within the Eastern European immigrant Jewish community. It is also understood that the medium of the Yiddish press could be used as a cultural bridging mechanism, enabling its readers to reappropriate their past experiences and education for the purpose of better understanding their new communities and acclimatizing themselves in their new home.[2] A particularly illuminating example of this process in action can be seen in Montreal in the early part of the twentieth century.

The *Keneder Odler* was Montreal's Yiddish-language newspaper, beginning in 1907, and its views, and those of its publisher, Hirsh Wolofsky (1878–1949), were of considerable importance for the city's Eastern European immigrant Jewish community.[3] Among the many articles and columns Wolofsky wrote for *Keneder Odler* in the course of his career, three of which were printed in book form after appearing first in the newspaper,[4] perhaps the most interesting are his series of columns entitled *Oyf Eybiken Kvall: Gedanken un batrachtungen fun dem hayntigen idishen leben un shtreben, in likht fun unzer alter un eybig-nayer tora, eingeteylt loyt di parshiyos fun der vokh*.[5] ["From the Eternal Source: Thoughts and Observations from Contemporary Jewish Life and Aspirations in the Light of Our Old and Eternally New Torah, Organized according to the Weekly {Torah} Portions"; hereinafter "*EK*"]. In this series of weekly columns, written throughout the Hebrew calendar year 5689 [1928–29],[6] Wolofsky attempted to create nothing less than a contemporary commentary or homily [*drush*] on the Pentateuch. The form the book took, commentary, as well as its division according to the weekly synagogue Torah readings, reflected a respect for the Judaic tradition. It also appropriated that tradition so as to shed new light on the dynamics of the contemporary Jewish community, whose "life and aspirations" Wolofsky wished to reflect.

Wolofsky, as publisher of *Keneder Odler*, has for a long time been understood by scholars as a significant factor in the rise and development of the Eastern European Jewish community in Montreal in the first half of the twentieth century. He is well known to researchers of Montreal Jewish history for his book of memoirs, *Mayn Lebens Rayze*. His other books, however, including EK, have attracted hardly any scholarly attention.[7] In the case of EK, at least, this is quite a pity, since an analysis of its contents will enable us to achieve an important insight into Wolofsky's thought, and, perhaps more importantly, into some of the directions in which he felt Montreal Jewry was headed in a crucial period in its history.

In his introduction to EK, Wolofsky began by consciously placing his work in the tradition of the ancient midrashic and later homiletic [*drush*] literature of Judaism. These premodern works, he asserted, sought to explain contemporary problems in terms of the Torah, using the literary means of allegory, fantasy, and imagination. These elements were added to the true story of Torah[8] in order to affect the hearts of the audience. This process was precisely what Wolofsky wished to follow, only in the twentieth century and "according to the American version [*nusakh*]."[9] He further attempts to define what he means by the "American version" by stating that in "America," everything is characterized by the slogan "hurry up," and by a process of popularization that leads to the neglect of serious, classical music for jazz. Similarly, serious books do not have the audience appeal of "light" magazines. In such a cultural atmosphere, *drush* also needs to become different. There is no twentieth-century audience for a homily lasting hours on end. Jews who are willing to listen at all to words of Torah want the speaker to come to the point in fifteen to twenty minutes without either elaborate introductions or difficult questions.[10] Having this situation in mind, Wolofsky was not about to create a "serious" commentary on the Torah in the old style. Rather, armed with his firm grasp of the text of the Torah, along with Rashi's commentary derived from his childhood education, he desired to satisfy his own curiosity about the Torah while writing a sort of Torah-based feuilleton on the problems of contemporary Jewish life.[11]

EK was, of course, a bit more than that. Wolofsky, in writing this work, thought of his enterprise in the context of the age-old Jewish custom of reviewing the weekly Torah portion [*ma'avir sedra zayn*] with the original biblical text read twice and the translation/interpretation [*targum*] once. At present, however, Wolofsky asserted that the original "text" of Jewish life has largely been forgotten and that therefore contemporary Jews are living their lives at a remove from the original [*targum-lebn*] in a world where practically nothing is "original" and all is *targum*. For Jews living in such a world, Wolofsky proposed to present a series of homilies that might, indeed, be more *targum* than original, but which were conceived by him to be in the spirit of the original.[12]

For Jews, historically, the Torah has been understood as containing within itself literally the entire cosmos.[13] It is no wonder, then, that Wolofsky, in considering the weekly portions of Torah, was able to find plenty of material to discuss everything that was on his mind, and that he thought would also be on the minds of his readers.

Prominent among these topics was what would later on be described as the "generation gap," that great lack of comprehension between the older, immigrant generation and the younger generation growing up in North America, who appeared to live in completely different worlds.[14] The older generation was portrayed in general terms as religiously traditional; the younger generation as in rebellion from that tradition. Thus the observance of the Jewish Sabbath,[15] and the observance of family purity laws[16] were portrayed as points of contention between the old and the new generations. The secular education of the young was understood as an important factor in this process. As Wolofsky stated, "'Wise' children [*hokhomim kinder*] who go to high school and college [and] already speak English with a correct accent," look down on their father, the "kike," with his foreign accent and conservative ways.[17] Young people with college educations grew ashamed of their Orthodox parents.[18] The curse recorded in Deuteronomy that "Your children shall be given over to a foreign nation and your eyes see"[19] refers, according to Wolofsky, to the non-Jewish cultures that the Jewish children will be drawn to without the parents being able to do anything about the situation.[20] Commenting on the fact that Joseph, in *Parshat va-Yehi*, visits his sick father without his Egyptian-born wife, Asenath, Wolosky states that, if he were a commentator like Rashi, he would say that Asenath was absent from the visit because she could not stand to go to the Jewish ghetto to see her father-in-law, the old Jew, the greenhorn. Wolofsky further comments to his readers on Asenath that, if such a thing has not happened in their family, it has certainly happened to their friends or acquaintances.[21] This anachronistic identification of "Egypt" as the locus of Jewish assimilation forms a sustained theme in *EK*. It is continued by Wolofsky in commenting on Pharaoh's offer to Moses in *parshas bo'* to let the adults out of Egypt but not the children. Wolofsky states in this instance that, as for the Jewish children, "Pharaoh must hold them under his influence and in his schools."[22]

Assimilation, not surprisingly, is one of Wolofsky's major themes in *EK*. Assimilation is a sin against the Torah and the Jewish people, as Jews shed their Jewish names,[23] exchange their holy tongue for the language of their country, their ancient literature for contemporary world literature, their *shabbes* and *yom tov* for Sundays and non-Jewish holidays. All of this, says Wolofsky, is a sort of modern "sacrifice" brought by Jews in place of the animal sacrifices ordained by the Torah. Unfortunately, the sacrifices of assimilation do not effect expiation of sin, as the sacrifices of ancient times did; instead, they bring in their wake the persecutions of anti-semitism.[24]

Wolofsky's proffered remedy for the plague of assimilation was support for Jewish education, and, more specifically, for the religious education of the Talmud Torah.[25] Though many felt that, in America, the cause of Jewish education was hopeless,[26] and sending Jewish children for Hebrew education after a long day in public school was far from being an ideal situation,[27] not educating children Jewishly at all was going to do them and society as a whole a great deal of harm. Wolofsky thus stated:

Visit a Reformatory and you will not find there any children who attended Talmud Torah. Go to Juvenile Court and you will find there only Jewish children who did not attend Talmud Torah and have no Jewish education.... Children who did not get a Jewish education are like snakes who bite and poison their parents and their people.[28]

But though a Talmud Torah education was the absolutely necessary foundation for the Jewish future,[29] support for the Talmud Torahs was very weak, especially in contrast to the building of fine synagogues. Thus Wolofsky put in his commentary to the words of Balaam, blessing the Children of Israel:

"How goodly are your tents"[30] ... how beautiful are your synagogues and your private dwellings, but how puny is your childrens' education. What a troubled Talmud Torah you have.[31]

Balaam's "blessing" inspired Wolofsky to express a note of caution with regard to gentile praise of the Jews. Previously, he had mentioned that every gentile who says a good word about the Jews is feted by them.[32] In the case of Balaam, Wolofsky pointed out that when Jews call upon a gentile to bless them, whether in a synagogue or at a Jewish national event, their blessing is an expression of Balaam's psychology, whose ultimate purpose is assimilation with the daughters of Moab.[33]

The state of the Talmud Torah was not dissimilar to the disarray Wolofsky found in other Jewish communal institutions. Their leaders were all too often not true Jews ['emese 'iden] and were prone to quarrel.[34] At times such "leaders" were suspected of mishandling communal funds.[35] The rabbis of the community were also likely to be the focus of controversies. Thus in *Parshas Toldos*, Rebecca, during her pregnancy when Jacob and Esau were contending in her womb, went "to seek God." "Probably," Wolofsky opined, "she [went to seek God] among the rabbis. But there she also found a conflict [*a vayisrotsetsu*]."[36]

The conflict among rabbis was at times between older, European-born rabbis and younger men who could speak the language of the country and, deviating from age-old Jewish tradition dared to actually preach in churches.[37] More often, however, the conflict was to be found among the older rabbis themselves, and the problem started with economics: rabbis simply had a hard time making ends meet. Rabbis, Wolofsky stated, needed to make an honourable living. When complaints are made that rabbis are not doing enough to meet communal needs, the question should first be asked whether the community was providing for them sufficiently. They do not have the time to do the things expected of rabbis, such as studying, visiting the Talmud Torah, or the sick, because they needed to make a living by providing people with kosher certifications, divorces, or *etrogim*.[38] Wolofsky had "a message for the rabbis: Do no injustice in a judgment....

If you have a congregation, do not flatter the members ... and do not spill your colleague's blood."[39] The rabbis' freedom within their congregations to reproach sins like desecration of the Sabbath was limited by the fact that the congregants who pay their salaries were themselves largely Sabbath desecrators.[40] As preachers, they often did not know what to say or how to say it.[41] Most of all, however, Wolofsky found that the rabbis went wrong because they abandoned their spiritual work to be sunk in the mire of the controversy over kosher meat.[42]

The kosher meat wars of Montreal, and of other North American Jewish communities of the era, caused all sorts of trouble, such as the sin of "bearing false witness," which Wolofsky interpreted for contemporary times in this way: "Do not make kosher stamps to sell non-kosher [*treyfe*] meat."[43] So-called kosher butchers were capable of more than deceit. They also were capable of forming a "trust" and engaging in bribery in two ways. The consumers were bribed with meat at one cent cheaper (per pound), and the rabbis were bribed so that they could not and would not pay any more attention to matters of *kashrut*.[44]

Wolofsky dealt in his commentary with other contemporary issues of likely interest to his readers. These included some of the great ideological issues of his time, including Zionism, Marxism, and the conflict between Torah and Science. He was writing in the context of the Zionist struggle to make the Jewish National Home promised in the Balfour Declaration a reality. Arab opposition, which, in the Fall of 1929, was to get violent, seemed to threaten the progress the Zionists had made in building a Jewish national homeland.[45] Zionism and its difficulties were thus very much on Wolofsky's mind as he reread the Torah. In commenting on Abraham's purchase of a burial place in Hebron, he thus stated, "Just as Abraham payed the full price for land in Hebron, we [Jews] pay the highest prices for the worst land [in Palestine]."[46] In imagining the spies sent out by Moses to travel to the Land of Canaan, in *Parshas Shelah*, Wolofsky had contemporary Zionist commissions, as well as ordinary tourists to Palestine, in mind. Thus among the questions the "commission" of spies is asked to report on, in Wolofsky's version, is: "Does the land have malarial swamps to be drained?"[47] Most of the Biblical spies spread a bad report about the land, like many contemporary "spies," who take one look at the land and run away. Commenting on contemporary Jewish opposition to the Zionist project, he stated "then [in biblical times] there were also Jewish Arabs⁴⁸ ... who say we have no right [to Palestine]." Only Caleb, described as an "enthusiastic [*heisser*] Zionist" and Joshua saw the land with true Jewish eyes.⁴⁹

One of the great problems facing the Zionists in that era was the fact that the Arabs formed a great majority of the total population of Palestine. Then as now, Wolofsky remarked, "the [non-Jewish] peoples in the Land of Israel are in an overwhelming majority over us.... [Nonetheless,] God is with you and not with those authorities [*ḥakhomim*] who say that all rights belong to the majority." Wolofsky understood that the Zionists were attempting to effect a fundamental transformation in the Jewish character, and he expressed some reservations in this regard. He felt, for instance, that Zionism's emphasis on physical strength and vindication of Jewish pride had somehow lessened respect for traditional Jews, who were predominantly non-bellicose.⁵⁰

While Wolofsky had his reservations concerning Zionists, he was thoroughly condemnatory of the ideology of Marxism, though it was founded, as he said, by a descendent of the biblical Jacob by the name of Karl Marx.⁵¹ Marx's followers included many Jewish young people whose sacrifices were performed "outside" the Jewish polity [*shehutei ḥuts*].⁵² Like the worshippers of the Golden Calf, they had dared to "put God on trial";⁵³ in Russia, Jewish communists persecuted Judaism.⁵⁴

Wolofsky, however much he played with the ideas and connections he found in the Torah, was no skeptic. All the biblical characters, like Abraham, Rachel, Miriam, and Moses, seem to have been thought of by Wolofsky as essentially historical.⁵⁵ That does not mean, however, that he was immune from the perceived conflicts between science and religion that concerned so many in his generation. In two instances in his book, he wondered aloud about the contradiction between a Jewish calendar that marked only 5,689 years and fossils that scientists claimed to be millions of years old. Showing that he had learned something from either Rabbi Hirsh Cohen, his friend, or Rabbi Yudel Rosenberg, his nemesis, or, perhaps both, he attempted to resolve the conundrum by quoting the Talmud and the *Zohar* on the worlds previous to our own, which God had created and then destroyed.⁵⁶ Similarly, the difficulty that the history of the Chinese seems to extend prior to Noah's flood was countered by

Wolofsky with the statement that if, as the ancient rabbis stated, the Land of Israel was not affected by the Flood, perhaps other lands were spared as well, such as China.[57]

In writing this book, Wolofsky, for all his individuality, was not unique in Jewish Montreal in the early twentieth century. In fact he found himself in the mainstream of a cohort of contemporaries in Montreal and elsewhere in North America,[58] who, through their teaching and publication, attempted to use the hallowed resources of the Jewish past, including Midrash, and Mishna, to recreate a thriving and culturally innovative Jewish community through the medium of Yiddish. As David Roskies described these people, they took for granted that the old Judaic culture had to be reinvented. If the original had become inaccessible to the average Jew in the street, then a compelling Jewish life in *targum* had to be established both intellectually and institutionally.[59] Like Wolofsky, these Jewish communal intellectuals were not unaware of the uphill struggle they faced.[60] Like him as well, they were essentially optimists. At the very end of *EK*, Wolofsky gave vent to this optimism. Having previously presented Egypt as the symbol of the perils of Jewish assimilation, he concluded his modern commentary on the Torah "in the American version" by stating that the Torah is the heritage of the Jewish people and a monument to Moses that will outlive the Egyptian pyramids and sphinx.[61]

· 9 ·

Afterword

Now with the rabbis [the situation] is certainly not a happy one. However without the rabbis it would be truly sad. – Rabbi Hirsh Cohen (1934)[1]

In conclusion, there is one major point that needs to be made. This book commenced with a discussion of the rabbis and *shoh̲tim* of Montreal at the beginning of the twentieth century that describes them as "forgotten men." They were forgotten, first of all, by those who wrote the histories of the Montreal Jewish community, who were both naturally more interested in and found more material relating to the non-religious sector of the immigrant community. I also stated that, within the Orthodox community itself, these are largely forgotten men. If you consider the Orthodox Jewish community of present-day Montreal, it is fair to say that its historical memory begins in 1941, with the arrival of the first European refugee rabbis in Montreal on one of the last ships crossing the Pacific from Shanghai prior to Pearl Harbor.[2] Thus the historical memory of Montreal Orthodox Jews begins with people like Rabbi Pinchos Hirschprung and Rabbi Leib Kramer. There is certainly justice in remembering these distinguished rabbis, who made their mark on their adopted community. However, it is equally important to point out that the rabbis who arrived in 1941 did not find a *tabula rasa*. They did not find Montreal without a unified – if flawed – rabbinical structure, or without a coherent – if flawed – *kashrut* supervision authority. There was also a considerable Jewish educational structure, with all its faults, in place when they came.

This book of studies in the Eastern European Immigrant Orthodox rabbinate of Montreal in the early decades of the twentieth century is not designed as a comprehensive history of the Montreal rabbinate in that era. It does, however, shed light on a number of individuals, organizations, and issues that were instrumental in the development of Orthodox Judaism in Montreal in this era. Furthermore, it has shown how presenting the Montreal rabbis not as individuals, but as part of a larger community, can provide us with added dimensions in our comprehension of the development of the Eastern European immigrant community of Montreal. This has important implications for the understanding of other major North American Jewish communities in the first half of the twentieth century. In all of them, immigrant Orthodox rabbis came, interacted with each other and with their communities, and painstakingly built up an institutional structure.

Had the refugee rabbis arriving in Montreal in 1941 not found an existing structure upon which they could build, they would have certainly not desisted from their task. However, theirs would have been a longer, harder, more uphill struggle than it was. In other words, this book has been discussing an era that ends with the onset of World War II. Of the rabbis we have discussed in any detail, Rabbi Crestohl died in 1928; Rabbi Rosenberg in 1935; and Rabbi Laxer in 1942. Rabbi Cohen died in 1950 but had been out of commission for a considerable time before that. Only Rabbi Herschorn remained active in the Montreal rabbinate after World War II. He died in 1969, though he, too, was incapacitated for most of the last decade of his life.[3]

A new generation of rabbinical leadership arrived in the 1940s, of whom Rabbi Hirschprung ultimately became the most prominent. But, important as it was that Montreal acquired Rabbi Hirschprung and the others, it was of equal, if not greater, importance that when Rabbis Hirschprung, Kramer, and their companions came to Montreal, there was someone to meet them at the station.

Glossary

Agudath ha-Rabbonim	Organization of Eastern European immigrant Orthodox rabbis in the United States and Canada founded in 1902.
Agudath ha-Shoḥtim	Guild of kosher slaughterers. In Montreal, it was organized as a labour union.
Agunot	(singular *Aguna*) Women halakhicly prohibited from remarrying.
Aliyah	Honour of being called up for the reading of the Torah in a synagogue.
Arba Minim	Four species used in ceremonial for the holiday of Sukkot, including *Lulav, Etrog, Hadas,* and *'Arava* (willow branches).
Batlanim	Literally "idlers." Sometimes used to describe those whose fulltime occupation is Torah study.
Beth Din	Rabbinic court.
Bimah	Raised area in synagogue from which services are led.
Chillul ha-Shem	A desecration or disgrace of God's name.
Din Torah	Case brought before a rabbinic court (*Beth Din*)
Etrog	Citron. One of the *'Arba Minim* used on Sukkot.
Gasos	Large animals, e.g., sheep and cattle.
Gemarah	Talmud.

Hadas	Myrtle branch. One of the *'Arba Minim* used on Sukkot.
Haftara	Public reading of selections from the prophetic books of the Hebrew Bible in synagogue.
Haggada	Text of the service of the Passover Seder.
Hakafa	Ceremonial procession of the Torah in synagogue on the holiday of *Simhat Torah*.
Halakha	Judaic law.
Hamets	Leaven. Food item not permitted to Jews during the holiday of Passover.
Haskala	Movement for the Westernization of Jews and Judaism.
Hassid	Adherent of the Hasidic movement.
Hazaka	In Judaic law, an acquired right.
Hechsher	Certification of the kosher status of food items.
Heder	Traditional Jewish elementary school.
Heter	Permission.
Hoshen Mishpat	One of the four sections of the Judaic legal code, *Shulkhan 'Arukh*, dealing with rabbinic court procedure.
Issur	Prohibition.
Kashrut	Fitness of food for consumption by Jews.
Kehilla	Organized Jewish community.
Keren ha-Yessod	Zionist fundraising organization.
Landsmanschaft	Organization of Jewish immigrants from the same town or district for self help and sociability.
Lulav	Palm branch. One of the *'Arba Minim* used on Sukkot.
Matza	Unleavened bread for Passover.
Mashgiah	(plural *Mashgihim*) Supervisor of the implementation of the laws and regulations regarding kosher food.
Meharsho	Rabbi Samuel Edels, commentator on the Talmud.

Mikveh	Ritual immersion pool.
Mitnaged	Opponent of the Hasidic movement.
Mizrahi	Organization of Orthodox Zionists.
Nudnik	Busybody.
Oifes	Poultry.
Parsha	Publicly read portion of the Torah.
Poalei Zion	Labour Zionists
Pushke	Charity box.
Rosh ha-Shana	Judaic new year's festival.
Sandek	Person who holds infant during circumcision ceremony.
Semikha	Rabbinic ordination.
Sha'atnez	Mixture of linen and wool prohibited by the Torah.
Shehita	Slaughtering of animals in accordance with the laws of *kashrut*.
Shohet	(plural *Shohtim*) Slaughterer of animals in accordance with the laws and regulations regarding kosher food.
Shabbes	Sabbath.
Shabbes Goy	Non-Jew who performs actions on behalf of Jews on the Sabbath.
Shevarim	One of the sounds emanating from the Shofar.
Sholom	Peace.
Shul	Synagogue.
Shule	Jewish school with a non-religious, *Yiddishist* orientation.
Shulkhan 'Arukh	Judaic legal code of the sixteenth century.
Simhat Torah	Last day of *Sukkot* holiday, in which the reading of the Torah is completed.
Sukkah	A temporary shelter used by Jews during the festival of Sukkot.

Talmud	Basic document of Rabbinic literature, which forms the intellectual basis for Rabbinic Judaism.
Talmud Torah	In North America, a school teaching Hebrew and Judaic subjects, which supplements public school instruction.
Tefilin	Ritual objects worn by Jewish men in weekday morning services.
Teruah	One of the sounds emanating from the Shofar.
Treifah, Treyf	Non-kosher.
Va'ad ha-'Ir	Jewish Community Council.
Wurst	Sausage.
Yohrzeit	Yearly memorial day for deceased relatives.
Yeshiva	Rabbinic academy.
Yiddishist	A person who believes that Yiddish is, or can be, the basis for Jewish culture and continuity.
Yidn	Jews.
Yishuv	Jewish community in Palestine under British Mandate.
Yishuvnik	Jew who lives in a small settlement, often with minimal Judaic education.
Yom Kippur	Day of Atonement.
Yom Tov	Jewish holiday.
Yoreh Deah	One of four sections of *Shulkhan 'Arukh*.
Zedaka	Charity.

Notes

CHAPTER ONE

1 Leo Jung, *Toward Sinai! Sermons and Addresses* (New York: Pardes, 1929), p. 276. I am grateful to my student, Dr. Maxine Jacobson, for bringing Rabbi Jung's statement to my attention.
2 See Chapter 6.
3 For a necessarily sketchy account of the history of the Montreal Jewish community, see Ira Robinson and Mervin Butovsky, *Renewing Our Days: Montreal Jews in the Twentieth Century* (Montreal: Véhicule Press, 1995), pp. 9–29. For the Canadian Jewish community as a whole during this era, see Gerald Tulchinsky, *Taking Root: The Origins of the Canadian Jewish Community* (Toronto: Lester, 1992), Parts III and IV.
4 An example of this is Tulchinsky. *Taking Root*'s index does not list an entry for Montreal's synagogues after page 35 and thus has no discussion of synagogues after the first half of the nineteenth century. Cf., however, Sara Ferdman Tauben, "Aspirations and Adaptations: Immigrant Synagogues of Montreal, 1880s to 1945," M.A. thesis, Department of Religion, Concordia University, 2004.
5 It is well documented that the American press reported the news of the destruction of European Jewry but tended to keep it off the front-page and "buried" in the inner pages. The Yiddish press, on the contrary, gave these news items great publicity. See Deborah Lipstadt, *Beyond Belief: The American Press and the Coming of the Holocaust, 1933–1945* (New York: Free Press, 1986).
6 See, among others, Arthur Morse, *While Six Million Died: A Chronicle of American Apathy* (New York: Random House, 1968); David Wyman, *Paper Walls: America and the Refugee Crisis, 1938–1941* (Amherst, MA: University of Massachusetts Press, 1968); Henry Feingold, *The Politics of Rescue: The Roosevelt Administration and the Holocaust* (New Brunswick, NJ: Rutgers University Press, 1970).
7 On this organization, see Jeffrey Gurock, "Resistors and Accommodators: Varieties of Orthodox Rabbis in America, 1886–1983," in *American Jewish Orthodoxy in Historical Perspective* (Hoboken: KTAV, 1996), pp. 1–62.

8   The most thorough analysis of the "Rabbis' March" is in Efraim Zuroff, *The Response of Orthodox Jewry in the United States to the Holocaust: The Activities of the Vaad-ha-hatzala Committee, 1939–1945* (New York and Hoboken: Yeshiva University Press and KTAV Publishing House, 2000), pp. 257–64. Cf. Raphael Medoff, "The Day the Rabbis Marched," http://www.wymaninstitute.org/special/rabbimarch/index1.php.

9   Cited in Aaron Rakeffet-Rothkoff, *The Silver Era in American Jewish Orthodoxy: Rabbi Eliezer Silver and His Generation* (Jerusalem and New York: Yeshiva University Press and Feldheim Publishers, 1981), p. 219.

10 Historians have emphasized the issue of basic change on the part of Jews in the nineteenth century. Two good example of this emphasis are the titles of David Sorkin, *The Transformation of German Jewry, 1780–1940* (New York: Oxford, 1987), and Gerald Sorin, *Tradition Transformed: The Jewish Experience in America* (Baltimore: Johns Hopkins University Press, 1997).

11 Michael Kazin, "The Grass-Roots Right: New Histories of U.S. Conservatism in the Twentieth Century," *American Historical Review* (February, 1992): 136.

12 Cf. Jenna Joselit, "What Happened to New York's 'Jewish Jews'?: Moses Rischin's *The Promised City* Revisited," *American Jewish History* 73 (1983): 163–72.

13 For exceptions to this neglect, see especially Charles Liebman, "Orthodoxy in American Jewish Life," in Marshall Sklare, ed., *The Jewish Community in America* (New York: Behrman, 1974), pp. 131–74. Aaron Rothkoff, *Bernard Revel: Builder of American Jewish Orthodoxy* (Philadelphia: Jewish Publication Society, 1972); Aaron Rakeffet-Rothkoff, *The Silver Era in American Jewish Orthodoxy: Rabbi Eliezer Silver and His Generation* (Jerusalem and New York: Yeshiva University Press and Feldheim Publishers, 1981); Jonathan Sarna, *People Walk on Their Heads: Moses Weinberger's Jews and Judaism in New York* (New York: Holmes and Meier, 1981); Gurock, *American Jewish Orthodoxy in Historical Perspective*; Kimmy Caplan, *Orthodoxy in the New World: Immigrant Rabbis and Preaching in America, 1881–1924* (Jerusalem: Zalman Shazar Center for Jewish History, 2002); idem., "In God We Trust: Salaries and Income of American Orthodox Rabbis, 1881–1924," *American Jewish History* 86 (1998): 77–106.

14 Louis Bernstein, *Challenge and Mission: The Emergence of the English Speaking Orthodox Rabbinate* (New York: Shengold, 1982), p. 7.

15 Dan Miron, *The Image of the Shtetl and Other Studies of the Modern Jewish Literary Imagination* (Syracuse: Syracuse University Press, 2000), p. 8. Recent scholarship has done much to illuminate the world of nineteenth-century Eastern European Orthodoxy. Cf., among others, Immanuel Etkes, *Rabbi Israel Salanter and the Mussar Movement: Seeking the Torah of Truth* (Philadelphia: Jewish Publication Society, 1993); idem., *The Gaon of Vilna: The Man and his Image* (Berkeley: University of California Press, 2002); Shaul Stampfer, *ha-Yeshivah ha-Lita'it be-hithavutah* (Jerusalem: Merkaz Zalman Shazar, 1995).

16 Simon Belkin, *Le Mouvement ouvrier juif au Canada, 1904–1920*, traduit du yiddish par Pierre Anctil (Sillery: Septentrion, 1999).

17 Israel Medresh, *Montreal fun Nekhtn* (Montreal: Keneder Odler, 1947); *Montreal of Yesterday: Jewish Life in Montreal, 1900–1920*; translated from the Yiddish by Vivian Felsen (Montreal: Véhicule Press, 2000); *Le Montréal juif d'autrefois*, trans. Pierre Anctil (Sillery: Septentrion, 1997); idem., *Tsvishn Tsvei Velt Milhomes* (Montreal:

Keneder Odler, 1964); *Between the Wars: Canadian Jews in Transition*; translated from the Yiddish by Vivian Felsen (Montreal: Véhicule Press, 2003).

18 Hirsh Wolofsky, *Mein Lebens Rayze* (Montreal: Keneder Odler, 1946).

19 Belkin, *Le Mouvement ouvrier juif au Canada, 1904–1920*, "Introduction," p. 17ff.

20 Medresh, *Le Montréal juif d'autrefois*, p. 38.

21 For an interesting insight into the life and ideals of a prominent yiddishist activist, see Mervin Butovsky and Ode Garfinkle, trans., *The Journals of Yaacov Zipper, 1950–1982: The Struggle for Yiddishkeit* (Montreal and Kingston: McGill-Queen's University Press, 2004).

22 For some sense of the volume and variety of the writings of North American Orthodox rabbis of this era, see www.hebrewbooks.com, a website devoted to bringing their thousands of published writings to public attention.

23 A partial exception to this rule was Ben Zion Eisenstadt, who published a book of biographical sketches of contemporary rabbis entitled *Dorot ha-Aharonim* (New York: Rosenberg, 5675 [1914/5]; reprinted New York, 1941, and Ashdod, 1997). He also published *Le-Toledot Yisrael ba-Amerika* (New York, 1917), and *Anshe ha-Shem be-Artsot ha-Berit* (St. Louis, 1933).

24 Yosef Haim Yerushalmi, *Zakhor: Jewish History and Jewish Memory* (Seattle: University of Washington Press, 1982). Cf. Jacob J. Shacter, "Haskalah, Secular Studies and the Close of the Yeshiva in Volozhin in 1892," *Torah u-Madda Journal* 2 (1990): 76–133.

25 Cf. Moses Rischin, *The Promised City: New York's Jews, 1870–1914* (Cambridge, MA: Harvard University Press, 1962); Irving Howe, *World of Our Fathers* (New York: Harcourt, Brace, Jovanovitch, 1976). This stance has been criticised by Jenna W. Joselit, "What Happened to New York's 'Jewish Jews'?" See note 12 above.

26 Bernstein, *Challenge and Mission*, p. 9.

27 But see Ira Robinson, "Kabbalist and Community Leader: Rabbi Yudel Rosenberg and the Canadian Jewish Community," *Canadian Jewish Studies* 1 (1993): 41–58; Stephen Speisman, *The Jews of Toronto: A History to 1937* (Toronto: McClelland and Stewart, 1979), p. 281ff.; and Moshe Stern, "Winnipeg Kashruth: A History," *The Nathan Lockshin Memorial Journal*, ed. Moshe Stern (Winnipeg: 1982), pp. 61–77.

28 Jeffrey Gurock, "Resisters and Accommodators."

29 On this issue, see Ari Ackerman, "'Judging the Sinner Favorably': R. Hayyim Hirschensohn on the Need for Leniency in Halakhic Decision-Making," *Modern Judaism* 22 (2002): 261–80.

30 Jonathan Sarna, *People Walk on Their Heads: Moses Weinberger's Jews and Judaism in New York* (New York: Holmes and Meier, 1982); idem, "The Myth of No Return: Jewish Return Migration to Eastern Europe, 1881–1914," *American Jewish History* 71 (1981): 256–68.

31 Aaron Rothkoff, "The American Sojourns of Ridbaz: Religious Problems within the Immigrant Community," *American Jewish Historical Society Quarterly* 57 (1968): 557–72. Cf. also Abraham J. Karp, "The Ridwas: Rabbi Jacob David Wilowsky, 1845–1913," in Arthur A. Chiel, ed., *Perspectives on Jews and Judaism: Essays in Honor of Wolfe Kelman* (New York: Rabbinical Assembly, 1978), pp. 215–37.

32 (Warsaw, 1913). Cf. Lloyd Gartner, "Jewish Migrants en Route from Europe to North America: Traditions and Realities," in Moses Rischin, ed., *The Jews of North America* (Detroit: Wayne State University Press, 1987), pp. 25–43.

33 Cf. Ira Robinson, "The Prehistory of a Legal Classic: The Origins of the *Mishnah Berurah*," unpublished paper presented at the Canadian Society for the Study of Religion, 2003.

34 Moses M. Yoshor, *The Chafetz Chaim: The Life and Works of Rabbi Yisrael Meir Kagan of Radin* (Brooklyn: Mesorah Publications, 1984), p. 342.

35 An example of this change of attitude has to do with a letter, written in 1864 by Rabbi Zadok ha-Kohen of Lublin, in which he expresses the opinion that "almost all those who come to those lands [America] throw off the yoke of Torah and commandments." When that letter was published in 1922, the anonymous editor inserted the following comment: "However now in our own days the situation has changed for the better and many of our brethren the children of Israel in America are occupied in Torah, [divine] service, charity and good deeds." *Poked 'Akarim* (Lublin, 1922), pp. 54–55.

36 For issues concerning the consumption habits of Eastern European Jews in North America, see Andrew Heinze, *Adapting to Abundance: Jewish Immigrants, Mass Consumption, and the Search for American Identity* (New York: Columbia University Press, 1990).

37 Ewa Morawska, *Insecure Prosperity: Small Town Jews in Industrial America, 1890–1940* (Princeton: Princeton University Press, 1996), p. 155.

38 Ibid., p. 14.

39 Joshua Ha-Levi Hirschorn, *Memainey Jeshuah: Responsa and Treatises on Talmudic Law* [Hebrew] (Montreal: 1959), p. 24a, ff.

40 Cf. Jeffrey Gurock, "Twentieth-Century American Orthodoxy's Era of Non-Observance, 1900–1960," *Torah u-Madda Journal* 9 (2000): 87–107. An organization called the Jewish Sabbath Alliance of America was active in the early part of the twentieth century whose purpose was, among other things, to attempt to secure jobs for Sabbath-observant Jews.

41 One must consider the prevalence of Jewish people observing the laws of *kashrut* at home, while ignoring them when outside the home. On the situation in Montreal with respect to Religious Observance, see Israel Medresh, *Montreal of Yesterday: Jewish Life in Montreal, 1900–1920*, trans. Vivian Felsen (Montreal: Véhicule Press, 2000), pp. 34–39.

42 Cf. Riv-Ellen Prell, *Fighting to Become Americans: Jews, Gender and the Anxiety of Assimilation* (Boston: Beacon Press, 1999).

43 Rakeffet-Rothkoff, *The Silver Era*, pp. 24–25.

44 Irving Howe and Kenneth Libo, *How We Lived: A Documentary History of Immigrant Jews in America, 1880–1930* (New York: Richard Marek, 1979), p. 99.

45 Louis Rosenberg, *Canada's Jews: A Social and Economic Study of the Jews of Canada* (Montreal: Canadian Jewish Congress, 1939), pp. 9–17.

46 On the impact of this demographic transformation, see Tulchinsky, *Taking Root*, p. 129ff.

47 Solomon Frank, *Two Centuries in the Life of a Synagogue* (Montreal: Spanish and Portuguese Congregation, 1968).

48 See Wilfred Schuchat, *The Gate of Heaven: The Story of Congregation Shaar Hashomayim in Montreal, 1846–1996* (Montreal and Kingston: McGill-Queen's University Press, 2000).

49 Thus Rabbi Harry Stern of Temple Emanu-El contributed greetings to the commemorative booklets issued at the time of the seventieth anniversaries of both Rabbi Hirsh Cohen and Yudel Rosenberg. *Souvenir Dedicated to Rabbi Jehuda Rosenberg Vice Chairman of Orthodox Rabbis of Montreal on the Occasion of His Seventieth Anniversary Jubilee* (Montreal, 1931), p. 16.
50 Yosef Eliyahu Bernstein, "ha-Yehudim ba-Kanada," ha-Melits 20, no. 31 (5 May 1884), p. 527. This article has been translated into English as *The Jews in Canada* (in North America: *An Eastern European View of the Montreal Jewish Community in 1884*, trans. Ira Robinson [Montreal: Hungry I Books, 2004]).
51 Cf. David Rome, *The First Jewish Literary School, Canadian Jewish Archives*, n.s. 41 (Montreal: Canadian Jewish Congress, 1988), p. 4.
52 Ephraim Shimoff, *Rabbi Isaac Elchanan Spektor: Life and Letters* (New York: Yeshiva University, 1959).
53 Cf. Caplan, *Orthodoxy in the New World*, p. 123.
54 Gilbert Klaperman, *The Story of Yeshiva University: The First Jewish University in America* (New York, Macmillan, 1969).
55 On the issue of rabbinical salaries, see Kimmy Caplan, "In God We Trust: Salaries and Income of American Orthodox Rabbis, 1881–1924," *American Jewish History* 86 (1998): 77–106.
56 Cf. Sarna, *People Walk on Their Heads*.
57 Abraham J. Karp, "New York Chooses a Chief Rabbi," *Proceedings of the American Jewish Historical Society* 44 (1955): 126–84.
58 See Michael S. Berger, *Rabbinic Authority* (New York: Oxford, 1998).
59 See Jacob Katz, "Rabbinical Authority and Authorization in the Middle Ages," *Divine Law in Human Hands: Case Studies in Halakhic Flexibility* (Jerusalem: Magnes Press, 1996), pp. 128–45.
60 See Jacob Katz, "The Dispute between Jacob Berab and Levi ben Habib over Renewing Ordination," *Divine Law in Human Hands: Case Studies in Halakhic Flexibility*, pp. 146–70.
61 Yoshor, *The Chafetz Chaim*, p. xxii.
62 Cited in Immanuel Etkes, *The Gaon of Vilna: The Man and His Image* (Berkeley: University of California Press, 2001), p. 224.
63 Cited in Abraham Karp, "The Ridwas: Rabbi Jacob David Wilowsky, 1845–1913," *Perspectives on Jews and Judaism: Essays in Honor of Wolfe Kelman* (New York: Rabbinical Assembly, 1978), p. 228.
64 Examples of such conflictual situations are given in Hannah Sprecher, "Let Them Drink and Forget Our Poverty: Orthodox Rabbis React to Prohibition," *American Jewish Archives* 43 (1991): 135–79.
65 Rakeffet-Rothkoff, *The Silver Era*, pp. 29–30.
66 Bernstein *Challenge and Mission*, p. 13.
67 Aaron Rakeffet-Rothkoff, *The Silver Era in American Jewish Orthodoxy: Rabbi Eliezer Silver and His Generation* (Jerusalem and New York: Yeshiva University Press and Feldheim Publishers, 1981), pp. 33, 74–75, 322.
68 E.g., Rakeffet-Rothkoff, *The Silver Era*, pp. 69–70. Cf. Jeremiah J. Bernstein, *Shehita: A Study in the Cultural and Social Life of the Jewish People* (New York: Bloch, 1941).

69 Bernstein, *Challenge and Mission*, p. 93. Cf. Harold P. Gastwirt, *Fraud, Corruption and Holiness: The Controversy over the Supervision of Jewish Dietary Practice in New York City, 1881–1940* (Port Washington, NY: Kennikat Press, 1974).
70 On the Eastern European Heder, see Shaul Stampfer, "'Heder' Study, Knowledge of Torah, and the Maintenance of Social Stratification in Traditional East European Jewish Society," *Studies in Jewish Education* 3 (1988): 271–89.
71 Cf. Klaperman, *Story of Yeshiva University*, p. 12ff.

CHAPTER TWO

1 *Souvenir Program Dedicated to Rabbi Hirsch Cohen/Chief Rabbi of Montreal and President of the Federation of Rabbis of Canada* (Montreal, 1930), p. 6.
2 On Cohen, see N. Gottlieb, *Sefer Ohole Schem* (Pinsk, 1912), p. 312. Cf. Steven Lapidus, "To Speak or Not to Speak: The Dilemma of Preaching for Rabbi Tzvi Hirsch Cohen," paper presented at "'A Skilled Tongue': Sermon and Society in the Canadian Jewish Experience," Concordia University, 2004.
3 Bernard Figler, *Canadian Jewish Profiles: Rabbi Dr. Herman Abramowitz, Lazarus Cohen, Lyon Cohen* (Ottawa: 1968), p. 93. On Volozhin, see Shaul Stampfer, *The Lithuanian Yeshiva* [Hebrew] (Jerusalem: Zalman Shazar Center for Jewish History, 1995).
4 *Jewish Times*, April 11, 1902, p. 146.
5 J.I. Segal, "Ha-rov Zvi Hakohen z'l," *Keneder Odler*, November 19, 1950.
6 M. Ginzberg, *Keneder Odler* 11/19/50. Gaetanne Blais, "Analyse du fonds et de la correspondence du Rabbin Cohen" (Ottawa: Canadian Postal Museum, 1999), p. 1.
7 On Lazarus Cohen, see Figler, p. 93ff.
8 *Keneder Odler*, September 14, 1930.
9 *Tog*, November 19, 1950.
10 Ginzberg.
11 *JT* 5/11/1900, p. 179.
12 *JT* 4/11/02. Mentions class as "about five years ago." In his memoir, Hirsh Wolofsky mentions that the house that served as Chevra Shas' home on Cadieux Street, faced Bnai Jacob, the most important Eastern European congregation of its time. *Mayn Lebens Rayze: Un demi-siècle de vie yiddish à Montréal 1946* (Sillery: Septentrion, 2000), p. 107.
13 Cf. Moshe Sherman, *Orthodox Judaism in America: A Biographical Dictionary* (Westport, CT: Greenwood Press, 1996), pp. 21–23.
14 *Jewish Times*, May 12, 1899, p. 177, specifies February 1866.
15 That he did not graduate from medical school seems to have been due to health problems stemming from exhaustion. David Rome, *The First Jewish Literary School*, *Canadian Jewish Archives*, n.s. 41 (Montreal: Canadian Jewish Congress, 1988), p. 16.
16 Beside Bnai Jacob, Rabbi Ashinsky was apparently also affiliated with Chevra Kadisha Congregation, as from 1898–1901 he signed the vital records of that congregation. "Database of Rabbis of Quebec"; www.jewishgen.org/Rabbinic/databases/quebec.htm.
17 *Jewish Times*, 1899, 207–8; 12/6/01, p. 12. Cf. Benjamin G. Sack, *History of the Jews in Canada* (Montreal: Harvest House, 1965), p. 247, n. 2.

18 *Jewish Times*, 2/4/98; 12/23/98.
19 John Kalbfleisch, "Rabbi was impressed by Montreal's piety," *The Gazette* (Montreal), February 4, 2001.
20 *Jewish Times*, August 4, 1899, p. 275.
21 *Jewish Times*, May 17, 1900.
22 *Jewish Times*, June 21, 1901. Cf. Rome, *First Literary School*, pp. 16–17.
23 *Jewish Times*, June 7, 1901, pp. 211, 213.
24 Rome, *First Literary School*, p. 18.
25 *Jewish Times*, December 20, 1901, p. 23. The Talmud Torah's monthly budget at this time was approximately $200.00, of which approximately $60.00 came from the students' tuition fees. Sack, p. 247, note 2.
26 *Jewish Times*, August 26, 1904, p. 340.
27 1 Tavo, 5664 [1904].
28 Rabbi Sprince, besides being the rabbi of Bnai Jacob, also had an affiliation to the Austro-Hungarian Congregation. He signed the vital records of both congregations. He last signed a vital record in Montreal in 1908. "Rabbis of Quebec Database" www.jewishgen.org/Rabbinic/databses/quebec.htm.
29 *Jewish Times*, April 11, 1902, p. 146. Ironically, because he had served for several years as rabbi in Paris, Rabbi Sprince would likely have known something of Montreal's other official language.
30 *Jewish Times*, November 7, 1902, p. 412.
31 Sunday, *toldot*, 5666. In another letter, *behar-behukkotai*, 5666 [1906], it seems that Rabbi Cohen's total income from kashrut supervision was $25.00 per week.
32 Often known as the "Roumanian Shul."
33 *Jewish Times*, July 27, 1906, p. 281.
34 Rome, *First Literary School*, p. 19. The identity of the "certain party" referred to is not specified, but, from the other evidence presented in this chapter, it is not unlikely that it was Rabbi Cohen and his supporters.
35 See Chapter 3.
36 For Wolofsky's evaluation of Cohen, see his autobiography, *Mayn Lebens Rayze*, p. 344ff.
37 In a letter dated 8 Nissan, 5673 [1913], Rabbi Cohen indicated that he thought of himself as the pre-eminent rabbi of the city. His rabbinical colleagues, he stated, were "either idlers [*batlonim*] or half or entire modernists [daytshen]."
38 See Chapter 4.
39 *erev pessah*, 5667 [1907]. This letter seems to indicate that tension between Rabbis Cohen and Ashinsky dated back to Rabbi Ashinsky's residence in Montreal.
40 *Canadian Jewish Times*, May 29, 1908, p. 215.
41 *Keneder Odler*, October 2, 1908.
42 For a description of his condition in his last years, see Harry P. Fierst to H.R. Biron, July 27, 1950. Hirsh Cohen file, Canadian Jewish Congress National Archives.
43 Rabbi Cohen published many of his sermons and opinion pieces in the *Keneder Odler*. He apparently did not publish anything beyond the newspaper, though, in a letter of 15 Tammuz, 5691 [1931], he spoke of the possibility of such a publication.
44 Cf. M. Ginzberg, *Keneder Odler*, November 19, 1950.
45 In a letter dated Thursday, *ha'azinu*, 5665 [1905], he mentioned that on Rosh ha-Shana and Yom Kippur that year, he preached in two synagogues a day.

46 10 Sivan, 5671.
47 M. Ginzberg, *Keneder Odler*, November 19, 1950.
48 7 Tammuz, 5667 [1907].
49 Friday, behar, 5693 [1933].
50 Rabbi Samuel Edels (1555–1631) Commentator on the Talmud.
51 3 hol ha-mo'ed pesach, 5670 [1910].
52 8 Adar I, 5692 [1932].
53 8 Nissan, 5673 [1913]. For Rabbi Cohen, "German" meant "modernized."
54 12 Nissan, 5687 [1927]. *Yoreh Deah* and *Hoshen Mishpat* are sections in the standard Code of Jewish Law, the *Shulhan Arukh*.
55 17 shvat, 5666 [1906].
56 12 Nissan, 5691 [1931].
57 5 ha'azinu 2, 5665 [1904]. Also twice on Yom Kippur.
58 *issru hag shavuot*, 5666 [1906].
59 *rosh hodesh tammuz*, 5691 [1931].
60 2 Teze, 5664 [1904]. He also eulogized Herzl in a "sephardic" synagogue Saturday night, devarim, 5664.
61 Undated 1920s?
62 The man Rabbi Cohen recommended was Rev. Hyman Goldstick. "History of the Birth of Edmonton and Calgary Jewish Communities"; Letter of Hirsh Cohen, 11 Av, 5666 [1906]. Jewish Archives and Historical Society of Edmonton and Northern Alberta.
63 1 hol ha-mo'ed sukkot, 5668 [1907]. He had been doing business with Weinstock at least since 1907. Or le-yom erev rosh ha-shana, 5667. 2 ekev, 5665, mentions ordering special etrog from Palestine for himself.
64 5 ha'azinu 2, 5665.
65 2 ha'azinu, 5666.
66 erev yom kippur, 5686 [1925].
67 20 Tammuz, 5666.
68 11 Adar, 5697 [1937].
69 Saturday night va-yeshev, 5685.
70 14 nissan, 5677.
71 Saturday night va-yeshev, 5685.
72 The reference is to Reform Temples. 1 lekha, 5686 [1925].
73 22 sivan, 5685 [1925].
74 Cited in Sharon Gubbay, "The Jewish Public Library: 1914–1952," Master's thesis, McGill University, 1983, p. 82.
75 Purim Night, 5667 [1907].
76 4 shevat, 5691 [1931].
77 For a similar contemporary rabbinic view of geological discoveries on the age of the earth, cf. Abraham Isaac Kook, *Igrot RAY"H* (Jerusalem: Mossad ha-Rav Kook, 1985) vol. 1, p. 104.
78 Maimonides' halakhic code, otherwise known as *Mishneh Torah*.
79 1 *Devarim*, 5685 [1925]. Cf. Ira Robinson, "'Practically, I Am a Fundamentalist': Twentieth Century Orthodox Jews Contend With Evolution and Its Implications", in Geoffrey Cantor and Marc Swetlitz, eds., *Jewish Tradition and the Challenge of Darwinism* (Chicago: University of Chicago Press, 2006), pp. 71–86.

CHAPTER THREE

1. Simon Glazer, translator, Maimonides *Book of Mishnah Torah: Yod Ha-Hazakah* (New York: Maimonides Publishing, 1927), Hebrew pagination, p. 47.
2. See the discussion of Rabbi Ashinsky in Chapter 2.
3. See Chapter 2.
4. Rabbi Glazer's first name in Hebrew was not *Shimon*, the Hebrew equivalent of Simon, but rather *Yeshaya* (= Isaiah). Though there is no evidence whatsoever to explain this anomaly, it may be that he did not like the rhyming sound of the name "Isaiah Glazer" in English. Glazer's name is inconsistently spelled in English as "Glaser" and "Glazer." On Rabbi Glazer, see Moshe Sherman, *Orthodox Judaism in America: A Biographical Dictionary and Sourcebook* (Westport, CT: Greenwood Press, 1996), pp. 75–78. Cf. David Rome, "Rabbi Simon Joshuah Glazer," *Canadian Jewish Archives*, n.s. 37 (Montreal: Canadian Jewish Congress, 1986): 51–82. An autobiographical account of his life prior to his arrival in America is contained in his Hebrew preface to his translation of Maimonides' *Book of Mishnah Torah: Yod Ha-Hazakah* (New York: Maimonides Publishing, 1927), pp. 1–48. On his career after he left Montreal, see Joseph P. Schultz and Carol L. Klausner, "Rabbi Simon Glazer and the Quest for Jewish Community in Kansas City, 1920–1923," *American Jewish Archives* 35 (1983): 13–25.
5. *The Jews of Iowa* (Des Moines: Koch, 1904).
6. Toledo, 1907.
7. *Jewish Times*, June 25, 1907, cited in David Rome, *The Immigration Story II: Jacobs' Opponents, Canadian Jewish Archives* 37, p. 52.
8. *Jewish Times*, October 23, 1903.
9. M. Ginzberg, *Keneder Odler*, November 19, 1950. Ginzberg cites Rabbi Cohen to the effect that he advocated Talmud study in the Talmud Torah "so that a generation of Karaites would not arise."
10. *Jewish Times*, May 19, 1904.
11. Rabbinical Court (Hebrew).
12. David Rome gives expression to this feeling when he wrote about Rabbi Glazer, "He came without the respect for social authority; without readiness to cooperate with his predecessors who had won leadership by many years of service; without acceptance of the traditions of many centuries of Canadian civilization and convention." *Canadian Jewish Archives* n.s. 37, p. 51.
13. Emphasis mine.
14. *Jewish Times*, April 15, 1908, p. 166.
15. *Jewish Times*, April 29, 1908, p. 179; August 21, 1908, p. 336.
16. Louis M. Singer to Simon Glazer, November 29, 1913. AJA Glazer Papers 1/14.
17. "The Kosher Meat Squabble," *Jewish Times*, August 21, 1908, p. 336.
18. Maxwell Goldstein, "Jewish Affairs in Canada," *Jewish Chronicle*, July 16, 1909, p. 16.
19. In an undated handbill having to do with butchers selling unapproved meat, Glazer signed along with three other rabbis: Jacob b. Benjamin Cohen, Moshe Gedaliah b. Menahem Dov, Simha Garber b. Mordecai. Eirann Harris, personal collection. Only Rabbi Garber is heard from again in Montreal rabbinical politics in later years.
20. "Killer" is a literal translation of the Hebrew *shohet*, but it has decidedly negative implications in English, which may have been intended.

21　This seems to be an exaggerated figure.
22　David Rome, *CJA* 37: 61–62. Rome notes that Glazer was similarly subjected to violence on January 29, 1909.
23　Thus in the thirty year period between 1901 and 1931, Montreal's Jewish population had grown from under 7,000 to over 60,000.
24　Cf. Harold Gastwirt, *Fraud, Corruption and Holiness: The Controversy over the Supervision of Jewish Dietary Practice in New York City, 1881–1940* (Port Washington, NY: Kennikat Press, 1974).
25　*Vaad Hoir Bulletin* 1 (March 9, 1933): 2.
26　For Bangor, see Judith S. Goldstein, *Crossing Lines: Histories of Jews and Gentiles in Three Communities* (New York: William Morrow, 1992), p. 128. For Johnstown, see Ewa Morawska, *Insecure Prosperity: Small-Town Jews in Industrial America, 1890–1940* (Princeton: Princeton University Press, 1995), p. 159. For Madison, see Hasia Diner, *Hungering for America: Italian, Irish and Jewish Foodways in the Age of Migration* (Cambridge, MA: Harvard University Press, 2001), p. 183.
27　Diner, *Hungering for America*, pp. 182–83. Cf. Andrew R. Heinze, *Adapting to Abundance: Jewish Immigrants, Mass Consumption, and the Search for American Identity* (New York: Columbia University Press, 1990).
28　I.e., of doubtful kashrut.
29　Glazer to Beth David Congregation, 2 Kislev, 5669 [November 26, 1908]. Herschorn Papers. Photocopy in possession of the author.
30　Hirsh Wolofsky, *Mayn Lebens Rayze*, p. 124.
31　Rabbi Glazer did receive some good press in the *Jewish Times* in 1912. Cf. Rome, *Jacobs' Opponents II*, pp. 74–75, 88.
32　In 1909, Rabbi Glazer sued Wolofsky and his newspaper for libel. He claimed $20,000 for an alleged libel arising out of a dispute between butchers and *shoḥtim*. It was settled out of court with the defendant agreeing to pay the legal costs of both sides and to publish a retraction. "Memorandum of Agreement," April 19, 1909, American Jewish Archives, Glazer Papers 1/18. Cf. *Jewish Times*, April 23, 1909, p. 429; April 30, 1909, p. 455.
33　American Jewish Archives, Glazer Papers, 2/7.
34　Rome, *Jacobs' Opponents II*, pp. 71–73. Cf. Sherman, *Orthodox Judaism*, p. 76; Gerald Tulchinsky, *Taking Root: The Origins of the Canadian Jewish Community* (Toronto: Lester, 1992), p. 227.
35　Food not fit for consumption by Jews during Passover.
36　The names have been omitted but are included in the original document.
37　President.
38　Honour of marching with the Torah scroll.
39　Honour of being called to the reading of the Torah.
40　*C* had the same surname as *B*.
41　AJA, Glazer Papers 269/1/6. According to his "Diary," he received a fee of $5.00 for this case.
42　*Jewish Times*, April 1, 1910, p. 5.
43　Which, presumably, had been baked on the Sabbath.
44　AJA Glazer papers, 269/2/7.
45　Just as his opponents had called him *Mr.* Glazer.
46　The nephew of Rabbi Hirsh Cohen.

47 From a document enumerating chicken slaughterers in Montreal dated September 5, 1923, it appears that Lamdan arrived in Montreal in 1905 and had received his certification to slaughter chickens in the same year. Canadian Jewish Congress National Archives, Va'ad ha-'Ir Collection, file 4.
48 On this incident, see Rome, *Jacobs' Opponents II*, p. 64ff.
49 Keinosuke Oiwa, "Tradition and Social Change: An Ideological Analysis of the Montreal Jewish Immigrant Ghetto in the Early Twentieth Century," doctoral dissertation, Cornell University, 1988, p. 66.
50 Tulchinsky, *Taking Root*, p. 251; David Rome, *The Plamondon Case and S.W. Jacobs, Canadian Jewish Archives*, n.s. 26 (Montreal: Canadian Jewish Congress, 1982): 62–63.
51 On the Plamondon case in general, see David Rome, *The Plamondon Case*.
52 Cf. Rome, "Rabbi Simon Joshuah Glazer," pp. 125–26.
53 This list is derived from Rabbi Glazer's 1909 diary. American Jewish Archives. An additional source of information consists of the official record books of births maintained by the congregations. According to these, Rabbi Glazer was the primary rabbinic signatory for Congregations Tifereth Israel (appears in 1912 list), Temple Solomon (also in 1912 list) and Achavas Achim (appears on no other list). "Rabbis of Quebec Database" www.jewishgen.org/Rabbinic/databases/quebec.htm.
54 *JT*, February 16, 1912, p. 7.
55 David Rome, *The Plamondon Case*, p. 62.
56 Maimonides, *Book of Mishneh Torah*, v–ix.
57 The date of the event was June 11, 1911. AJA, Glazer papers 269/2/7.
58 Interestingly, Rabbi Glazer secured for this book a copyright not merely for the United States and Canada, but also for England.
59 It is thus reminiscent of Maimonides' *Moreh Nevukhim/Guide of the Perplexed*.
60 On Maimonides' *Mishneh Torah*, see Isadore Twersky, *Introduction to the Code of Maimonides (Mishneh Torah)* (New Haven, CT: Yale University Press, 1980).
61 Pp. vi–vii.
62 P. 176.
63 Simon Glazer, *Sermons* (New York: Star Hebrew, 1930), www.hebrewbooks.org., unpaginated.
64 Glazer, *Sermons*.
65 Glazer, *Sermons*.
66 Glazer Papers, American Jewish Archives. 269/1/6.

CHAPTER FOUR

1 An earlier version of this chapter was published in *Canadian Jewish Studies* 1 (1993): 41–58.
2 *Idisher Journal* (Toronto), March 23, 1916.
3 Many of the details of Rosenberg's biography are taken from a biographical sketch published in a souvenir program for a banquet celebrating Rosenberg's seventieth birthday, edited by Dr. Zvi Cohen and entitled *Sefer ha-Zikkaron le-Hag Yovel ha-Shiv'im shel ... R.Yehuda Rosenberg* (Montreal, 1931), pp. 5–6. Cf. also the memoir of his daughter, Leah Rosenberg, *The Errand Runner: Reflections of a Rabbi's Daughter* (Toronto: John Wiley, 1981). I am presently preparing a comprehensive biography

of Rosenberg entitled "A Kabbalist in Montreal: The Life and Times of Rabbi Yudel Rosenberg."

4 See Chapter 2.

5 On the study of Russian by rabbis in that period, see Azriel Shohat, *The "Crown Rabbinate" in Russia: A Chapter in the Cultural Struggle between Orthodox Jews and "Maskilim"* [Hebrew] (Haifa: University of Haifa Press, 1975), p. 132. Cf. Immanuel Etkes, "The Relationship between Talmudic Scholarship and the Institution of the Rabbinate in Nineteenth Century Lithuanian Jewry," in Leo Landman, ed., *Scholars and Scholarship: The Interaction between Judaism and Other Cultures* (New York: Yeshiva University Press, 1990), pp. 107–32.

6 For instances of Rosenberg's interest in these secular subjects, see Leah Rosenberg, *Errand Runner*, pp. 22, 65. Cf. also Yudel Rosenberg, *Nifla'ot ha-Zohar*, p. 6.

7 In this aspect, Rabbi Rosenberg stands in sharp contrast with Rabbi Cohen, whose publications were limited to "op-ed" pieces in the *Keneder Odler*.

8 *Yaddot Nedarim* (Warsaw: F. Baumritter, 1902). In citing Rosenberg's works, only the date of the first edition will be given. It should be noted that nearly all his works were published in several editions and that most of his Hebrew works were translated into Yiddish. I am presently preparing a comprehensive bibliography of Rosenberg's writings in conjunction with the biography. For the present, see David Rome, *A Selected Bibliography of Jewish Canadiana* (Montreal: Canadian Jewish Congress and Jewish Public Library, 1959) "Religion," pp. 16–18.

9 This volume is listed in the biographical sketch cited in note 2 above as being in manuscript under the title of *"Allufei Yehuda."* It was to have been printed as the second half of his work *'Omer va-Da'at*. It exists in page proof (Piotrkow, Ḥanokh Henikh Folman, 5694), but, to my knowledge, it was never printed during Rosenberg's lifetime. Rosenberg also published the following response: *Dvar Halakha 'im Muttar le-She'ol ba-Goral, Sefer Goral ha-'Assiriot*, ed. Meir Yehoshua Rosenberg [Yudel Rosenberg's son] (Warsaw: Baumritter, 1904), pp. 19–23; *Me'or ha-Hashmal* (Montreal, 1924).

10 *Peri Yehuda* (Bilgoraj, Poland, 1935).

11 *Kol Torah* (Warsaw, 1908). Only one volume of this periodical was published. Approximately half of the material published was written by Rosenberg.

12 *Sefer ha-Keriah ha-Kedosha* (New York, 1919); *Sefer Ateret Tiferet* (New York, 1931); *Mikveh Yehuda* (Toronto, 1914?); *Seder Hakafot* (Montreal, 1919); *Seder ha-Prozbul* (Piotrkow, 1910); *Darsha' Zemer u-Fishtim* (Piotrkow, 1912); *"A Brivele Fun di Zisse Mame Shabbes Malkesa zu Ihre Zin und Tehter fun Idishn Folk"* (Montreal, 1924); *Sefer Refuat ha-Nefesh u-Refuat ha-Guf* (Warsaw, 1913). Cf. Ira Robinson, "A Letter from the Sabbath Queen: Rabbi Yudel Rosenberg Addresses Montreal Jewry," *An Everyday Miracle: Yiddish Culture in Montreal* (Montreal: Véhicule Press, 1990). pp. 101–14.

13 *Sefer Refael ha-Malakh* (Piotrkow: Belkhatovski, 1911). He also translated a work on homeopathic medicine (Piotrkow, 1912). Cf. Ira Robinson, "The Tarler *rebbe* of Ùłd and His Medical Practice: Towards a History of Hasidic Life in Pre-First World War Poland," *POLIN: Studies in Polish Jewry* (London and Portland, OR: Littman Library of Jewish Civilization, 1998), vol. 11, pp. 53–61.

14 *Sefer Divrei ha-Yamim le-Shlomo ha-Melekh* (Piotrkow: Kleiman, 1914).

15 *Sefer Eliyahu ha-Navi* (Piotrkow: Zederboim, 1910).
16 *Tiferet MAHAR'EL mi-Shpoli* (Piotrkow: Folman, 1912). Cf. Ira Robinson, "The Zaddik as Hero in Hasidic Hagiography," in Menachem Mor ed., *Crisi and Reaction: The Hero in Jewish History* (Omaha, NE: Creighton University Press, 1995), pp. 93–103; idem., "Hasidic Hagiography and Jewish Modernity," *Jewish History and Jewish Memory: Essays in Honor of Yosef Haim Yerushalmi*, ed. Elisheva Carlebach, John M. Efron, and David N. Myers (Hanover and London: Brandeis University Press, 1998), pp. 405–12.
17 *Der Greidizer* (Piotrkow: Sholomovitz, n.d.). Ira Robinson, "The Uses of the Hasidic Story: Rabbi Yudel Rosenberg and His Tales of the Greiditzer Rebbe," *Journal of the American Association of Rabbis* l (1991): 17–25.
18 *Sefer Nifla'ot ha-MAHARAL im ha-Golem*. On the subject of the Maharal of Prague, Rosenberg also wrote *Haggadat ha-MAHARAL mi-Prag* (Warsaw, 1905) and *Sefer Hoshen ha-Mishpat shel ha-Kohen ha-Gadol* (Piotrkow, 1913). He claimed to base all three works on manuscripts from the "Royal Library of Metz." However, it is apparent from a perusal of these works that they constitute Rosenberg's original writings. Ira Robinson, "Literary Forgery and Hasidic Judaism: The Case of Rabbi Yudel Rosenberg," *Judaism* 40 (1991): 61–78. See also the following note.
19 Joseph Dan, "The Beginnings of Hebrew Hagiographic Literature" [Hebrew], *Jerusalem Studies in Jewish Folklore* 1 (1981), p. 85. Cf. Gershom Scholem, *On the Kabbalah and Its Symbolism* (New York: Schocken, 1965), p. 189, note 1; Arnold L. Goldsmith, *The Golem Remembered, 1909–1980* (Detroit: Wayne State University Press, 1981), p. 40; Joachim Neugroschel, *Yenne Velt: The Great Works of Jewish Fantasy and Occult* (New York: Stonehill, 1976), vol. 1, p. 351. Gershon Winkler attempts to defend the veracity of Rosenberg's account of the Golem, arguing that a rabbi who could publish halakhic works would never knowingly state such a falsehood. See his *The Golem of Prague* (New York: Judaica Press, 1980), p. xi. Cf. also Eli Yassif, ed., *The Golem of Prague and Other Tales of Wonder* [Hebrew] (Jerusalem: Mossad Bialik, 1991), introduction, pp. 7–72; Shnayer Z. Leiman, "The Adventure of the Maharal of Prague in London: R. Yudl Rosenberg and the Golem of Prague," *Tradition* (2002): 1–63.
20 *Zohar Torah*, seven volumes. Vols. 1–2 (Montreal: 1924); vol. 3–5 (New York: Trio Press, 1924–1925). The first volume, on Genesis, was published in Warsaw in 1905 under the title *Sha'arei Zohar Torah*. Volumes 6 and 7, entitled *ha-Zohar ha-Kadosh* and comprising the Zohar on Psalms, Song of Songs, Proverbs, and Ecclesiastes, were published in Bilgoraj, Poland, 1929–30). Rosenberg also published a bilingual (Hebrew-Yiddish) edition of legends of the Zohar under the title *Nifla'ot ha-Zohar* (Montreal, 1927) Cf. the critical remarks of Isaiah Tishby, *Mishnat ha-Zohar* (Jerusalem: Mossad Bialik, 1982), vol. 1, p. 113, note 7.
21 Rosenberg, *Errand Runner*, p. 59. Cf. also the numerous letters of greeting from around the world published in Cohen, *Sefer ha-Zikkaron*.
22 Cf. Harold Gastwirt, *Fraud, Corruption and Holiness: The Controversy over the Supervision of Jewish Dietary Practice in New York City, 1881–1940* (Port Washington, NY: Kennikat Press, 1974); Abraham J. Karp, "New York Chooses a Chief Rabbi," *Proceedings of the American Jewish Historical Society* (1954): 129–98; Aaron Rothkoff, "The American Sojourns of Ridbaz: Religious Problems within the Immigrant

Community," *American Jewish Historical Quarterly* (1968): pp. 557–72; Ira Robinson, "The Education of an American Orthodox Rabbi: Mayer Joshua Rosenberg Comes to Holyoke, Massachusetts." *Judaism* 40 (1991): pp. 543–51; idem., "The First Hasidic Rabbis in North America," *American Jewish Archives* 44 (1992), pp. 501–15; idem., "Toward a History of Kashrut in Montreal: The Fight over Municipal Bylaw 828 (1922–1924)," in *Renewing Our Days: Montreal Jews in the Twentieth Century* (Montreal: Vehicule, 1995), pp. 30–41. See Chapter 1 of this book.

23 Stephen A. Speisman, *The Jews of Toronto: A History to 1937* (Toronto: McClelland and Stewart, 1979), p. 281.
24 Rosenberg, *Errand Runner*, p. 64.
25 See Chapter 3.
26 American Jewish Archives, Glazer Papers.
27 See Chapter 7.
28 *Keneder Odler*, January 24, 1919.
29 Ibid., pp. 39, 65–66; Speisman, *The Jews of Toronto*, pp. 166–67, 173–74.
30 Cf. Rosenberg, *Errand Runner*, p. 67. Cf. Ira Robinson, "The Kosher Meat War and the Jewish Community Council of Montreal, 1922–1925," *Canadian Ethnic Studies*. 22 (2) (1990): pp. 41–53. See Chapter 6 and seven of this book.
31 The account of this period in *The Errand Runner*, p. 67, is misleading, though reference is made to a demonstration against Rosenberg in front of his home. The unfolding of events, heavily prejudiced against Rosenberg, may be followed in the pages of the *Keneder Odler*, and outlined in my article "The Kosher Meat War," as well as my article, "Toward a History of Kashrut in Montreal" and in Chapter 7 of this book. Cf. Quebec Superior Court, District of Montreal, case no. 3312 Laxer et al. vs. Jewish Butchers Society of Montreal et al., March 18, 1925.
32 Rosenberg, *Peri Yehuda*, p. 34. For a similar remark by a European Hasidic leader, Moshe of Kozienice, see the citation in Raphael Mahler, *Hasidism and the Jewish Enlightenment: Their Confrontation in Galicia and Poland in the First Half of the Nineteenth Century* (Philadelphia: Jewish Publication Society, 1985), p. 246.
33 "A Brivele," p. 11. Despite this, Rosenberg seems to have maintained amicable enough relations with the local Reform rabbi, Harry Stern, as evidenced by Stern's letter included in the souvenir program for Rosenberg's seventieth birthday.
34 Cf. Ira Robinson, "Because of Our Many Sins," p. 39.
35 Rosenberg, "A Brivele," p. 7. Other contemporary Jewish leaders such as Cyrus Adler, President of the Jewish Theological Seminary of America, likewise looked to the forty-hour week as the solution to the problem of sabbath observance. Cf. Ira Robinson, ed., *Cyrus Adler: Selected Letters* (Philadelphia: Jewish Publication Society, 1985), vol. 1, pp. 183–85.
36 Ibid., p. 6.
37 Ibid.
38 Ibid., pp. 14–15.
39 Rosenberg, *Me'or ha-Hashmal*, p. 3. In this responsum, Rosenberg ruled that turning electric lights on and off was forbidden on the Sabbath but permissible during holidays. Cf. pp. 7–9.
40 Ibid., p. 13.
41 Rosenberg, "A Brivele," p. 14. Rosenberg also discusses the phenomenon of *kaddish* as a spur to synagogue attendance on pp. 4–5.

42 Rosenberg, *Peri Yehuda*, p. 16. On the phenomenon of the non-observant "Orthodox" Jew, see Jeffrey Gurock, "The Winnowing of American Orthodoxy," *American Jewish Orthodoxy in Historical Perspective* (Hoboken: KTAV, 1996), pp. 299–313.
43 Rosenberg, *Mikveh Yehuda*, p. 3. Cf. Israel Meir Kahan, *The House of Israel* (New York, 1934), pp. 32–33. An illustration of contemporary "modern" attitudes toward mikveh can be found in Anna Shtrernshis, *Soviet and Kosher: Jewish Popular Culture in the Soviet Union, 1923–1939* (Bloomington: Indiana University Press, 2006), pp. 152–53.
44 Rosenberg, "*Der Krizis fun Lodz Warsaw*" (Piotrkow, 1912), pp. 2–3. This pamphlet is a Yiddish version of *Darsha' Zemer u-Fishtim*.
45 Rosenberg, *Peri Yehuda*, p. 56.
46 Ibid.
47 Ibid., pp. 34–35. The reference is to the Biblical story recounted in Genesis 32, 25–29. For a similar evaluation by a contemporary European rabbinic figure, see Elhonon Wasserman, *Ma'amar Ikvete de-Meshiha* (New York, 1937).
48 45 Cf. Gershom Scholem, *Major Trends in Jewish Mysticism* (New York, 1971), pp. 341ff. Cf. Mahler, *Hasidism and the Jewish Enlightenment*, p. 282.
49 46 Rosenberg, *Zohar Torah*, vol. 1, title page: The Book of the *Zohar* will be revealed to the inhabitants of the lower world in the end of days and for its sake "Each of you shall return to his possession...." Cf. Rosenberg, *Nifla'ot ha-Zohar*, p. 159. A similar sentiment is expressed in the title page of Zvi Hirsch Khotsh's *Nahalat Zvi*, a Yiddish translation of the *Zohar* first published in 1711: "It [the *Zohar*] will be understood by great and small [alike]. And in this merit we will merit to go to Jerusalem."
50 Cited in letter of H. Medini, *Zohar Torah*, vol. 1, p. 3.
51 Ibid., p. 9.
52 Ibid., p. 3.
53 Ibid., p. 9.
54 Rosenberg, *Nifla'ot ha-Zohar*, p. 6.
55 Cf. Ira Robinson, "Torah and Halakha in Medieval Judaism," *Studies in Religion* 13 (1984): 47.
56 E.g., Rosenberg, "*Krizis*," pp. 1, 7; "*Me'or ha-Hashmal*," pp. 5–6. Cf. note 8 above.
57 Rosenberg, "*A Brivele*," pp. 3–4.
58 Rosenberg, *Seder Hakafa*, advertisement on last page.
59 Rosenberg, *Peri Yehuda*, p. 5.
60 Ibid., p. 7.
61 Ibid., p. 6.
62 Rosenberg, *Nifla'ot ha-Zohar*, pp. 145–46.
63 Ibid., pp. 126–27.
64 Ibid., p. 147. Cf. also p. 146.
65 Ibid., p. 159.
66 I am aware of at least four editions: Montreal, New York, and Bilgoraj, 1924–31; New York, 1955; Jerusalem, 1967; New York, 1970. There are presumably others of which I am not yet aware.
67 Adin Steinsaltz, *The Thirteen-Petalled Rose* (New York: Basic Books, 1980); Aryeh Kaplan, *Mediation and Kabbala* (York Beach, ME: Samuel Weiser, 1982).
68 See Leo Levi, *Torah and Science: Their Interplay in the World Scheme* (New York: Association of Orthodox Jewish Scientists, 5743 [1983]).

CHAPTER FIVE

1. Herzig was a *shohet* and cantor in Montreal. American Jewish Archives, Herzig Family Correspondence, 1914–1940.
2. See the discussion of rabbinical ordination in Chapter 1.
3. There is a tradition current in the Laxer family that Getsel Laxer hated the sight of blood.
4. Aaron Rakeffet-Rothkoff, *The Silver Era in American Orthodoxy* (Jerusalem and New York: Feldheim and Yeshiva University Press, 1981).
5. Cf. Robinson, "The First Hasidic Rabbis in North America," *American Jewish Archives* 44 (1992): 501–15, and Chapter 4 of this book.
6. Cf. Ismar Schorsch, "The Emergence of the Modern Rabbinate," *From Text to Context: The Turn to History in Modern Judaism* (Hanover and London: New England Universities Press, 1994), pp. 9–50.
7. Hutchins Hapgood, *The Spirit of the Ghetto*, ed. Moses Rischin (Cambridge, MA: Harvard University Press, 1967), p. 60ff.
8. Cf. Harold Gastwirth, *Fraud, Corruption and Holiness: The Controversy over the Supervision of Jewish Dietary Practice in New York City, 1881–1940* (Port Washington, NY: 1974).
9. While this story concerns a somewhat later era, it nonetheless illustrates the narrow range of choices available to these men. On Rabbi Feinstein's expertise in slaughtering, see Moshe Dovid Tendler, *The Responsa of Rav Moshe Feinstein*, Vol. 1, *Care of the Critically Ill* (Hoboken: KTAV, 1986), pp. 11–12. On Rabbi Feinstein in general, see Ira Robinson, "Because of Our Many Sins: The Contemporary Jewish World as Reflected in the Responsa of Moses Feinstein," *Judaism* 35 (1986): 35–46.
10. Louis Rosenberg, *Canada's Jews*, pp. 197–98.
11. *Sefer Heker Davar* (Montreal: 1960). On Crestohl see Ira Robinson, "Hyman Meyer Crestohl," *Dictionary of Canadian Biography* 15 (Toronto: University of Toronto Press, 2005), p. 240.
12. That this phenomenon was not confined to Montreal is confirmed in the story of Rabbi Naphtali Levy, who corresponded with Charles Darwin, wrote the first Hebrew book on Darwin's theories, and, after his emigration from Radom, Poland to London, worked as a *shohet*. See Ralph Colp, Jr. and David Kohn, "'A Real Curiosity': Charles Darwin Reflects on a Communication from Rabbi Naphtali Levy," *The European Legacy* 1 (1996): 1716–27.
13. Both volumes were extensions of columns he wrote for the *Keneder Odler*.
14. His articles on Maimonides were collected into a volume: *Der Rambam: Zein lebn un shafn* (Montreal, 1933).
15. *Likkutei Beit Aharon* (New York: 1954).
16. *Sefer 'Edut be-Yisrael* (Montreal: 1943).
17. *Sefer Hutim ha-Meshulashim* (Montreal: 1953).
18. The section of this chapter on Laxer is largely based upon the Laxer Papers. These documents were originally lent to me by Laxer's granddaughter, Ms. Soryl Naymark of St. Laurent, Quebec, in 1997. Their contents, written in several ledgers and notebooks as well as numerous detached sheets include several works of Torah scholarship, the longest of which extends well over a hundred pages in manuscript, as well as notes for sermons and a limited amount of correspondence, mainly related to kashrut

and Torah scholarship. The Laxer Papers are presently housed in the Canadian Jewish Congress Archives in Montreal.

19 The dates are contained in a family reminiscence entitled "Laxer Saga," by Lily Laxer Bernstein (June, 1999), pp. 3, 23.
20 The name appears in his marriage document dated Adar, 5658 [1898]. Laxer Papers [LP].
21 Draft of Letter to Meir Shapira, 1930 LP.
22 Laxer, "Laxer Saga," p. 3.
23 Draft of Laxer to Hirsh Cohen, LP.
24 Laxer, "Laxer Saga," pp. 8–10.
25 Louis Rosenberg, *Canada's Jews* (Montreal, 1939), p. 308.
26 Laxer signed the vital records of that congregation from 1916 to 1919. "Rabbis of Quebec Database" www.jewishgen.org/Rabbinic/databases/quebec.htm. That synagogue was founded in 1905 and was located at 5390 St. Urbain. See the unpublished paper of Sara Tauben, "The Urban Synagogues of Montreal: A Survey of Synagogues Established in Montreal Up to 1945" (1999), p. 5.
27 Cf. Rosenberg, *Canada's Jews*, p. 309.
28 Cf. Isaiah, Chapter 58.
29 His daughter comments that he was "highly principled and very puritanical about carrying out the Orthodox ritual" and that "he did not suffer fools too well." "Laxer Saga," pp. 5, 7.
30 These include hazzanim, *shohtim*, and teachers who did not have, or did not wish to use rabbinic credentials. The significance of this title needs further elucidation.
31 Others may have been lost when the bulk of his library was sold upon his death. "Laxer Saga," p. 2.
32 On the Tosafists, see Ephraim Urbach, *The Tosafists: Their History, Writings and Methods* [Hebrew] (Jerusalem: Bialik Institute, 1968).
33 The following is a list of the major works preserved in the mss:
Gal Likkutim mi-Ba'alei Tosafot – an alphabetically arranged anthology of citations from the Tosafistic commentary on the Talmud (Minute Book, pp. 368–265 [writing in minute book goes in reverse to the pagination]; Colossus Notebook 15b–21b, 23a–32b; High School Exercise Book, 1a–38b; Ledger Book, 1–53).
Commentary on *Pirkei Avot*, which consists of an extensive system of sources from throughout rabbinic literature, bearing upon each and every word or phrase of the tractate (Colossus Notebook, 1a–14b, 37a–45a; The Classic Notebook 1b).
Commentary on the Prayerbook (The Classic Notebook).
Supercommentary on Rashi on Genesis and Part of Exodus (Classic Notebook).
Commentary on *hilkhot terefot* (The Colossus Notebook-Sefer Zikkaron, 1a–25b).
Commentary on Tractate *kallah rabbati* (The Colossus Notebook-Sefer Zikkaron, 27b–32b, 35a–37a; The Colossus-Sefer Sho'el ka-'inyan).
Hiddushei Torah (Novellae on the Pentateuch) (The Colossus-Sefer Sho'el ka-'inyan, 1a–27a
yafeh la-bedika responsa – questions only (Homespun Notebook).
Notes for sermons on special Torah readings of Adar (each has 4 sections) (Minute Book, 55–38).
34 Though Laxer wrote an introduction to several of his commentaries, it is basically the same text recycled.

35 I Samuel 10, 11–12; 19, 24.
36 Genesis 25, 23.
37 Notebook "The Colossus – *Sefer Sho'el ka-'inyan*," 6b–7a. LP.
38 Joshua Hershorn to Laxer, 22 and 29 August 1938. LP.
39 David Roskies, "Yiddish in Montreal: The Utopian Experiment," in Ira Robinson et al., eds., *An Everyday Miracle: Yiddish Culture in Montreal* (Montreal: Véhicule Press, 1990), p. 22ff. In general, the phenomenon of Orthodox publishing in North America in general bears additional analysis.
40 These were the East Side, West End, Davis, and Canada Packing slaughterhouses.
41 Ira Robinson, "Toward a History of Kashrut in Montreal: The Fight Over Municipal By-law 828 (1922–1924)," in Ira Robinson and Mervin Butovsky, eds., *Renewing Our Days: Montreal Jews in the Twentieth Century* (Montreal: Véhicule Press, 1995), pp. 38–39. For further details on this and other court cases in which Laxer was involved, cf. "Laxer Saga," p. 19ff. See Chapter 7.
42 The article appeared in *Keneder Odler* editor Hirsh Wolofsky's daily page one column, *"gut morgen,"* on May 30, 1922.
43 Significantly, Wolofsky allowed a reply by the "establishment" rabbi, Hirsh Cohen, in his *"gut morgen"* column of June 8, 1922. On the handbills, see Robinson, "The Kosher Meat War and the Jewish Community Council of Montreal, 1922–1925," *Canadian Ethnic Studies* 22 (1990): 48, n. 75 Cf. "Laxer Saga," p. 39.
44 On the reverse of the page is a circular letter dated 7 Adar, 5682.
45 On the term, "local rabbis," see Robinson, "Kosher Meat War," p. 44.
46 Advertisements for Borden's milk with Rabbi Rosenberg's certification of its kashrut for Passover were published in the *Keneder Odler* on April 7, 9, 12, and 16, 1922.
47 Cf. Robinson, "Kosher Meat War," pp. 43–44.
48 On Shapira, see *Encyclopedia Judaica*, vol. 14, cols. 1299–1300. His published book of responsa, *Or ha-Me'ir* (1926), was too early to have included a response to this question.
49 Lamentations 5, 8.
50 It is worth noting that part of the tension between them and the Jewish Community Council may have been ethnic differences given that the "chief rabbi," Hirsh Cohen, was of Lithuanian origins. See Robinson, "Kosher Meat War," p. 43.
51 Cf. Amos 6, 4.
52 Cf. *Mishna Sota* 9, 15.
53 Yudel Rosenberg, *Yeheveh Da'at*, responsum 26, pp. 105–6. This volume remained in page proofs. A copy is in the possession of the author.
54 Interview with Leah Rosenberg, who asserts that thereafter the two men would not speak to each other.
55 Thus the "Laxer Saga" (p. 22) recounts a family tradition that Laxer once bested the chief rabbi of Palestine, Abraham Isaac Kook, in a dispute over kashrut.
56 L. Tapper, *Archival Sources for the Study of Canadian Jewry* (Ottawa: National Archives of Canada, 1987), p. 22. Cf. Ira Robinson, "Crestohl, Hyman," in *Dictionary of Canadian Biography*, Vol. 15, *1921–1930* (Toronto: University of Toronto Press, 2005), p. 240.
57 "Revered Scholar Passes," *Canadian Jewish Chronicle*, May 11, 1928, p. 9.
58 *Canadian Jewish Chronicle*; "*ha-rov Hayyim Meir Crestohl shtarbt plutsling,*" *Keneder Odler*, May 6, 1928, p. 1.

59 Tapper, *Archival Sources*, p. 22.
60 *Canadian Jewish Chronicle*, May 11, 1928.
61 Tapper, *Archival Sources*, p. 22.
62 *Canadian Jewish Chronicle*, May 11, 1928.
63 Tapper, *Archival Sources*, p. 22; Letter from Rabbi Reines to the American *Mizrahi* leadership, CJC National Archives.
64 Crestohl, *Sefer Heker Davar* (Montreal: 1960). It was noted that the ms. was written in Brooklyn, NY, in 1910.
65 Email and attached document from Micah Males, September 3, 2002.
66 Tapper, *Archival Sources*, p. 22.
67 This is yet another example of the old adage of students of North American Jewish history that the word "Shalom" [peace] in a congregational name bespeaks conflict.
68 Guy W.-Richard, *Le Cimetière juive de Québec: Beth Israîl-Ohev Sholom* (Sillery: Septentrion, 2000), p. xxiii.
69 Simon Glazer, Diary, February 9, 1909. American Jewish Archives, Cincinnati, Ohio 269/2/1.
70 "Jewish Conditions in Quebec," *Jewish Times*, May 27, 1910.
71 Cohen to Crestohl, dated the day after *Yom Kippur*, 5677. NAC. Cf. the discussion of Rabbi Cohen's trade in these items in Chapter 2.
72 According to Chaim Leib Fox, this newspaper appeared in the years 1911–12. *100 Years of Yiddish and Hebrew Literature in Canada* [Yiddish] (Montreal: Adler Printing, 1980), p. 66.
73 *Bavli, Shabbat*, 34a.
74 This sort of charge against North American rabbis of this era was commonplace. Cf. Aaron Rakeffet-Rothkoff, "The Eastern European Immigrant Rabbinate in Its Formative Years, 1880–1910," *Gesher* 5 (1976): 135, 146.
75 Tapper, *Archival Sources*, p. 22.
76 CJC National Archives Crestohl file. Clipping from *Keneder Odler*, n.d. (1960?).
77 Cohen to Crestohl, 24 Shevat, 5678.
78 Tapper, *Archival Sources*, p. 22. The Crestohl papers in the National Archives of Canada contain a letter of appointment as rabbi of the congregation, dated November 1, 1920.
79 It is perhaps noteworthy that in his Quebec City letterhead, he called himself "Rabbi" in English and "rabbi and slaughterer" in Hebrew.
80 *Keneder Odler*, May 6, 1928.
81 In the minutes of the *Va'ad ha-'Ir* "Religious Committee," dated February 14, 1923, it is recorded that Rabbi Hirsh Cohen had discovered that Rabbi Crestohl was slaughtering chickens as well as cattle and had warned him that "he should be one or another." Canadian Jewish Congress National Archives, Va'ad ha-'Ir Collection.
82 *Canadian Jewish Chronicle*, May 11, 1928.
83 Quebec City Jews were often derisively referred to by Montreal Jews as *"yishuvnikes"* ["country bumpkins"]. David Rome, *Jacobs' Opponents II, Canadian Jewish Archives* 41 (Montreal: Canadian Jewish Congress, 1988), p. 64.
84 *Canadian Jewish Chronicle*, May 11, 1928.
85 Crestohl, *Sefer Heker Davar*.

CHAPTER SIX

1. This chapter is an expansion and adaptation of my article, "The Foundation Documents of the Jewish Community Council of Montreal," *Jewish Political Studies Review* 8, nos. 3–4 (1996): 69–86.
2. Ibid., p. 86.
3. "Community Council" (Hebrew).
4. On the American Jewish Committee, see Naomi Cohen, *Not Free to Desist: A History of the American Jewish Committee, 1906–1966* (Philadelphia: Jewish Publication Society, 1972).
5. See Naomi Cohen, "The Ethnic Catalyst: The Impact of the Eastern European Immigrants on the American Jewish Establishment," in David Berger, ed., *The Legacy of Jewish Immigration: 1881 and Its Impact* (Brooklyn: Brooklyn College Press, 1983), pp. 131–48.
6. On the governance of North American Jewish communities, see Daniel Elazar, *Community and Polity: The Organizational Dynamics of American Jewry* (Philadelphia: Jewish Publication Society, 1995).
7. On this movement, see Arthur Goren, *New York Jews and the Quest for Community: The Kehilla Experiment, 1908–1922* (New York: Columbia University Press, 1970). Cf. idem., "The New York Kehillah: A Response," *American Jewish History* 80 (1991): 535–46.
8. The concept of the *kehilla* in Europe was also undergoing an important change because of the pressures of modernization and emancipation. Cf. Jacob Katz, "Ideological Differences over the Status of the Kehila: The Jewish Community in the Age of Emancipation," in Alfred Ivry, Eliot Wolfson, and Alan Arkush, eds., *Perspectives on Jewish Thought and Mysticism* (Amsterdam: Harwood, 1998), pp. 457–69.
9. A *landsmanschaft* was a group of Jews coming from the same town or area in Europe. Thus people coming from Vilna might form a *Vilner landsmanschaft*. Sometimes this group founded a synagogue, sometimes not. These organizations typically offered healthcare, insurance, and death benefits for their members. In an era in which there was no "social safety net" to speak of, immigrant Jews created their own. Cf. Daniel Soyer, *Jewish Immigrant Associations and American Identity in New York, 1880–1939* (Cambridge, MA: Harvard University Press, 1997).
10. On the Philadelphia Kehilla, see Ira Robinson, "Two North American Kehillot and their Structure: Philadelphia and Montreal," *Proceedings of the Eleventh World Congress of Jewish Studies, Division B, The History of the Jewish People*, vol. 3, *Modern Times* (Jerusalem: World Union of Jewish Studies, 1994), pp. 139–46.
11. See Gerald Tulchinsky, *Taking Root: The Origins of the Canadian Jewish Community* (Toronto: Lester, 1992), p. 261ff.
12. For a history of Canadian Jewish organizations, see Ira Robinson, "They Work in Faithfulness: Studies in the Constitutional Documents of Canadian Jewish Organizations Other than Synagogues," in Daniel Elazar, Michael Brown, and Ira Robinson, eds., *Not Written in Stone: Jews, Constitutions and Constitutionalism in Canada* (Ottawa: University of Ottawa Press, 2003), pp. 111–51.
13. On Caiserman, see Bernard Figler and David Rome, *Hannaniah Meir Caiserman: A Biography* (Montreal: Northern Printing and Lithographing, 1962).

14 On the Jewish school question in Montreal, see Arlette Corcos, *Montréal, les juifs et l'école* (Sillery: Septentrion, 1997), pp. 69–150.
15 See Chapter 2 of this book.
16 See Chapter 3 of this book.
17 See Chapter 4 of this book, as well as Ira Robinson, "Kabbalist and Community Leader: Rabbi Yudel Rosenberg and the Canadian Jewish Community," *Canadian Jewish Studies* 1 (1993): 41–58.
18 Ira Robinson, "The Kosher Meat War and the Jewish Community Council of Montreal, 1922–1925," *Canadian Ethnic Studies* 22, no. 2 (1990): 44. Cf. letter of Rabbi Hirsh Cohen, 16 Iyyar, 5683 [1923], Canadian Jewish Archives, Montreal.
19 On Wolofsky, see his autobiography, *The Journey of My Life* (Montreal: Eagle Publishing, 1945). Cf. Pierre Anctil, "Introduction du traducteur," Wolofsky, *Mayn Lebens Rayze: Un demi-siècle de vie yiddish à Montréal, 1946* (Sillery: Septentrion, 2000), pp. 15–38.
20 The complete English text of this pamphlet is published in Robinson, "Foundations Documents," pp. 80–86.
21 Cf. Figler and Rome, *Hannaniah Meir Caiserman: A Biography*, p. 146.
22 A desecration of [God's] Name (Hebrew).
23 Non-kosher sausage (Yiddish).
24 Begging (Yiddish).
25 Rabbinical Court (Hebrew).
26 In that era, all Montreal Jewish schools were supplementary. Their students derived their secular education in the Protestant school system.
27 Bernard Figler and David Rome, *Hannaniah Meir Caiserman: A Biography*, p. 145.
28 The presidium of three has been retained by the Jewish Community Council to the present day.
29 Then estimated to include between 40,000 and 45,000 people.
30 Hirsh Wolofsky, *Mayn Lebens Rayze* (Montreal, 1946), p. 113. In the English translation of this book, done by A.M. Klein, the following phrase, which is not extant in the original Yiddish, is added: "which [i.e. the Jewish community of Palestine] had already afforded some excellent examples of this type of internal communal administration." *The Journey of My Life* (Montreal, 1945), p. 86. Pierre Anctil, in his French translation, *Mayn Lebens Rayze: Un demi-siècle de vie yiddish à Montréal, 1946*, trans. Pierre Anctil (Sillery: Septentrion, 2000), p. 177, mistranslates "name" [*nomen*] as "idée."
31 National Council (Hebrew).
32 Paltiel Dickstein, *Toldot Mishpat ha-Shalom ha-'Ivri* (Tel-Aviv: Yavne, 1964); Ronen Shamir, *Colonies of Law: Colonialism, Zionism and Law in Early Mandate Palestine* (Cambridge: Cambridge University Press, 2000). Another influence was undoubtedly the establishment of a Jewish court of arbitration, known in Hebrew as *Beth Mishpat ha-Shalom*, in New York City in 1920. The composition of the New York court, with its three member panel consisting of a rabbi, a lawyer, and a businessman, is similar to the way in which the Montreal court was formed. See Samuel Buchler, *"Cohen Comes First" and Other Cases: Stories of Controversies before the New York Jewish Court of Arbitration* (New York: Vanguard Press, 1933), p. xiii.
33 Jewish Community Council of Montreal Papers, Canadian Jewish Congress National Archives.

34 See Chapter 7, and Ira Robinson, "Kosher Meat War."
35 See Chapter 5.

CHAPTER SEVEN

1 This chapter is an adaptation and an expansion of my article, "The Kosher Meat War," *Canadian Ethnic Studies* 22 (1990): 41–53.
2 Va'ad ha-'Ir Collection, Canadian Jewish Congress Archives, Montreal.
3 See Chapter 6.
4 See Chapter 5.
5 It is important to note that they were called "Jewish," and not "Kosher" butchers. Regardless of the greater or lesser strictness of the *kashrut* of their establishments, in the literature of the era, Jews went to "Jewish" butchers.
6 For American examples of the same phenomenon, see Hasia Diner, *Hungering for America: Italian, Irish, and Jewish Foodways in the Age of Migration* (Cambridge, MA: Harvard University Press, 2002), p. 206. It is worth noting that even though there is a perfectly good Hebrew/Yiddish word for butcher, "*katsev,*" the only term ever employed in the Montreal Yiddish documents from this era I have examined is "*butcher.*"
7 See Chapter 3.
8 See Chapter 4.
9 See Ira Robinson, "The Kosher Meat War and the Jewish Community Council of Montreal, 1922–1925."
10 See Chapter 3.
11 See Chapter 4.
12 Leah Rosenberg, *The Errand Runner: Reflections of a Rabbi's Daughter* (Toronto: Wiley, 1981), p. 68.
13 *Keneder Odler,* March 1, 1923. Cf. *Canadian Jewish Chronicle,* March 2, 1923. This, of course, goes beyond the normal harassment that bearded Jews faced from non-Jews on the street, particularly from children. Cf. Leah Rosenberg, *The Errand Runner,* p. 50; Moses Rischin, *The Promised City: New York's Jews: 1870–1914* (New York: Harper and Row, 1970), p. 91; Sydney Stahl Weinberg, *The World of Our Mothers: The Lives of Jewish Immigrant Women* (Chapel Hill, NC: University of North Carolina Press, 1988), p. 95.
14 On the Jewish Community Council, see Ira Robinson, "The Foundation Documents of the Jewish Community Council of Montreal," *Jewish Political Studies Review* 8, nos. 3–4 (1996): 69–86.
15 *Keneder Odler,* March 8, 1923.
16 "Arrest Butchers in Assault Case," *Montreal Star,* March 10, 1923.
17 March 15, 1923.
18 Jewish Community Council of Montreal Papers, Canadian Jewish Archives, Montreal, box 23.
19 On the infiltration of underworld elements in the kosher meat industry of New York City at this time, see Aryeh Goren, *New York Jews and the Quest for Community: The Kehilla Experiment, 1908–1922* (New York: Columbia University Press, 1970), p. 79; Harold Gastwirth, *Fraud, Corruption and Holiness: The Controversy over the Supervision of Jewish Dietary Practice in New York City, 1881–1940* (Port

Washington, NY: Kennikat Press, 1974), pp. 44–54. Joseph Belsky, *I the Union: Being the Personalized Trade Union Story of the Hebrew Butcher Workers of America* (New York: Raddock & Brothers, 1952), p. 48.
20 Rabbinical Council affiliated with the Jewish Community Council.
21 Literally "greased."
22 The reference is to the rabbinic usage in which the Hebrew word *damim* can signify either "blood" or "money."
23 *Keneder Odler*, April 29, 1923, p. 5.
24 One period is sixteen weeks and the other is seventeen weeks.
25 It is likely that payments in this category were up because the shifting loyalties of kosher butcher shops during the kosher meat war necessitated more supervisory manpower on the street.
26 See Chapter 6.
27 The Executive Secretary of the *Va'ad ha-'Ir*.
28 Mr. Fitch, the *Va'ad*'s lawyer, was later to be elected to the Quebec Legislative Assembly on the Union Nationale ticket.
29 In the Laxer family history, there is a recollection of Rabbi Laxer debating with Rabbi Kook, and, according to the memoir, besting Rabbi Kook in the argument.
30 On the School Question, see David Rome, *Canadian Jewish Archives*, new series, vols. 2 and 3 (1975); Arlette Corcos, *Montréal, les Juifs, et l'école* (Sillery: Septentrion, 1997).
31 *Keneder Odler*, September 16, 1923, p. 1. Rabbi Rosenberg had in 1922 initiated a process limiting licensed kosher chicken abattoirs in Montreal to eight. This measure was passed by the Montreal City Council in 1923, after Rabbis Rosenberg and Cohen had fallen out and the Kosher Meat War had commenced. Immediately the *Va'ad ha-'Ir* moved to get the licences for all eight abattoirs in its own hands. Thus rabbis Rosenberg and Herschorn, having been shut out of the kosher chicken market, protested to the Mayor. Ira Robinson, "Toward a History of Kashrut in Montreal: The Fight Over Municipal By-law 828 (1922–1924)," in Ira Robinson and Mervin Butovsky, eds., *Renewing Our Days: Montreal Jews in the Twentieth Century* (Montreal: Véhicule Press, 1995), pp. 30–41.
32 Approbation.
33 Under the law of that era, married women could not sue in court without their husbands' permission.
34 The volume of minutes from this period has had its pages ripped out.
35 The four-month period is prior to the outbreak of the kosher meat war. The eleven-month period is prior to the solution of the conflict.
36 See Chapter 5.
37 See Chapter 2.
38 Leah Rosenberg, *The Errand Runner: Reflections of a Rabbi's Daughter* (Toronto: Wiley, 1981), p. 114; Interview with Leah Rosenberg.
39 *Vaad Hoir Bulletins* 1–2, March 9, 1933; April 28, 1933. Canadian Jewish Congress National Archives, *Va'ad ha-'Ir* Collection, file 17.
40 Chicken slaughterers.
41 Slaughterers of large animals (i.e., cattle).
42 The situation of chicken slaughtering continued to plague the *Va'ad* in 1933. *Keneder Odler*, December 28, 1933.

43 On a similar phenomenon in New York City, see Paula Hyman, "Immigrant Women and Consumer Protest: The New York City Kosher Meat Boycott of 1902," *American Jewish History* 69 (1980): 91–105. Cf. also Diner, *Hungering for America: Italian, Irish, and Jewish Foodways in the Age of Migration*, p. 206.
44 Canadian Jewish Congress National Archives, Jewish Community Council of Montreal, file 19b. The handbill is undated. It is in a file of newspaper clippings from late 1933 and early 1934. The date of the mass meeting is Monday, November 20. In 1933, November 20 falls on a Monday, so the incident most likely occurred in that year.
45 See Tulchinsky, *Taking Root*, pp. 204–30.
46 Steven Lapidus, "The Jewish Community Council: The Evolution of Sectarianism in a Montreal Organization," 2006 Biennial Scholars' Conference on American Jewish History, http://www.cofc.edu/~jwst/pages/Lapidus,%20Steven%20-%20Sectarianism%20in%20Montreal%20+.pdf.

CHAPTER EIGHT

1 I would like to acknowledge the encouragement of Prof. Richard Menkis of the University of British Columbia in the conception of this chapter.
2 On the rise of the Yiddish press in New York, see Arthur Goren, "The Jewish Press," in Sally M. Miller, ed., *The Ethnic Press in the United States: A Historical Analysis and Handbook* (Westport, CT: Greenwood Press, 1987), pp. 203–29; Ronald Sanders, *The Downtown Jews: Portrait of an Immigrant Generation* (New York: Harper and Row, 1969); Isaac Metzker, ed., *A Bintel Brief: Sixty Years of Letters from the Lower East Side to the Jewish Daily Forward* (Garden City, NY: Doubleday, 1971).
3 On this newspaper, see Pierre Anctil, ed., *In the Eye of the Eagle* (Montreal: Véhicule Press, 2001); Louis Levendel, *A Century of the Canadian Jewish Press: 1880s–1980s* (Ottawa: Borealis Press, 1989), pp. 17–22; David Rome, "Men of the Yiddish Press," *Canadian Jewish Archives* n.s. 42 (1989).
4 The first book he published was *Eyrope un Erets Yisroel nokhn velt krieg* (Montreal, 1922). The second, *Oyf Eybiken Kvall* (Montreal: Eagle Publishing, 1930). The last was his autobiography, *Mayn Lebens Rayze* (Montreal: Eagle Publishing, 1946). This memoir was translated into English as *The Journey of My Life* (Montreal: Eagle Publishing, 1945), and into French as *Mayn Lebens Rayze: Un demi-siècle de vie yiddish à Montréal 1946*, trans. Pierre Anctil (Sillery: Septentrion, 2000).
5 Montreal: Eagle Publishing, 1930.
6 For internal evidence, see *EK*, p. 11.
7 They are mentioned briefly in Chayim Leyb Fox, *100 Years of Yiddish and Hebrew Literature in Canada* [Yiddish] (Montreal: Adler Printing, 1980), pp. 102–3. They are not mentioned in Pierre Anctil's introduction to his translation of the memoirs.
8 It is clear from a careful reading of *EK* that Wolofsky believed in the essential historicity of the narratives of the Torah. See note 53 below.
9 *EK*, pp. 2, 5. It is worth noting that, for the most part, Wolofsky speaks of "America," and does not seem to be looking at a Canadian specificity in the situations he depicts.
10 In this Wolofsky was, of course, reacting similarly to many contemporary rabbis. See Kimmy Caplan, *Orthodoxy in the New World: Immmigrant Rabbis and Preaching in America, 1881–1924* (Jerusalem: Zalman Shazar Center for Jewish History, 2002).

11   *EK*, p. 6.
12   *EK*, p. 7.
13   Cf. Moshe Idel, *Absorbing Perfections: Kabbalah and Interpretation* (New Haven, CT: Yale University Press, 2002), p. 26ff.
14   *EK*, p. 176.
15   *EK*, p. 82.
16   *EK*, p. 103.
17   *EK*, p. 112.
18   *EK*, p. 29.
19   Deuteronomy 28, 32.
20   *EK*, p. 176.
21   *EK*, p. 49.
22   *EK*, p. 62.
23   *EK*, p. 179.
24   *EK*, p. 95, cf. p. 100.
25   There is no mention here of the yiddishist "radical" schools. In another context, he also seemed to include those schools in his support for Jewish education. See Ira Robinson, "The Foundation Documents of the Jewish Community Council of Montreal," *Jewish Political Studies Review* 8, nos. 3–4 (1996): 81.
26   *EK*, p. 21.
27   *EK*, p. 92.
28   *EK*, p. 56. This point is reiterated on p. 163.
29   *EK*, 61.
30   Numbers 24, 5.
31   *EK*, p. 149. Further on Wolofsky's criticism of the synagogal "edifice complex," see pp. 69, 80.
32   *EK*, p. 132.
33   *EK*, p. 149.
34   *EK*, p. 67.
35   *EK*, pp. 85–86.
36   *EK*, p. 29.
37   *EK*, p. 30, cf. also p. 160.
38   *EK*, pp. 76–77. This point is reiterated on p. 92.
39   *EK*, p. 109.
40   *EK*, p. 106.
41   *EK*, p. 129.
42   *EK*, p. 133. Cf. Ira Robinson, "The Kosher Meat War and the Jewish Community Council of Montreal, 1922–1925," *Canadian Ethnic Studies* 22 (1990): 41–53.
43   *EK*, p. 68.
44   *EK*, p. 71.
45   *EK*, p. 37. On the impact of these events in the United States, see Naomi Cohen, *The Year After the Riots: American Responses to the Palestine Crisis of 1929–30* (Detroit, Wayne State University Press, 1988).
46   *EK*, pp. 25–26.
47   *EK*, p. 134.
48   The reference is apparently to Jewish anti-Zionists, who took up the cause and the arguments of the Palestinian Arabs.

49 *EK*, pp. 135–36.
50 *EK*, p. 49.
51 *EK*, p. 32.
52 *EK*, p. 107. The reader of the columns could not miss the reference to the issue of kosher meat coming into the city from outside, which was an issue among Montreal rabbis, as it was in many contemporary North American communities. Cf. p. 184.
53 *EK*, p. 80. On these trials in the Soviet Union, see Anna Shternshis, *Soviet and Kosher: Jewish Popular Culture in the Soviet Union, 1923–1939* (Bloomington: Indiana University Press, 2006), p. 93ff.
54 *EK*, p. 178.
55 Cf. note 8 above.
56 *EK*, p. 11. Cf. chapters 2 and 4 of this book.
57 *EK*, p. 15.
58 Cf. Ira Robinson, "Hasid and Maskil: The Hasidic Tales of an American Yiddish Journalist," in Steven Engler and Gregory P. Grieve, *Historicizing "Tradition" in the Study of Religion* (Berlin: Walter de Gruyter, 2005), pp. 283–96.
59 David Roskies, "Yiddish in Montreal: The Utopian Experiment," in Ira Robinson et al., eds. *An Everyday Miracle: Yiddish Culture in Montreal* (Montreal: Véhicule Press, 1990), pp. 22–38.
60 Cf. Ode Garfinkel and Mervin Butovsky, "The Journal of Yaakov Zipper," in Ira Robinson et al., eds., *An Everyday Miracle: Yiddish Culture in Montreal* (Montreal: Véhicule Press, 1990), pp. 53–68.
61 *EK*, p. 188.

CHAPTER NINE

1 Hirsh Cohen, Report to the Annual Meeting of the *Va'ad ha-'Ir*, ḥanukkah, 5695 [1934].
2 An illustration of the passenger list of the S.S. *President Pierce*, which departed Shanghai for San Francisco on September 29, 1941, and which includes the names of Rabbis Hirszprung, Kramer and others is published in Efraim Zuroff, *The Response of Orthodox Jewry in the United States to the Holocaust: The Activities of the Vaad-ha-hatzala Committee, 1939–1945* (New York and Hoboken: Yeshiva University Press and KTAV Publishing House, 2000), after p. 128.
3 Interview with Michael Herschorn, Rabbi Herschorn's son.

Index

abattoirs, chicken 113, 155
Abraham 124–25
Abramovitz, Shalom 5, 21, 32
Abramowitz, Herman 32, 39, 46
Achavas Achim (congregation) 143
Adath Yeshurun (congregation) 26
Adler, Cyrus 146
Agudath ha-Rabbonim 2–3, 8, 17–18, 129
Agudat ha-shoḥtim (Montreal) 75–77, 79–81, 84, 129
Alberta 30
Amalek 63
American Jewish Committee 88–89
American Jewish Congress 92–93
Americanization 90, 119
Anctil, Pierre 5, 156
anti-Semitism 38, 47, 93, 122
Arabs 124, 157
Aramaic 59
arba' minim. See Sukkot
Arbeiter Ring Shule 106, 108
Arye Leib of Shpole 58
Asenath 122
Ashinsky, Aaron Mordecai 22–26, 35–36, 54, 138–39
Aspler, Jonah 78
Association of Jewish Butchers of Montreal. *See* Jewish Butchers' Society of Montreal
Austria. *See* Austro-Hungarian Empire

Austrian-Hungarian Congregation (Shaarei Tefilla) 44, 47, 139
Austro-Hungarian Empire 72, 78

Balaam 122
Balfour Declaration 55, 91, 124
Bangor, Maine 42
Baron de Hirsch Institute (Montreal) 23, 29, 46, 99
Belkin, Simon 5
Bernstein, Louis 4, 6
Bet Din. See rabbinic court
Beth David (Roumanian Congregation) 25, 29, 43, 48
Beth Israel (Montreal) 25, 29
Beth Israel (Quebec City) 48, 82–83
Beth Judah (congregation) 48
Beth Mishpat ha-Shalom (New York) 153
Beth Solomon (congregation) 48, 143
Bialik, Chaim Nahman 21
Bible (Hebrew) 33, 38, 53, 59, 75, 120–21, 124, 147
  commentaries 72
  translation 121, 126
Blumenthal, B. 41
B'nai B'rith 92
Bnai Jacob (congregation) 13, 23, 25–26, 48, 138–39
Board of Jewish Education (New York) 91
Boer War 23

Borden Milk Company (Montreal) 77, 111, 150
Boston 89
Boucher, Madame 109
British Empire 38
Brooklyn, New York 36, 55
Bryan, William Jennings 33
Budwicz 21
Bukovina 72
Bund, Jewish Socialist 9
Butchers' Association (Montreal) 25

Cahan, Abraham 11
Caiserman, H.M. 93
Caleb 125
Calendar, Jewish 66
Canada 22, 69, 72, 82, 92, 143
  Census 12, 72
  Customs 31, 45–46
  Governor General 28
  Jewish community 59, 92–93, 95
  Jewish immigration 12–13
  "Jewish religious services" 71
  Sunday Laws 28
Canadian Jewish Chronicle (Montreal) 44, 93
Canadian Jewish Congress 93, 95, 98
  National Archives 27
Canadian Packing Company 107, 150
Canadian Zionist Federation 23, 92
Canadianization 90, 93
cantors 69, 72
Catholics 72, 83
Chatham, New Brunswick 73
Chevra Kadisha (congregation) 47–48, 138
Chevra Shas (congregation) 22, 48, 138
Chicago 8, 12, 22, 49, 87
chicken dealers 112
China 125–26
Christians 61
Coderre, Louis 113
Cohen, Ania 28
Cohen, Fishel 22
Cohen, H. 106
Cohen, Hirsh x, 21, 24–35, 38, 41–42, 44–46, 48, 53, 57, 59–60, 69, 74–75, 77, 82, 85, 93, 101, 103, 106–7, 109, 115–16, 125, 127–28, 137, 139–41, 144, 150–51, 155
Cohen, Jacob 141
Cohen, Lazarus 22, 24
Cohen, Leizer 29
Cohen, Lyon 46
Cohen, Myer 84
Cohen, Sarah Kreindel 27
Columbus, Christopher 66
Communism 94, 125
Concordia University Institute for Canadian Jewish Studies ix
Consumers' League 106–7
Copernicus, Nicholas 66–67
Crestohl, Hyman x, 69, 72, 81–85, 128, 151

Dan, Joseph 58
Darrow, Clarence 33
Darwin, Charles 67, 148
democracy 92
Denver 91
Depression (1930s) 7, 29, 33, 115
Des Moines, Iowa 37
de Sola, Meldola 23, 39
Detroit 22–23
din Torah 36, 59, 79, 103, 129. *See also* rabbinic court
Dorchester Street Synagogue. *See* Beth Israel
Dorshei Zion Society (Quebec City) 84

East End Slaughterhouse (Montreal) 73–74, 150
education, Jewish 18, 37–38, 49, 60, 90–91, 93, 97, 111, 122, 127, 153
  parochial (day) school 97–98
Egypt 54, 121–22, 126
Elijah (Gaon of Vilna) 49
Elijah (prophet) 58
England 13, 143
  Chief Rabbi 38–39
  Jewish community 39
  United Synagogue 38–39
English language 19, 22–23, 25, 31, 37–38, 48–51, 55, 61, 72–73, 93, 104, 121
Epstein, Ḥayyim Fishel 110

Erzwillig, Lithuania 36
Esau 123
etrog. See Sukkot
Europe 13
European literature 81
evolution 33, 54, 67, 148

Federation of Zionist Societies of Canada 84
federations of Jewish charities 89–91
Feinstein, Moses 71, 148
Fitch, Louis 109, 155
Folks Shule (Jewish People's School) 99, 101, 106, 108
Forward (New York) 94
fossils 125
Frankfurt 49
Freiheit (New York) 94
French language 49
Friedlaender, Elias 24
Friedman, Julius 113
Fundamentalism 34, 53–54

gangsters 107, 116, 154
Garber, Simcha 93, 141
Gemara 15, 32. *See also* Talmud
generation gap 121
George V, King 48
Germany 88
Glazer, Simon x, 26, 28, 35–55, 59, 69, 75, 82–84, 93, 105–6, 141–43
Gloversville, New York 82
Goldstein, Maxwell 41
Goldsman, Wolf 41–42
Goldstick, Hyman 140
Golem of Prague 58, 145
Gordon, Eliezer 16
Gordon, Jacob 40
Guaranteed Milk Company (Montreal) 111
Gurock, Jeffrey 7
Guttmacher, Elijah 58

hadassim. See Sukkot
hagiography 58
halakha 7–8, 10, 57–58, 62, 65, 71, 78, 83–84, 105, 130, 146

family purity 121
Halifax, Nova Scotia 47, 84
hamets. See Passover
Hapgood, Hutchins 70
Hanukkah 51–53
Harlem (New York) 55
Harris, Eirann 141
Hasidism. *See* Judaism, Hasidic
Haskala 57, 130
Haverim Kol Yisrael (congregation, Papineau) 48
hazaka 76, 84, 130
Hebraism 4
Hebrew 19, 21, 24, 31, 50, 53, 57–59, 68, 73, 84
literature 58
teachers 72
Hebron 124
heder 18, 23, 130
Heller, Nachman 24
Herschorn, Michael 158
Herschorn, Sheea (Joshua Halevi) 10, 75, 101, 104–5, 100, 112, 114–15, 128
Herzig, Leibush 69, 78, 148
Herzl, Theodore 30
High Holy Days 62, 112. *See also* Rosh ha-Shana and Yom Kippur
Hirschprung, Pinchos 127–28
Holocaust 2, 133
homeopathy 144
Hoshen Mishpat. See Shulhan 'Arukh
Humboldt, Alexander von 33

Idishe Velt 82
Isaac Elchanan Theological Seminary 14, 17
Israel, State of 100
Israel Baal Shem Tov 49
Israel Meir ha-Kohen (Hofets Hayyim) 8, 16

J.J. Joubert Milk company (Montreal) 111
Jacob 123, 125
Jacobs, S.W. 46
Jacobson, Maxine 133
jazz 120
Jerusalem 25

Jewish Butchers' Employees Association (Montreal) 44
Jewish Butchers' Society of Montreal 76, 104, 106, 110, 114
Jewish Chronicle (London) 41
Jewish community
  North America 3, 7, 87–88, 119, 128
Jewish Community Council (Montreal) xi, 1, 60, 78–81, 86–88, 93, 98, 100–117, 132, 150, 153, 155
  Finance Committee 105, 111
  Mishpat ha-Shalom 100
  rabbinical council 80, 114–16
Jewish Compromiser (Toledo) 37
Jewish Herald (Des Moines) 37
Jewish Immigrant Aid Society 99
Jewish People's Library. *See* Jewish Public Library
Jewish People's School. *See* Folks Shule
Jewish Public Library (Montreal) ix, xi, 33
Jewish Sabbath Alliance of America 136
Jewish Times (Montreal) 24–26, 38, 40, 82, 142
Johnstown, Pennsylvania 42
Joseph, Jacob 11, 14
Joseph, Montefiore 82
Joshua 125
Judaism 96, 125
  Ashkenazic 12, 15, 49, 110
  Conservative 4
  Eastern European 9–10, 50, 64, 89, 91
  Hasidic 5, 49, 55, 57, 64, 72, 130
  modern 68
  Montreal 75, 82, 128
  North American 4, 18, 48–49, 51, 128
  Orthodox 4, 8–9, 36, 38, 48, 61, 68, 88, 90
  Rabbinic 4, 6, 15
  Reform 4, 13, 38, 49–50, 61
  Russian 21
  Sephardic 12
Jung, Leo 1, 133

kabbala 34, 57, 64, 66, 68
  Lurianic 66
kaddish 146
Kansas City 54–55

Kaplan, Aryeh 68
Kaplan, Bernard 23
Karaites 141
Karo, Joseph 15
Kashrut (kosher) 10–11, 18–19, 26, 35, 40, 59–60, 63, 76, 91, 111–12, 123, 130, 148, 158
  Montreal 76, 85, 91, 95, 97, 101, 104–5, 112, 127, 136
  North America 91
Kazin, Michael 3
Kehal Yeshurun (congregation) 47
Kehillah 87, 89–93, 95, 97–100, 130, 152
  New York 92
  Philadelphia 92, 152
Keneder Odler (Montreal) 26, 29, 43–44, 59, 72, 76, 93–94, 104–5, 107, 109–10, 112–14, 119–20
Kerem Israel (congregation) 48
Keren ha-Yessod 33, 130
Kingston, Ontario 30
Kishinev pogrom 88
Klein, Mr. 116
Kook, Abraham Isaac 110, 150, 155
Kosher butchers 39–40, 43, 104–6, 109–12, 114, 116, 142, 154–55
Kosher meat
  Chicago 22
  England 39
  Montreal xi, 25, 39–43, 71, 76–78, 81, 85, 93, 99, 102–3, 108–10, 113–14, 124, 155
  North America 11, 42–43, 59, 71, 124
  Toronto 40
kosher slaughtering. *See shehita*
kosher slaughtering. *See shohet*
Kramer, Leib 127–28
Kruger, Hayyim 72
Ku Klux Klan 54

Labour movement 61, 117
  Jewish 6, 44, 90, 96, 100
Lachavitsky, A. 107
Lamdan, Solomon 46, 143
Land of Israel (Palestine) 30, 36, 54–55, 91–93, 100, 115, 124–26
  Jewish community (*yishuv*) 100, 132, 153

landsmanschaft 90, 97, 130, 152
Latin 49
Laxer, Getsel x, 69, 71–76, 78–81, 84–85, 101, 104–5, 107, 110, 114–15, 128, 148–49, 155
Leavitt (Halifax) 47
Le Soleil (Quebec City) 47
Levinthal, Bernard 110
Levy (Montreal Alderman) 39
Levy, Naphtali 148
Lida, Yeshiva of 82
Lithuania 7, 13, 36, 55, 150
Lodz 58
Loewe, Judah 58
London 148
Lublin 58, 78
lulavim. See Sukkot

Macaroffsky 41–42
Maccabees. See Haukkah
Maclennan 114
Madison, Wisconsin 43
Maimonides 34, 47, 49–50, 65, 72
Manischewitz Company 45
Marx, Karl 125
Marxism 124–25
Mary, Queen 48
Mashgiah 99, 101, 105, 108, 130
matza 45–46
Medresh, Israel 5
Meharsho (Rabbi Samuel Edels) 28, 130
Mendele Mokher Seforim. See Abramovitz, Shalom
Mendelssohn, Moses 49
Mesopotamia 54
Messiah 50, 65
midrash 120, 126
mikveh 62, 131, 147
Milton Street Synagogue. See Beth David
Miriam 125
Miron, Dan 4–5
Mishna 15, 74, 126
Mishpat ha-Shalom ha-'Ivri 100
mitnaged 55
Mizrahi. See Zionism, religious
Moab 123

Mohilever, Samuel 81
Montreal 10, 58–59, 69, 72, 84–85, 93, 95, 113
  Board of Kashruth 26
  City Council 39–40, 155
  City of 114
  Federation of Jewish Charities 33, 90, 92–93, 99
  Jewish community 1, 11–12, 23–24, 26, 33, 38, 46, 59, 75, 82, 85–88, 92–93, 96, 98, 101, 105, 115–17, 119–20, 126, 127, 142
  Jewish education 60
  Jewish Home and Orphan Asylum 44
  Jewish religious services 71
  Jewish school question 27–28, 93, 98, 111
  Protestant School Board 61, 93, 98, 153
  Religious Community Council 93–94
  slaughterhouses 150
  St. Lawrence Market 46
  synagogues 133
  "Uptown" 98
  Va'ad ha-Kashrut 103
Montreal Herald 41–42
Montreal Star 26, 106
Monument Nationale (Montreal) 33
Morgen Zhurnal (New York) 94
Moses 15, 122, 124–26
Moshe of Kozienice 146
Moshe Gedaliah ben Menahem Dov 141
Mount Vernon, New York 27, 32
Muslims 61
Mussolini 21, 29

Nadler, Mr. 109, 111, 114
Naymark, Soryl 148
Neanton, Abraham 41
New York City 7–8, 10–12, 14, 30, 36, 49–50, 55, 59, 72, 81–82, 87–88, 91, 93, 156
  Jewish "ghetto" 70
Noah 62, 125
non-observant Orthodox 147
North Bay, Ontario 10
Nova Scotia 47

Ohabei Shalom (Quebec City) 82–83
Oiwa, Keinosuke 46
Ottawa 30, 48

Palestine. *See* Land of Israel
Papineau Synagogue 85
Passover 29, 44, 111, 130
Paterson, William 46
Pearl Harbor 127
Peretz Shule 99, 101, 106, 108
Philo of Alexandria 4
Pittsburgh 24, 36
Philadelphia 49, 88, 91, 110
philosophy, Jewish 72
Pilpul 49–50
Pirkei Avot 74
Plamondon Case 46–47
Poalei Tsiyyon. See Zionism; Labour
pogroms 7
Poland 21–22, 55, 57–58, 81
Purim 77

Quebec (City) 45–46, 81–83, 85, 151
Quebec (Province) 69
   education system 93
   labour laws 76
   Quiet Revolution 1
   Superior Court 39, 60, 113

rabbinic court 39, 41, 97, 129
rabbinic literature 74
Rabbinical Council of America 4
Rabbinate 73, 81, 87, 124, 156
   Canada 7, 57, 63, 69
   Eastern European 1, 5, 14, 18, 70
   Lithuanian 14, 16
   Montreal x, 2, 5–7, 19, 21, 23, 25, 35, 73, 77–79, 81, 93, 97, 99, 101–3, 108, 113, 116–17, 127–28
   North American immigrant 4, 6–7, 14, 17, 19, 37, 59, 69–70, 72, 110–11, 123, 128
   ordination. *See semikha*
   Orthodox 30, 57, 71
   Quebec 84
   rabbinical students 81
   small communities 72
   Toronto 40
   Western European 70
Rabbis' March 2–3, 134
Rachel 125
Radom 57, 148
Rashi (Solomon ben Isaac) 120, 122
rebbe (Hasidic) 5
Rebecca 123
Reines, Isaac 81
responsa 58
"Reverend" (para-rabbinic title) 73, 85
Roback, A. 26
Rockefeller, John D. 104
Romania 85
Rome
   Jewish catacombs 4
   persecution of Jews 15
Rome, David 98
Roosevelt, Franklin 2–3
Rosenberg, Aaron 72
Rosenberg, Leah 59, 106, 150
Rosenberg, Louis 71
Rosenberg, Yudel ix, 26, 55–70, 72, 75, 77–80, 85, 93, 101–3, 105–6, 109–15, 125, 128, 137, 143, 145–46, 150, 155
Rosenman, Samuel 3
Rosh ha-Shana 10, 29, 112, 131
Roskies, David 75, 126
Russia 7, 11, 36, 71, 88, 125
   military draft 36
Russian language 21, 57, 144
Russian-Polish Hadrath Kodesh Congregation (Montreal) 85
Russo-Japanese War 7

Saadia Gaon 72
Sabbath 61–62, 65, 69, 73, 75, 83, 121–22, 124, 131, 136, 142, 146
St. Louis 91, 110
Samuel, Maurice 31
San Francisco 158
Sanhedrin (Synhedrion) 52
Sarasohn, Kasriel 37
Scholem, Gershom 67–68
science 54, 58, 65–68, 124–25
Scopes, John 33
Seattle 54

Segal, J.I. 21
Segal, Moshe Nochum 7
semikha 14–17, 22, 58, 69, 81, 131
sermons 73
Shaar Hashomayim (congregation) 12–13, 22–25, 32, 39, 46
sha'atnez 63
shabbes goy 75, 131
Shanghai 127
Shapiro, Meir 78
Shearith Israel (Spanish and Portuguese Congregation) 12, 23, 25, 39
shehita 43, 47, 60, 69–70, 76–78, 99, 131
Sherbrooke 30, 72
shofar 32
shohet (shohetim) 11, 22, 30, 40, 43, 46, 59, 69, 71–75, 77–85, 99, 101–8, 110, 113, 115–16, 127, 131, 141–42, 148–49
  chicken 115–16
Shomrim Laboker (congregation) 48
shtetl 5
Shulhan 'Arukh 15, 29, 84, 130–31
sick benefit societies 97–98, 100
Siedlice 81
Silver, Eliezer 70
Simchat Torah 44, 131
Sinai 15
Skaryszew 57
Socialism 94
Society for the Prevention of Cruelty to Animals 47
Sokolow, Nahum 81
Solomon, King 58, 67
Spector, Isaac Elchanan 13–14
Sprince, Solomon Baer 25, 139
S.S. President Pierce 158
Standard Oil Trust 104
Steinsaltz, Adin 68
Stern, Abraham 72
Stern, Harry 137, 146
Stern (Montreal) 43
Sukkot 30–31, 82, 123, 129, 131
Sunday schools 37–38
synagogues 123, 146
  East European immigrant 70
  Montreal 12–13, 22, 44
  North American 69

Syracuse 22

Talmud 21–22, 34, 38, 46, 53–54, 58, 72, 83, 125, 132, 141
  minor tractates 74
  Tosafistic commentary 74, 149
Talmud Torah 18–19, 23, 38, 132
  Anshe Sfard (Montreal) 44
  Montreal 23–25, 27, 31, 35, 96, 99, 101, 105, 108, 112, 122–23, 139, 141
Tarlow 58
tefilin 84, 132
Temple Emanuel-El 13, 24–25, 137
Tifereth Israel (congregation, Mile End) 48, 73, 143
Tog (New York) 94
Toledo, Ohio 26, 37–38
Torah 18–19, 33, 44, 53, 58, 61–63, 65, 68, 77, 119–22, 124, 126, 148
  oral 69
Toronto 30, 40, 45–46, 48, 58–60
Totris 72

Ukraine 5, 9
Union of American Orthodox Congregations 8
United Hebrew Community of Montreal, Canada. See United Orthodox Congregations
United Orthodox Congregations (Montreal) 26, 38–39, 41, 55, 59, 105
United Orthodox Synagogues. See United Orthodox Congregations
United States 69, 71, 88, 143, 157
  Department of State 2
  Eastern European Jews in 89–91
  German Jews in 89–92
  government 55, 88, 91
  Jewish community 13, 88–89, 92, 95
United Synagogue. See United Orthodox Congregations

Va'ad ha'Ir. See Jewish Community Council
Va'ad Leumi 100
Valcartier, Quebec 84

Vilkomir 21
Vilna 14, 49–50, 152
Vineberg, Hattie 113
Volozhin 21

Warsaw 49, 58, 81, 87
Weinreb, Joseph 40
Weinstock (Toronto) 45
Weinstock, Boruch 30, 140
Weitzman, Rose 81
Weizmann, Chaim 33, 81
Widrevitch (New York) 17
Willowski, Jacob (Ridbaz) 8, 16, 22, 59
Winnipeg 23
Wise, Stephen 32
Wolofsky, Hirsh xi, 5, 26, 43–44, 87, 93–101, 103, 105, 108, 119–26, 142, 150, 156–57
Woloz, Leib Simon 113
Women, Jewish 11, 100
World Jewish Congress 2
World War I 7–8, 50, 59, 84, 91–92
World War II 128

Yerushalmi, Yosef Haim 6

yeshiva 8, 21, 28, 99, 106, 132
Yeshiva University 14
Yiddish
  education 75, 96, 101, 106, 157
  language 3, 5, 11–12, 19, 23, 31, 37, 43, 48, 50, 58, 68, 70, 72, 84, 104, 119, 126
  literature 4, 21
  press 2, 26, 36, 76, 93, 119, 133
Yiddishe Gazetten (New York) 36
Yiddishism 4–5, 33, 75, 132
yohrzeit 62, 132
Yom Kippur 10, 30, 73, 106, 112, 132
Yoreh De'ah. See Shulḥan 'Arukh

Zadok ha-Kohen of Lublin 136
Zalmanovitz, Rabbi 93
Zionism 4, 32–33, 51, 81, 124–25
  anti-Zionism 91, 125, 157
  in Canada 23, 84
  Labour 5–6, 98, 131
  in Montreal 5
  in North America 91–92
  non-Zionism 91
  religious 23, 81–82, 85, 131
Zohar 58, 64, 66–67, 125, 145, 147

www.ingramcontent.com/pod-product-compliance
Lightning Source LLC
Chambersburg PA
CBHW052100300426
44117CB00013B/2222